TV-Philosophy in Action

TV-Philosophy

Series Editors:
Sandra Laugier, Martin Shuster, Robert Sinnerbrink

Television with Stanley Cavell in Mind
edited by David LaRocca and Sandra Laugier (2023)

TV-Philosophy: How TV Series Change our Thinking
Sandra Laugier (2023)

TV-Philosophy in Action: The Ethics and Politics of TV Series
Sandra Laugier (2023)

TV-Philosophy in Action

The Ethics and Politics of TV Series

SANDRA LAUGIER

UNIVERSITY
of
EXETER
PRESS

First published in 2023 by
University of Exeter Press
Reed Hall, Streatham Drive
Exeter EX4 4QR
UK

www.exeterpress.co.uk

Copyright © Sandra Laugier 2023

The right of Sandra Laugier to be identified as author of this
work has been asserted by her in accordance with
the Copyright, Designs and Patents Act 1988.

Series title
TV-Philosophy

This book has received funding from the European Research Council (ERC)
under the European Union's Horizon 2020 research and innovation programme
(grant agreement N° 834759)

British Library Cataloguing in Publication Data
A catalogue record for this book is available
from the British Library.

https://doi.org/10.47788/QOOC5977

ISBN 978-1-80413-092-6 Hardback
ISBN 978-1-80413-093-3 ePub
ISBN 978-1-80413-094-0 PDF

Cover image © iStockphoto/paseven

Every effort has been made to trace copyright holders and obtain permission to
reproduce the material included in this book. Please get in touch with any enquiries
or information relating to an image or the rights holder.

Typeset in Adobe Caslon Pro by S4Carlisle Publishing Services, Chennai, India

Contents

Foreword by William Rothman — vii
Introduction and Acknowledgements — 1
1 Perfectionism — 10
2 The Second Wave: Gender, Race, and Class — 53
3 Spoilers, Stories, Stars — 107
4 Metaphysics — 133
5 Serial Care — 169
Bibliography — 199
Serigraphy and Filmography — 201
Index — 205

Foreword

William Rothman

This book, and its companion volume, *TV-Philosophy: How TV Series Change our Thinking*, both draw on the author's 2019 book *Nos vies en séries*, and her weekly columns for French newspaper, *Libération*—and together prove Sandra Laugier to be a philosophically sophisticated theorist, and insightful and engaging critic, of twenty-first-century television series.

Laugier, a philosophy professor at the University of Paris 1 Panthéon-Sorbonne, is the author of thirteen—and editor or co-editor of an astonishing twenty-five (and counting)—books on moral philosophy, political philosophy, philosophy of language, gender studies, and popular culture. She has also translated into French nine books by Stanley Cavell, her own professor of philosophy and mentor, as he was mine. We are far from alone in recognizing Cavell as the greatest and most important modern American philosopher. That this judgement is shared by a large and growing community of scholars in so many countries and so many academic fields is in no small part thanks to the inspiring international conferences Laugier has organized over the years and to her own writing and teaching.

When I published my first books in the 1980s, academic film study in America was in the grip of the delusion that by embracing what it called 'theory', a fledgling field groping for assurance of its legitimacy could acquire, in a single bold stroke, the authority of a science—an authority unattainable by acts of criticism accountable to a critic's experience. When the field turned to 'theory', it turned away from philosophy—and from criticism. Students were taught that to think seriously about film they had to break their attachment to the movies that were meaningful to them, as if movies were pernicious ideological constructs to be decoded and repudiated, not works of art capable of teaching us how to think about them. But if we stop loving movies, stop letting them move us, we cannot think about their value, why we seek our attachments to them, how they attract us, what rightful call they make upon us. That is, we cannot think seriously at all about the movies in our lives.

That is not how Cavell wrote about film—or the way Laugier writes about television series. She writes in ways that are open and responsive to the ways television series themselves think, as I like to put it, and to her ways—our ways—of incorporating series into our lives with others in the world. In writing about television series, she aspires to align herself philosophically with Cavell's understanding that we cannot acknowledge the worth of a work of art, or its meaning, without finding words we are prepared to stand behind, words that give voice to our experience even as they acknowledge the work's ways of expressing its ideas in its own artistic medium.

Laugier's work stands on its own, but it takes inspiration and guidance from Cavell in many ways. Cavell is considered, not wrongly, an ordinary language[1] philosopher in the tradition of J.L. Austin (his own professor of philosophy) and the Ludwig Wittgenstein of *Philosophical Investigations*. But he's an ordinary language philosopher like no other. From the early essays that comprise *Must We Mean What We Say?*, his first book, to his last writings, Cavell not only skilfully employed the kinds of appeal to what we ordinarily do and do not say that are exemplary of ordinary language philosophy, but he was also engaged in investigating philosophically the very procedures his writings exemplified. Insofar as he treated the medium of his own philosophical writing as a subject for philosophy, I think of Cavell as the philosopher who, in a modernist spirit, raised ordinary language philosophy to an explicit self-consciousness.

Why the serious study of film calls for philosophy is a question at the heart of *The World Viewed: Reflections on the Ontology of Film*, Cavell's second book. And why thinking seriously about television series, too, requires the perspective of self-reflection that only philosophy is capable of providing is a question at the heart of Laugier's two books about television series.

In a 1999 colloquium at the Sorbonne—one of those events Laugier organized—Cavell remarked that the study of film—or television, Laugier would add—cannot be a 'worthwhile human enterprise' if it 'isolates itself' from the kind of criticism Walter Benjamin had in mind when he argued that 'what establishes a work as art is its ability to inspire and sustain criticism of a certain sort, criticism that seeks to articulate the work's idea; what cannot be so criticized is not art'. Laugier's book, *TV-Philosophy in Action* is that kind of criticism.

As the book's title implies, for Laugier as for Cavell, philosophy is not a realm of abstract and technical thought; it is an activity performed by human beings in the world—an activity, in principle open to all, that can play important roles in the human form of life. Indeed, as Cavell put it, 'any place in which the human spirit allows itself to be under its own question is philosophy' (Fleming and Payne, 59).

The World Viewed is such a place. As Cavell's writings about film demonstrate, a Hollywood movie can be such a place too. That there have been films that are great works of art, masterpieces, that are 'under their own question', that film is a medium *of* philosophy, is for Cavell what makes it a subject *for* philosophy. And it is at once the premise and conclusion of

---

1 See Laugier, Sandra. *Why We Need Ordinary Language Philosophy* (Chicago: Chicago University Press, 2013).

TV-Philosophy in Action that the television series Laugier loves, cares about, thinks about, and writes about are also 'under their own question'. For Laugier, the television series, like the feature film, is a medium of art that has produced its share of masterpieces, works worthy of the kind of philosophical criticism she devotes to them, criticism that reveals the television series, at least at its best, to be a medium of philosophy.

As Laugier points out in her Introduction to this book's companion volume, *TV-Philosophy: How TV Series Change our Thinking*, Cavell himself, in his 1982 essay 'The Fact of Television' (Cavell and Rothman, 59–86), denied that television was capable of producing artistic masterpieces, individual works that most fully reveal and acknowledge the conditions of the television medium. He distinguished between television, 'a current of simultaneous event reception', and film, defined in *The World Viewed* as 'a succession of automatic world projections'. The mode of perception that he claims is called upon by television's material basis is not viewing; it is monitoring (Cavell and Rothman, 72).

Between the 1980s and the beginning of the twenty-first century, television became something other than what it had been. Insofar as the experience of television no longer had to be tethered to monitoring, the arguments in 'The Fact of Television' for denying that television can be a medium of art were rendered moot. The untethering of television fiction from monitoring was a development whose possibility 'The Fact of Television' acknowledged. It was a development Cavell surely welcomed, as he welcomed the news that his son Benjamin had signed on as a screenwriter for the great—and quite Cavellian—series *Justified*, which premiered in 2010 and ran for six seasons.

And in his 1988 essay 'The Advent of Videos' (Cavell and Rothman, 145–52), Cavell considers some implications of the fact that since he published 'The Fact of Television' this had come to pass. The advent of digital video recorders (TiVo was introduced in 1999), in tandem with streaming video, made untenable the assumption of the evanescence of television series. What made digital recorders and streaming video so consequential is that it made it possible for television—television as it had become, that is, or what replaced television as it had been—to be an artistic medium capable of producing great works worthy of the kind of criticism that *TV-Philosophy in Action* exemplifies.

Buffy the Vampire Slayer, a 'teen' series like none that had come before it, which premiered in 1997 and ran for seven seasons, and *The West Wing*, which ran from 1999 to 2006, are two series that figure prominently in *TV-Philosophy in Action*, as do numerous other series that were made—and Laugier may have seen—before she started writing her columns for *Libération* in 2013. We might think of her original encounters with those series as taking place during a period in when Laugier, like millions of others, enjoyed a relation to the television series in her life that was comparable to Cavell's 'natural' relation to film in the quarter of a century in which going to the movies was a regular part of his week, as it was for millions, without his ever being moved to think philosophically about movies and their impact on his life.

Because the writing of *The World Viewed* was prompted by memories of movies that are 'strand over strand', as the book's first line puts it, with memories of his life, Cavell found himself feeling, upon completing the body of the book, that he had written a kind of memoir—not the story of the period of his life in which he enjoyed what he calls a 'natural relation' to movies but, rather, 'an account of the conditions that were satisfied by movies and movie-going' for all who enjoyed the relation to movies he had enjoyed—a relation that had become lost. Analogously, the columns and other short pieces in *TV-Philosophy in Action* can be characterized as providing an account of the conditions satisfied by television series for all who have enjoyed the relation to them that Laugier enjoyed.

What broke Cavell's 'natural relation' to movies, and what that relation was, such that its loss seemed to demand repairing or commemorating by taking thought, are questions Cavell addressed in *The World Viewed* as a whole. In Laugier's case, however, it wasn't the breaking of a prior relationship to television series, a break precipitated by a sense that television series had changed in ways that made it impossible for such a relationship to be sustained, that moved her to think and write philosophically about television series at a moment when numerous academics began publishing articles and books about television. She is writing as a fan, writing in praise of series she loves, series whose characters she cares deeply about, series that have something to teach her about being a human being in the world, series that care for their viewers, as she likes to put it, keeping hope alive in increasingly troubled times.

And yet television series, and the ways that they impact our lives, have not remained unchanged. *TV-Philosophy in Action* distinguishes three distinct waves of feminist series, for example, each wave exemplifying in its own way an Emersonian perfectionist moral outlook——the view that the human self is always becoming, as on a journey, a never-ending quest to attain (to paraphrase Emerson) an unattained yet attainable self.

And Laugier reflects on the causes and implications of the fact that in the years between *The West Wing* and *House of Cards*, which premiered in 2013, the year she started writing her columns, television series, like politics, had changed—and, it would seem, not for the better, from a perfectionist perspective, given that idealistic politicians in the earlier series morphed into all-too-familiar cynical opportunists—although Laugier nonetheless sees both series, in different ways, as exemplars of Emersonian perfectionist texts.

What broke Cavell's 'natural relation' to movies, and what that relation was that its loss seemed to demand repairing or commemorating by taking thought, are questions he wrote *The World Viewed* to answer. That the book's writing cannot be separated from what the writing is, that it is 'under its own question', is what makes it philosophy, as Cavell understood and practised

it. *TV-Philosophy in Action* has a different way of being 'under its own question'. In characterizing the book as a 'collection', Laugier has in mind Cavell's understanding that a proper collection, like a work of art worthy of serious criticism, is an expression of an *idea*. The idea that the columns and other short pieces in *TV-Philosophy in Action* collectively express is that, at least so far, Emersonian perfectionism, albeit in diverse and often surprising ways, has been ascendant in American television series in the twenty-first century, as it was in Hollywood movies of all genres in the New Deal years. The idea also reveals itself to be an idea about television series as an artistic medium and a medium of philosophy, and an idea as to why thinking and writing seriously about television series, like thinking and writing seriously about movies, calls for the perspective of self-reflection only philosophy is capable of providing.

In my Preface to *Cavell on Film*, I noted that in comparison with his preceding book *Contesting Tears* (his late book *Cities of Words* had not yet been published) some of the writings in the collection may seem to be slight, occasional pieces. Yet, as I wrote—and the same could be said about the pieces that make up *TV-Philosophy in Action*, as opposed to the longer, more overtly theoretical approach of its companion volume *TV-Philosophy: How TV Series Change our Thinking*—'Cavell's occasional pieces bring home, with special vividness, a crucial feature of his aspiration and achievement as a writer, namely, that every one of his writings is an occasional piece. Every one of Cavell's writings responds to, acknowledges, its particular occasion, an occasion inseparable from the writing's "cause".' This brings home, in turn, that any and every occasion may be found to call for philosophy.

For Laugier, as for Cavell, philosophy is a way of rising to its occasion. Every one of the pieces in *TV-Philosophy in Action* contains at least one new idea or thought, an idea or thought she expresses, puts into words, more fully there, on that occasion, motivated by her experience of that series, than anywhere else in the book.

Because Laugier understands that television series do not merely reflect cultural, social, and political change but, like philosophy when it is 'in action', are powerful agents of change that play significant roles in forming, and reforming how we live and how we think—how we think, for example, about television series and the roles they play in our lives. Between 2013 and 2022, television series continued to change in ways Laugier's monthly columns in *Libération* chart in 'real time', as it were. Although the book is not organized strictly chronologically, we can nevertheless sense how Laugier's thinking changes, deepens, as each series she writes about moves her to some new thought about their medium—and about her herself. In this way, *TV-Philosophy in Action* is not only a collection. Every piece is itself like an episode in a television series, a series we care about more and more as it goes on. There's much more I could say about this admirable book, but to avoid spoilers, I'll stop here.

Works cited

Cavell, Stanley, *Little Did I Know: Excerpts from Memory* (Palo Alto, CA: Stanford University Press, 2010).

———, *Cities of Words: Pedagogical Letters on a Register of the Moral Life* (Cambridge, MA: Harvard University Press, 2005).

———, *The World Viewed: Reflection on the Ontology of Film*, enlarged edition (Cambridge, MA: Harvard University Press, 1979).

———, *Must We Mean What We Say?* (New York and Cambridge: Cambridge University Press, 1969, 2002).

Cavell, Stanley and William Rothman, *Cavell on Film* (New York: State University of New York Press, 2005).

Fleming, Richard and Michael Payne (eds), *The Senses of Stanley Cavell* (Lewisburg, PA: Bucknell University Press, 1989).

Introduction

This volume, *TV-Philosophy in Action: The Ethics and Politics of TV Series*, is one of two books that result from a decade-long enterprise in writing about TV series. The project developed out of a monthly column for the French newspaper *Libération* (from 2013 to 2022), which led to a book *Nos vies en séries* (2019) and an ongoing European Research Council project 'Demoseries', which is exploring a corpus of 'security TV series' from conception to reception.

These two new books provide English speaking readers with access to my work on TV series for the first time. *TV-Philosophy: How TV Series Change our Thinking* is a theoretical monograph discussing the philosophical 'thought' of series—that is, the thought about the world that is produced and expressed through TV series—a 'Series-Philosophy' akin to the Film-Philosophy developed by Stanley Cavell, Robert Sinnerbrink, William Rothman, and others.

This book, *TV-Philosophy in Action: The Ethics and Politics of TV Series*, can be seen as Series-Philosophy put into practice. It provides readers with a selection of my columns from *Libération*, brought together with other writings from *AOC* (https://aoc.media/), *Le Monde*, and *l'Obs*. These pieces focus on individual series, or groups of related series, and films. Together, they may be taken as exemplars of a body of Series-Philosophy. The *Libération* columns in particular were often written in close proximity to the viewing experience, and are informal in tone: I write as a philosopher of ordinary language and a fan of series.

These two books—the more theoretical overview provided by *TV-Philosophy: How TV Series Change our Thinking* and the more specific and particularized *TV-Philosophy in Action: The Ethics and Politics of TV Series*—are envisaged as complementary. They can be read one after the other or in tandem, that is to say, dipping in and out of *TV-Philosophy in Action* for exemplars, while digesting the theoretical arguments of *TV-Philosophy*. An index of series, with references to all pages on which each one is mentioned, is included at the end of each book.

***

From the very first column, which welcomed the arrival of *House of Cards*, my pieces for *Libération* focused—as befits a newspaper column—on popular series or films of the moment and their political and moral relevance. The texts were brief and circumstantial (after all, life is made up of circumstances and contexts that offer vehicles for our personal expressions). The columns were often linked to political events, for which series have proved to be powerful tools of analysis and criticism. They were written during a period, fortunately now past, when it was important to philosophically defend television series as true works of art, or at least as works that had to be taken seriously—just as cinema had to be defended in the previous century, when it was considered entertainment for the uncultured.

My goal was not to produce a Series-Philosophy that would take series as its object, or to use the columns to showcase or support an ethics or a politics. This was because, first, I would argue that philosophy itself is completely transformed by our interest in these forms of popular culture, as it was by cinema, which (as Stanley Cavell showed) found its place in the world through its particular affinity with our ordinary experience; and secondly, as I demonstrate in *TV-Philosophy: How TV Series Change our Thinking*, popular series produce and express ethics in their own right. There is indeed a Series-Philosophy, akin to the Film-Philosophy set out by Cavell, Sinnerbrink, Rothman, and others.

The series I discuss here (and I analyse only series that strike a chord with my own tastes, so apologies for all those that are missing) create a new, collectively elaborated, public space and outlet of democratic life. They are not only a resource for reflection on the stakes of the present moment, but also a tool for moral, social, and political transformation. Education through series represents new hope in a world where anti-democratic values are implemented or promoted by many regimes and political actors, and where political discourses and commitments are sometimes emptied of their meaning. TV series now have such a place in the life of viewers that they cannot be reduced to, as some used to say, 'mirrors of society'. They also have a specific agency in and act upon the world—through the transformations they bring about in us. This is the method of analysis that I have adopted, not as an initial choice but rather by seeing meaning emerge from reading and perceiving particular series (and some films) that are representative of the way in which popular culture counts for us.

My guides in this Series-Philosophy are neither the philosophy of film nor TV criticism. I was educated in an eclectic tradition of criticism that was to be found in the newspaper *Libération*—my bible since I was a teenager in the 1970s, when I would go to the movies several times a week at a 'Cinéclub' where I absorbed American films, both classic and contemporary, and watched all available TV series (*Columbo*, *The Persuaders*, *Starsky and Hutch*, *Dallas*), and in the 1980s. My teachers at that time were the popular critics Serge Daney and Louis Skorecki. The latter was among the first to actually respect TV shows on the same level as films, and he wrote about them in a witty, joyful style.

From the beginning of the century, I contributed to *Libération* on a regular basis, submitting political op-eds (which were always welcomed, even when they were blatantly radical) and participating in a yearly issue, 'Le Libé des philosophes' for which a large number of French philosophers produced all the sections (politics, culture, international politics, etc.). I always chose to do the TV section, presenting the programmes of the day and recommending certain films and series, and I enjoyed doing this tremendously. However, it was on the basis of my philosophical and political work (which focuses on American philosophy, the ethics of care, gender, and democracy) that in 2013 the 'Idées' section of *Libération*, directed by Cécile Daumas, recruited me along with three other philosophers to write weekly philosophy columns (with each of us writing once a month). For reasons I still cannot fully explain, mine was from the very beginning a column on the TV shows I liked and found relevant for talking about the world in general, and my world in particular.

These shorter writings are more of a collection (in the sense Cavell gives the word in his extraordinary essay 'Collecting Things':[1] putting together things that matter to you, in no particular order) than a systematic discussion of themes. Nevertheless, in order to aid the reader, it seems useful to organize them loosely into chapters, or concepts; that is, variants of the series experience that emerged from the 'bottom up', so to speak, out of the topics of series that caught my interest, affection, or curiosity. They can be thought of as the proof of concept of the companion volume, *TV-Philosophy: How TV Series Change our Thinking*.

They are reflections on particular characteristics and dynamics of TV series on the basis of readings of specific examples from a broad set of shows (and some popular films) that, for me, constitute the background context and grammar of these series. These monthly columns in *Libération* were thus exercises in philosophical criticism of topical shows.

Moreover, the pieces brought together here are the outcome and expression of the politicization of series over the last decade—the fact that they have grasped the political through aesthetics, but also the fact that they have been taken up by politics and the world. They are also strongly and explicitly connected to a specific political context, be it American or French. They are themselves exercises in popular culture, all written for general-public outlets, and meant to call attention to the intellectual strength and pure cleverness of TV series, while at the same time demonstrating, in action, the power of popular culture to produce and transform values. This is what may be called series' realism—a realism than can shape a fiction or hypothetical time period. Here we may think of shows such as *For All Mankind* that, like *The Handmaid's Tale* or *The Leftovers*, teach their viewers much more about the actual world than do many other, explicitly present-moment, 'political' shows.

These columns were available online and widely read, and I often ran into strangers or friends who were following them faithfully, using them as recommendations for shows to watch—a service that proved of public interest at a time when shows were proliferating throughout the world, and when official TV criticism often merely echoed series' own promotional materials.

---

1   In Stanley Cavell, *Here and There* (Cambridge, MA: Harvard University Press, 2022).

And I never claimed to be doing TV criticism (which was the job of the excellent TV critics at *Le Monde, Télérama, L'Obs, Libération*).

Film criticism was a different story. I have often found myself at odds with the prestigious tradition of French film criticism when it focuses on popular cinema (and, more recently, on TV series). There is the tendency, denounced early on by Cavell, of critics to consider that they are the inventors of a film's or series' intelligence, and to imply that the producers of such cultural products would themselves be incapable of understanding the importance of their own creations. This is often the case with analyses in the form of 'the philosophy of' a series or a popular film. Too often, such 'philosophical' essays are dedicated to expressing certainty in the superiority of one's point of view. There is also an ongoing anxiety about the disappearance of film and of the mythical experience of the movie theatre—which neglects to take into consideration the fact that today, movie theatres, apart from the small and beloved 'Art et Essai' cinemas still active in the Paris Quartier Latin, are places where seeing a film is unaffordable for many. Cavell insisted on moviegoing as essential to the film,[2] but my point is that we have to look elsewhere for an actual and widely *shared experience*.

A theoretical discussion of TV series is pointless if it does not engage in analysis of how they affect us, as well as in the study of particular series. In *TV-Philosophy: How TV Series Change Our Thinking*, I detail the ways in which classic series constitute our personal and collective histories, our corpus, and our culture. In this book, I trace the singular experience and the political, moral, and sometimes metaphysical impact of the series that have shaped us in recent years, while also (in)forming and inventing new meanings of this 'us' (hence the forceful presence of the series *This Is Us* in my corpus).

The category of series we are dealing with here has revealed itself as an aesthetic form of the democratic ideal. Some element of moral exploration is at the heart of most TV shows rooted in everyday life. By enabling viewers to see their lives in sharper focus, and attain greater understanding of their own potential, series give us access to a form of democratic life that is based not on pre-existing and consensual values, but rather is rooted in inventing shareable values through the possibilities of the medium.

TV series may offer us common cultural referents that populate ordinary conversations and political debates. In this way, they create a new public space, or even a model for collectively re-elaborating democratic life. The study of TV series is therefore not only a resource for reflecting on current issues but also a tool for social and political transformation.

I covered all kinds of topics in this *Libération* column between 2013 and 2022. Sometimes, I discussed current events, frequently taking political stances on issues such as feminism, democracy, and care, particularly during the Covid-19 pandemic. The writing collected here represent only a small portion

---

2 Stanley Cavell, *The World Viewed* (Cambridge, MA: Harvard University Press, 1971), ch. 1.

of the approximately one hundred published columns. Additionally, during these years, I also often wrote about films that mattered to me.

Warshow placed cinema at the heart of popular culture and, therefore, the need for a specific sort of criticism for popular culture, stating:

> Such a criticism finds its best opportunity in the movies, which are the most highly developed and most engrossing of the popular arts, and which seem to have an almost unlimited power to absorb and transform the discordant elements of our fragmented culture.[3]

Today we can only read this as a comment on television series, which are certainly now, more than films, a compendium of all culture, absorbing and recycling elements of music, video games, classic television, and, of course, cinema. What Cavell claimed for popular Hollywood films – their ability to create a culture shared by millions of people – has been transferred to other corpora and practices, including television series, which have taken on, or even assumed, the task of educating the public. Television series are places for individual education, an education that resembles a form of subjective improvement through the sharing and discussion of public and ordinary material, integrated into the lives of individuals and a source of conversation.

The texts gathered here also evoke this global popular culture, symbolized today in series. Like William Rothman, I do not work from a hierarchy between TV and film, although I fully understand that it exists for many. There is now a corpus of true masterpieces in series, and it is important to me that this corpus exists, is known, seen and reviewed, and taught: series that, as Cavell says, express, represent, and invent exactly the possibilities of the medium. But the moral perfectionism that guides my reading comes from classical cinema, and this is what led me to keep in this volume a few film reviews that testify to this form of common life shared by series and films.

By allowing each viewer to increase the intensity of their life and the understanding of its possibilities, the series present us a form democratic life no longer based on pre-existing and consensual values, but inventing values that we can share by using the possibilities of the medium.. The series I am talking about here create a new public space and a form of democratic life to be elaborated collectively. They are not only a resource in the reflection on the present stakes, but also a tool for moral, social and political transformation. In rupture with some current narcissistic positions, accusing the series as a source of alienation – and undervaluing their audiences as well, held to be incapable of resisting the pressures and methods of platforms, I aim here to put this tool to practice.

---

3   Warshow, *The Immediate Experience*, p. xxxviii.

Despite the abundance of publications on series in the United States and Europe, it seems that research has not yet taken the measure of the role that series can and do play in the transmission and sharing of values, the development of democratic ideas, an awareness of risks (terrorist or climatic), and movement towards social inclusion, gender equality, and diversity. Yet it is clear that the cult series *Buffy the Vampire Slayer*, for example, has played a significant role in promoting gender and sexual equality; and the series *24*, launched in the aftermath of 9/11, raised awareness of the long-term risks of terrorism and of the moral degeneration of democracies engaged in a global fight against threats—while also preparing audiences for the sight of a black president.[4] *The West Wing* depicted a minority president as early as 2004, a character inspired at the time by a brilliant young senator from Illinois. In Europe, the series *Baron Noir* (France) and *La Casa de Papel* (Spain) sought to educate a public that has become somewhat cynical, and to re-enchant democratic life. The development of so-called post-apocalyptic series (*The Walking Dead*, *The Leftovers*, *The Handmaid's Tale*, *Station Eleven*, *Foundation*) brings greater attention to the risk of environmental and health disasters, and to the vulnerability of democratic value-systems and freedoms.

A shift in the cultural field and its hierarchies is underway, and global changes in attitudes towards television series, as sites of reappropriation and audience empowerment, are a mark of this. Culture was previously seen as a site for the expression of individual taste and status; now it is treated as an essential motor of political intervention and social innovation—and of democratization, if we understand democracy, as so many citizens (and theorists) do today, not only as an institutional system but as a call for equality and participation in public life.

This makes it possible to redefine popular culture as more than mere entertainment; as instead performing the work of moral and political education. The urgency and importance of the discourse of TV series lies in the way they act on and transform our conception of morality, something that became apparent with the advent of works that became sites for developing pluralist and conflicting ethics, including *The Sopranos*, *Six Feet Under*, *The Wire*, *Lost*, *Mad Men*, and *Breaking Bad*. Since as long ago as the 1990s, TV series have aspired to provide moral education. *ER* articulated the competing demands of private life and work, as well as the conflicts involved in caring for patients. Over its fifteen seasons, it raised numerous public health issues, including AIDS, inequality of access to care, disability, and end of life care. *The West Wing* was a powerful reflection on freedoms and democracy, topics that have recently returned to the fore in the United States. Today, many TV series continue to focus on political issues, whether this be violence against women in *Unbelievable*, racism in *When They See Us*, *Watchmen*,

---

4   See S. Allouche (ed.), *24h chrono et la naissance du genre sécuritaire* (Paris: Vrin, 2022).

Lovecraft Country, and *Lupin*, or the difficulties of care work in *Maid*. Each of these examples has pedagogical and transformative aims, and seeks to draw our attention to neglected or marginalized social concerns. Since the start of the twenty-first century, the range of characters depicted has proliferated: gay (*Buffy the Vampire Slayer*, *The Wire*) and trans (*The L Word*, *Transparent*, *Pose*) characters became mainstays long before they appeared in movies; and non-white characters have also become central to mainstream productions (*American Crime*, *This Is Us*, *Watchmen*, and, most spectacularly, *Lupin*). Series concerned with women's lives and female visibility have also burgeoned (*Six Feet Under*, *Orange is the New Black*, *The Handmaid's Tale*), and with even greater impetus since #MeToo. It is now a question of representing *all* humans, in their diversity, with the small screen offering a privileged field of expression for these new faces: *For All Mankind*, for instance, introduces fictitious female and black characters involved in the early conquest of space, opening up both the casting and the concept of mankind itself.

The democratic essence of television series lies in the way every viewer is empowered to trust their own judgement, which they can build and consolidate through access to these works. Series allow each viewer the freedom to master, or at least become confident in, their own cultural choices and perceptions—in line with the expectations we have of democratic decision-making today. Series thus embody the potential to render all series viewers competent—hence traditional criticism's difficulty with them. The potency of TV series lies in their integration into daily life and their capacity to offer us a narrative of progress, through attachment to characters over the course of their lives and ours; and to groups whose interactions include us and thus animate us.

This democratic conception of series as a source of education is alien to the view, still present in intellectual and media circles (especially in France), of 'mass' culture as the alienation, manipulation, or intoxication of viewers. As Jean-Paul Sartre would say, 'mass' is the others. Under the guise of criticism, this is an expression of contempt for the public, and is anti-democratic, since it assumes that the 'critic' is above this alienation. My claim (and what these essays seek to illustrate) is that audiences are intelligent enough to learn not to be manipulated.

Each of my essays seeks to elucidate the power of series, the singularity of their thought, not in the sense of what is thought about them, but how they think—or express a particular perspective on—the world we live in.

This book proceeds thematically, but also historically, starting with moral and political ambition and ending with the pandemic and lockdown. I start, in Chapter 1, by exploring the ways in which series discuss and illustrate moral perfectionism, often with reference to cinematographic models. I also address the political positioning of TV series and their capacity to analyse and criticize the world we live in, while giving voice and space to new categories of humans. As Chapter 2 reveals, series may also do the work of reparation (*When They See Us*, *Unbelievable*, *Lupin*, *Maid*, etc.)—work that popular cinema has sometimes failed to address, but which the hybrid format of the single-season series engages with. To achieve such goals, series assemble their own mythologies, on the model of contemporary myths, of which *Star Wars* is, of course, the great example (though the quality of the franchise has somewhat declined in the transfer to the TV series format—with the spectacular exception of *Andor*—it has also facilitated its own inventions, in particular through a significant cast of actors). This is tackled in Chapter 3, together with other material on the mechanisms of storytelling through series. As Chapter 4 investigates, by exploiting the possibilities of the serial timeframe and the diachronic complexity of their characters, TV series can take on the fields of metaphysics and scepticism, posing questions about mortality, sexuality, and human/non-human or living/non-living differences. They revisit such topics as outer space and what it means to be on Earth, proposing a metaphysics of the everyday, as well as an everyday metaphysics for a time of climate crisis. In Chapter 5, I consider how, during the pandemic—a prelude to other crises to come—series took care of their audiences, reciprocating the relationships of care that viewers have had with their characters for years.[5] In the midst of the COVID-19 crisis, it fell to series to invent, describe, and elicit forms of resilience through the renewed visibility and significance of the ongoing risk of terrorism, conceptualized as the paradigm for other crises and threats. Presenting us with vulnerable and fallible humans whom we learn to care about, series emerge as an art form for a vulnerable world.

Acknowledgements

I wish to thank all the friends who have shared with me the project of acknowledging the philosophical importance of television series, as well as innumerable conversations on specific shows: Martin Shuster, Paola Marrati, Daniela Ginsburg, Sylvie Allouche, Thibaut de Saint-Maurice, Pauline Blistène, Hugo Clémot, Jeroen Gerrits, Hent De Vries, Mathias Girel, Philippe Corcuff, Perig Pitrou, David LaRocca, and William Rothman. Special thanks to Simon (for *Game of Thrones*), Marie (for *Buffy*), Ulysse (for *The Wire*), and Jocelyn (for all the shows he didn't like but shared faithfully).

I am grateful to the whole 'Idées' team at *Libération*, particularly Cécile Daumas, for continuous stimulation and help with my monthly column (2013–2022); to Sylvain Bourmeau, who has encouraged and welcomed several longer essays in his renowned online journal *AOC* (*Analyse Opinion Critique*); to my dear friend Maxime Catroux at Editions Climats (Flammarion) who generously welcomed my first book on television, *Nos vies en séries* (2019).

---

5   See, e.g., Sandra Laugier, *Politics of the Ordinary: Care, Ethics, and Forms of life*, 2020; The Ethics of Care as a Politics of the Ordinary, *New Literary History*, 46, 2015, pp. 217–40.

Many thanks Daniela Ginsburg, to Louise Chapman and to Tatsiana Zhurauliova for their wonderful translations.

Last but not least, I am extremely grateful to my wonderful and smart editor, Anna Henderson, who supported this project, understood its ambition better than I did, and who, just like a super-capable producer, guided the two volumes of *TV-Philosophy* from their first concept, through the episodes, and to the final product.

1

Perfectionism

House of Cards, The End of Utopia

Enthusiasts of TV series, whom we shall hereinafter denominate seriphiles, may recall *The West Wing*, an exemplary series that could be seen on evening television in the early years of the present millennium. Initially aired on NBC from 1999 to 2006 (and a few months later on France's Channel 2), it presented the brilliant and cultured fictional American president, Jed Bartlet, winner of the Nobel Prize for Economics and fancier of Foucault. The series portrays Bartlet (played by Martin Sheen of *Apocalypse Now* fame) as a man animated by a sense of justice, commitment to social progress, and the defence of liberties. He, along with his team of advisers—C.J. Cregg, Josh Lyman, and Toby Ziegler (whose singular exchanges and modes of expression were orchestrated by Aaron Sorkin, a conversational style we gladly find again in *The Social Network*)—trained the public in democratic thinking and collective intelligence.

The world of *The West Wing* and its heroes was the bearer of an unfulfilled ideal through its representation of American politics, inverting the political reality of the time (reactionary, imbecilic, and characterized by warlike Bushism). Its presentation corresponded with a concept of democracy that, from the perfectionist perspective of Emerson and Thoreau, would be the utopia of a future world still to come—an object of both demand and hope. Accordingly, the last season of *The West Wing* (2006) ended with the election, after Bartlet's two terms in office, of Matt Santos, a minority candidate whose character was directly inspired by the young senator Barack Obama during his first election campaign of 2004.

By 2013, while Obama (the real one) was entering his second term in office, we were addicted to the distinctly different political world—still set in Washington DC, but now presented in a rather elitist format (Netflix in the US)—of *House of Cards*. This time, the hero, Francis Underwood (Kevin Spacey), is not the president (who is rather a flimsy character), but one of

---

* This article first appeared in *Libération*, 13 September 2013.

the key leaders of the House of Representatives, to where the action has moved. Cunning, manipulative, and even (spoiler alert) criminally cold, this central protagonist represents nothing as mild as the foibles of the characters in *The West Wing*.

Between 2006 and 2013, something happened in TV series that mirrored the public's new affection for unsavoury characters (*House*, *Dexter*, etc.) to whom we became attached by virtue of being around them. Both Underwood and the hero of *Boss*, another fascinating series that describes the world of Chicago City Hall, are political avatars of this trend: both aim for naked power without public ideals, private vulnerability (each has a wife who is at once a trophy, an accomplice, and a rival ready to betray him), or concern for others.

Between 2006 and 2013, something also happened in conceptions of politics. Democracy, so well embodied and expressed by Obama at the time of his election, remained in a state of mere verbal aspiration, and it is this disappointment that is reflected in the cruel irony of democratic rhetoric, from *Boss* to *House of Cards* where, in the morally gloomy world of the House, the citizen—excluded from political calculations—no longer enjoys any voice or representation.

House of Cards signals the end of politics based on government by the people—on both representativeness and being able to identify with one's leaders. Indeed, Underwood's marked connivance with the viewer is an explicit super-manipulation: through its allusions to its predecessor, *The West Wing*, the series signals the end of the utopian realist series that, from *The L Word* to *The Wire*, constructed an alternative reality designed to meet the hopes or demands of a better world.

What is there left to hope for when the other world no longer has any space, and is none other than the one we inhabit? 'There Is no Planet B', Occupy Wall Street protesters once chanted. Yet the democratic ideal remains, no longer in the institutions and powers of politics, but as a demand—in movements and revolts around the world—for transparency, and for the participation of all in public life. It remains, in short, in the dissatisfaction immanent in ordinary moral and political life.

Old, Ugly, and Nasty

Proud or closeted (if they're outside the 18–34 target audience), the fans of the sitcom *How I Met Your Mother* will remember a cult episode from season two where our favourite hero, Barney Stinson (Neil Patrick Harris), wants to lend a hand to his friend Marshall, who is terrorized by his super-stern constitutional law professor. Intrigued, Barney goes to observe Professor Lewis (Jane Seymour) and the other students, where he identifies Lewis as a cougar, a species whose basic traits he details for the viewer's education: forty-something, stylish mane, deep neckline, bright red claws, attracted to young men—seemingly easy prey for Barney, who finds himself trapped in a burgeoning sexual relationship. He will, nevertheless, fall short: Professor Lewis grades his performance 'C-'; she refuses to extend Barney's education, stating that she teaches all day and does not wish to continue at night. This dramatic and abrupt turn of events, which demystifies Barney's predatory status, signals the new hold of 'old ladies' on our screens.

TV heroines have changed a great deal since they won their first places in the credits. They are no longer very young or even very cute—Sarah Linden (Mireille Enos) is not super-sexy in her big jumpers in *The Killing*; nor is Birgitte Nyborg, the prime minister of the Danish series *Borgen*; nor Patty Hewes (Glenn Close) on *Damages*; nor even the great favourite, Carrie Mathison (Claire Danes), who is rather ravaged and unattractive at the end of the first season of *Homeland*. These women, like their *The West Wing* ancestor, C.J. Cregg (Allison Janney), are primarily characterized by intelligence, ambition (nay, professional monomania), and desire for personal perfection. With their own agendas, they lead their own lives without waiting for a Prince Charming, and, like Professor Lewis, have no time to lose.

These depictions are a far cry from the classic young-pretty-sympathetic-white-straight heroine such as Rachel (Jennifer Aniston) in *Friends*, Carrie (Sarah Jessica Parker) in *Sex and the City*, or Ally in *Ally McBeal*: endearing personalities whose lives are lived in expectation of the ideal encounter—or, in the case of *Desperate Housewives*, still defined by their family, relationships, or sentimental concerns.

The series of the 2010s, *Top of the Lake*, *Downton Abbey*, *House of Cards*, and *Game of Thrones*, begin to present us with 'old ladies' in important roles. Catelyn Stark, Claire Underwood, and Lady Mary are at once beautiful and disturbing, admirable and evil, sexual and cold, and compete with young girls in the public's fantasies by playing with ambivalence.

Admittedly, *Friends*' fans have aged twenty years, and one could say that series have followed. But it is not only that. Just as the Hollywood classics of the 1930s and 1940s gave women a voice and a place thanks to a generation of remarkable actresses from Katharine Hepburn to Barbara Stanwyck,

---

* This article first appeared in *Libération*, 6 December 2013.

so the series of the 2000s and 2010s are creating new female role models, and, through their mass distribution, are shaping collective intelligence and transforming life forms. This began with the *Buffy the Vampire Slayer* revolution, a cult series for teenagers that its creator (the brilliant Joss Whedon) conceived as a feminist work intended to educate and morally transform a co-ed audience. To do so, it puts on-screen an ordinary girl (Sarah Michelle Gellar) who pulverizes vampires, and, with them, stereotypes of the female heroine: either the little blonde girl who is cut up in the first fifteen minutes of horror films or the noisy teenager in high school shows.

But the eponymous Buffy, while atypical, was always kind and pretty in a manner similar to the heroines of *Alias* and *The L Word*, series that also put women in the spotlight. The series of the 2010s thus go further than *Buffy* by creating a gallery of female characters as dark and awful as their male colleagues. In the wake of *The Sopranos* and *House*, it is now women's turn to acquire the dignity of the villain, and thus enter a new stage of emancipation by leaving the maternal and sexual roles reserved for them by the cinema. The small screen offers a privileged field of expressivity for these new faces to display their defects, such as the credits of the new series *Orange Is the New Black*.

The arrival of leading roles featuring older women, who exist without procreation or marriage as a goal, but who are resolutely oriented towards a future grounded in other forms of achievement, is a milestone in the history of women.

Immanent Justice

In a harrowing scene in *Foxcatcher*, 1984 Olympic gold medal wrestler Dave Schultz (the always excellent Mark Ruffalo) is forced to praise the deranged billionaire (Steve Carell) who funds him, for the purposes of an infodrama documentary. The falsity of the sentiment causes Dave the utmost difficulty in pronouncing the words dictated to him on camera: 'He's my mentor.' This falsity sums up the tragedy of *Foxcatcher*.

The best season of *Buffy the Vampire Slayer*, the sixth, has an episode, 'Once More with Feeling', in which Buffy and her friends—Spike included—are irrepressibly driven to sing (in pure musical theatre style) whenever they have something to say. The grip of the musical voice compels them to express the truth of their feelings and lives in a touching manner (one thinks of Resnais' beautiful 1997 film, *On connaît la chanson*, where the voices coming from popular songs have this same revelatory effect).

Talking movies possess this remarkable capacity to make us hear the legitimacy of tone—and its opposite, falseness, which is not so much a lie as a radically shifted, inexpressive character of speech. Correctness and legitimacy are, then, defined by appropriateness to the context *and* appropriateness between subject and voice—the capacity, as Cavell would say after Wittgenstein, to signify what is said; that is, to make sense.

Television series, in particular the underrated format of the sitcom, are also constantly in search of the perfectionist tone of conversational exchange. The brief form offered by the text or tweet constitutes, on a smaller scale, an innovative framework for this exploration, an accuracy that has been collectively sought and constantly evaluated in the comments, speeches, and actions of recent weeks, following the attacks of 7 and 9 January, and subsequently, the demonstration of the 11th. Everyone is looking for the right words, without necessarily managing to sound right (especially when they claim to speak for everyone), but this desire for truthfulness—as a common demand on oneself, against the usual tendency to ask of others what one does not demand of oneself—was a novelty in the discourse of intellectuals, as well as of those in the government. It was rooted in the ordinary demand, presented by all the demonstrators on the 11th and beyond, for freedom and protection of expression; not necessarily of words—which, as Emerson said, can regularly 'grieve' us with their falsity—but specifically of the legitimacy that is common to musical performance, the words of conversation, friendly gestures.

The language philosopher J.L. Austin, author of *How to Do Things with Words* and also of *Sense and Sensibilia*, has explored this multiplicative capacity of ordinary language to 'fit', and to fit precisely, as well as to touch, arouse feelings, and refine perceptions, including acting on people, things, and

---

* This article first appeared in *Libération*, 30 January 2015.

performing acts (such as promising, marrying, and breaking up; humiliating, betraying, and consoling). For this, Austin distinguishes three well-known species of speech acts: locutionary (saying something), perlocutionary (having an effect by saying something, e.g., shocking someone with an expression), and illocutionary (doing something in the very act of saying something, e.g., calling for murder, approving it, inciting racial hatred).

All the ordinary judgements we make today are based on these fine distinctions that we must patiently learn to draw in ordinary language. Who decides whether an act of language humiliates or calls for murder? Is it the act of shocking or disturbing someone that is legally condemnable or morally questionable? We must make distinctions in each situation, whether it is regarding pornographic material or racist provocations, wherever they come from. The fact that our words and expressions are also acts of various kinds is precisely what allows for and articulates their accuracy; it is also undoubtedly what must make us rethink the effects, the strength, and the freedom of our expressions—as well as our defence of those of others.

Love, Marriage, and the KGB

Weisberg and Yost's *The Americans* is entering its third season (on FX and Canal+) as one of the best shows of the decade, or at least the most enjoyable. Though *The Leftovers* is a wonderful series, it is not easy to watch; *House of Cards*, also in its third season, remains interesting and enjoyable, but is now rather hollow and chilling. Meanwhile, *The Americans* manages to combine moral and political relevance with the intense charm of its characters, a couple of KGB agents, Philip (Matthew Rhys) and Elizabeth (Keri Russell), thereby proving once again that the strength of a TV series lies in our attachment to its fictional beings who become a part of our lives and experience.

Can the success of *The Americans* be explained by the fact that it is set in 1980s Reagan America? Nostalgic 50-somethings have noted, and appreciated, the recent proliferation of homage to the 1980s, including *A Most Violent Year* (J.C. Chandor, 2014), *Foxcatcher*, *Dallas Buyers Club* (Jean-Marc Vallée, 2013), not to mention *Argo* (Ben Affleck, 2012) or (I insist) *Guardians of the Galaxy* (James Gunn, 2014). The 1980s were a pivotal period that saw upheavals whose effects we are still experiencing, though they very much belong to the twentieth century—a world before the fall of the Wall, with its KGB, FBI, CIA, the Hitchcockian alphabet soup of *North by Northwest* (Alfred Hitchcock, 1959); before Afghanistan and Iraq, when the enemy was still well identified—in short, a world that is no longer. *The Americans* seeks to express the comparative moral and political questioning of our present, where the threat of terrorism has replaced the Cold War—though the dualism of the blocs remains, as is signalled by the moment in the third season of *House of Cards* where President Underwood confronts his terrifying Russian counterpart Petrov (played by Lars Mikkelsen, whom we immediately identify as Mads Mikkelsen's brother, aka Hannibal).

The Americans is part of the growing KGB spy genre—*Spies of Warsaw*, *Allegiance*—but its originality stems from its opening at the beginning of the Reagan years, a time of the end of the Détente, of anti-communist tension, and of a mini-resurgence of McCarthyism (under the influence of the former), in an America that still calls itself the 'free world' for the final few years that precede the disintegration of the East. Philip and Elizabeth Jennings, 'The Americans', live in a suburban neighbourhood of Washington with their two children, presenting the image of the perfect American family to the outside world... while secretly conducting intelligence missions, infiltrations, assassinations, and kidnappings. Nevertheless, the series has a singularity. The characters, despite their occasional doubts (Philip, especially, likes the capitalist way of life), are committed and sincere communists. The manner in which the series resolutely manages to place the viewer on the main characters' side, creating an attachment in the

---

* This article first appeared in *Libération*, 27 March 2015.

American public to spies, communists, atheists, killers, and (worst of all) occasional (professional) adulterers, demonstrates the moral power of the serial writing. Though the series of the 2000s have accustomed us to appreciating villains, *The Americans* arouses something else—a strange moral adherence, like a nostalgia for the good.

This is no doubt thanks to the device that gives the series its tension and its novelistic texture, the key event of the first episodes: Philip and Elizabeth, who, up to now, have coldly played the role of the perfect couple, genuinely fall in love with each other. The rest of the series deals with this transformation from which they never recover, as something that complicates their lives, their work, and their relationship with their children. We thus enter the territory of remarriage, a fundamental structure of Hollywood cinema (and of some series, from *Dream On* to *How I Met Your Mother*): the reconciliation of the couple as an image of political union. Just as in *The Philadelphia Story* (George Cukor, 1940), which stages a remarriage on the site of the American Declaration of Independence, the question of the private relationship constitutes a means of posing a political question: that of the link between humans and their society, and of the possibility of a true conversation and a common public life. In short, it is the question of the *State of the Union*—the title of another film illustrating the genre (Frank Capra, 1948), and an allusion to the president's annual policy speech to the nation. Elizabeth and Philip, through this serial reworking of the theme of remarriage, carry the perfectionist demand for a state (private or public) that can ensure a minimum of happiness for its citizens. Unlike Frank and Claire Underwood in *House of Cards*, our Americans carry this altruistically, divorced from all personal, material, symbolic, and moral benefit, reminding us that the search for happiness requires forgotten or invisible forms of political idealism.

Caring Democracy

The series *Designated Survivor* is pretty indefensible: clunky, poorly written, and splintered between too many narrative threads, it is a pale imitation of *The West Wing*—especially in its attempts to keep up with current political events, which, though repressed in the background of the series, are compromised from the outset by Trump's unforeseen election, which occurred after the series had started.

This situation is strangely reminiscent of the cult series *24*, which was launched around the time of 9/11: though programmed and written beforehand, it was oriented by reality itself towards the theme of the fight against terrorism. The parallel is only enhanced by Kiefer Sutherland in the role of President Tom Kirkman (*Designated Survivor*); though present in the corridors of the White House as Jack Bauer on *24*, this time he is promoted to president.

TV series are now places of hybridization of genres and models of genre (except for original creations, such as *Twin Peaks*, *Six Feet Under*, *24*, *Top of the Lake*, *Orange is the New Black*, and *The Leftovers*, which have become the exception), and so this mix of the classics such as *The West Wing* and *24*—with a touch of *Scandal* and *Homeland*—in *Designated Survivor* has a hard time asserting itself. This is in no small part because it is placed under the *West Wing* umbrella with the arrival of a new advisor with a nimble, sub-Sorkinian repartee (Lyor Boone) and a stronger focus on either recurring characters (Emily Rhodes, the chief of staff, is entitled to a character episode) or those passing through (the captain of the sinking submarine, Gregory Smith, from *Everwood*). The allusions to *The West Wing* multiply and confirm the moral positioning of the series, as expressed by the spokesman Seth Wright (a good and appropriate successor to C.J. Cregg), who is played by Kal Penn, a member of Barack Obama's White House team in real life.

What is striking about this rather average series about an average president is the ordinary ethical demands embodied by its hero, Kirkman. Unlike Jack Bauer, who had a few grey areas (his taste for torture—both active and passive—for obeying absurd orders, and for sacrificial self-destruction), and Josiah Bartlet (with his pride and the liberal snobbery of a Nobel Prize winner for economics), President Kirkman has only one rule of action: to do the right thing, or at least to do the best that he can. A *good enough* president.

We may recall *The West Wing* and the alternate reality that the series offered in the 2000s: Bartlet's fictional team, advised by Bill Clinton's real-life ex-team, expressed a good-natured liberalism and a conversational and geopolitical intelligence that contrasted remarkably well with Bush's warlike and reactionary rhetoric and policies.

---

* This article first appeared in *Libération*, 30 November 2017.

The realism of *The West Wing* was to propose, in a perfectionist way, the possibility of another world and the hope of its realization: Kirkman is not Bartlet, and Trump is not (even) Bush. We get the political series we deserve. Exactly like *The West Wing*, *Designated Survivor*—albeit in a more simplistic and crude way—displays *what is missing*: minimal ethics, a desire for the common good, and attention to the suffering of others.

I am thinking of the series' interesting treatment (s2e4) of the disputed question of the fate of monuments to the glory of the Confederacy, which contrasts pleasantly with the distressing declarations of the White House Secretary General, John Kelly, who described the fight to maintain slavery as 'courageous'. Trump's ignorance is not only a mark of a 'lack of culture' and a refusal of the history marked by the massacre of the American Indians and the struggles for civil rights, but an expression, first and foremost, of an active indifference to injustice and a deliberate absence of compassion and care—expressed explicitly in his contempt for women, American Indians, blacks, the poor, and the handicapped, who are ejected from a citizenship to which he would henceforth set the criteria of membership.

From this perspective, the most political series of the moment is *This Is Us*, which, also in its second season, introduces us to an average white family adopting a black child in the 1980s. Rebecca Pearson's (Mandy Moore) flashback at the very beginning of the second season brings us to the moment in the first (beautifully constructed) episode of the series when, having lost one of her triplets, she allows herself to be convinced by her husband Jack to adopt an abandoned black baby, born on the same day, at the same time, and in the same place: 'This stranger became my child, and this child became my life.'

This is the same spirit behind the remarkable, both cinematographically and politically, miniseries *The People v. O.J. Simpson: American Crime Story*, which revisits the traumatic acquittal of a rich and famous sportsman by a vengeful jury, aided by the racism of the police and a twisted judicial system (which, for once, is cynically reversed in favour of a black man). This Golden Globe-winning work has the strength to expose the effects of a profound rupture that Barack Obama has subsequently sought to repair. At the end of the series, the deputy prosecutor, Christopher Darden, accuses O.J. Simpson's lawyer, Johnnie Cochran: nothing will have changed for black people after the verdict.

Without sentimentality, the realistic (the characters' neuroses and imperfections make them endearing) portrayal in *This Is Us* affirms that America is mixed and multiple in its history and its present. In its us is an us that also figures the US(A) beyond the Pearsons—in the recognition of loss and the past (the series is inhabited by Jack's premature and mysterious death) as a source of self-confidence issues for its children. *This Is Us* (which was largely unpopular with French critics) creates an alternative reality, vulnerable and inclusive, to a world without mercy.

Adèle's Perfectionism

Stanley Cavell defines moral perfectionism as the idea of being faithful to oneself, or, more specifically, to the humanity that is in oneself: 'The soul taking the road (upwards, forwards)' and refusing society in the name of this requirement, and of a culture. Culture here is understood in the sense of *Bildung*—of education, and of the 'popular culture' that, as Cavell, following Emerson, has constantly demonstrated, assumed the task of transmitting and expressing the democratic aspiration—a society where everyone would have his or her rightful voice—whether in Hollywood comedies of remarriage or in dramas of 'unmarriage' and the 'unknown woman'. *Blue Is the Warmest Colour* [*La Vie d'Adèle*] (Abdellatif Kechiche, 2013) inherits both genres, while simultaneously radicalizing democratic stakes.

Everything has been said about *Blue Is the Warmest Colour*: the love, the sex, the suffering; the brutal emotion that the three-hour viewing of the film provokes. What has not been pointed out, however, is that this sharing of emotions is motivated not by any 'universality' of the singular lesbian passion that is told to us, but by what drives the heroine, Adèle, and us with her. It is this perfectionism—even before the encounter, and after the break-up, and beyond—this desire to go outside and ahead of oneself through the education brought about by the encounter with others or with works (Marivaux, as in Kechiche's 2003 film *L'Esquive*, from which *Blue Is the Warmest Colour* directly follows; or painting, as Emma is a student at the Beaux-Arts) that moves Adèle's desire and lack of another life, of a more accurate expression, of a true conversation. Cavell lists, in *Conditions Handsome and Unhandsome*, the fundamentals of perfectionism:

> A mode of conversation between friends (one older and one younger) / one of whom has intellectual authority; because his life is representative or exemplary of a life that is an attraction to the other; and the self recognizes itself chained in this attraction and discovers that it can turn around (convert, revolutionize); a process of education begins in which each self is drawn towards a more advanced state; which finds expression in the dream of a transformation of society.

This is the parallel and perfectionist scenario of *Blue Is the Warmest Colour*. Adèle quietly states—during the dinner scene at the home of Emma's super-tolerant and borderline condescending *bobo* parents—that her goal in life is to become a teacher. The temporality of the film is thus marked by the stages of the love story, but also of her journey from being a good student, to undertaking this profession that allows her to survive the emotions that 'run through her', and to exercise her ability to educate others—us as viewers, as well as her students. There is a dimension of

---

* This article first appeared in *Libération*, 6 November 2013.

friendship in the perfectionist encounter, as in the remarriage (Grant and Hepburn in Cukor's *The Philadelphia Story*): reciprocal moral education and egalitarian transformation of the two elements of the couple, which idealizes the democratic conversation. It is, on the contrary, the impossibility of such a conversation that we find in the (melo)drama genre, where perfectionism must manifest itself and be exercised in other ways—through self-confidence and singular expressiveness, a non-conformist reappropriation (for Adele, as for Ennis and Jack in Ang Lee's *Brokeback Mountain*) of the human. After Nietzsche and Schopenhauer as educators, Adèle as a perfectionist-educator teaches us, through her presence, the reversal of values. Perfectionism is also what allows for the transgression of social inequality inscribed in the credits (the unknown Adèle Exarchopoulos versus the rising star Léa Seydoux). The film highlights Emma's inability to honour the perfectionist demand—to allow herself to be educated reciprocally—and, not without cruelty, the conformism of her cultural discourse. A transgression that explains the controversy surrounding the film is this focus on Adèle's face and the inscription of the character in our experience, thus producing moral perfectionism, far from an abstract quest for the good—a form of life; the 'life' referred to in the film's French title; that is, that of the ordinary vulnerable living being, with its tears—through the miracle of what Cavell calls photogenesis, or the creation of a woman.

The realism of the film is also in this aesthetic, perfectionist, and democratic coup de force: the sharing of the Cannes Palme d'Or (with a jury presided by Steven Spielberg) between the director and the film's actresses, recognition of the collective nature of the work and demystification of the virile figure of the author. The fact that a major daily newspaper devoted its front page to the release of the film in cinemas, which some people were moved by, is recognition of its importance in public life and in our lives as viewers; this, as well as the popular and youthful success (more than 700,000 admissions) of a long and difficult film, including the shooting, is a sign that cinema can bring ethics to life and restore philosophy to its role, to quote Cavell again, of 'educating grownups' through a love of truth that is always revolutionary.

Buffy, Take 1: the Perfectionist Series

It is a happy coincidence that, in the midst of a presidential campaign, the now somewhat conventional Women's Rights Day coincided, on 8 March, with the twentieth anniversary of the first episode of the series *Buffy the Vampire Slayer*. *Buffy*, which managed to blend all the genres and elements of popular culture—vampire show, high school drama, love stories, rock, film and TV—was, first and foremost, a feminist work. Many subsequent series (*Alias, The Walking Dead, The West Wing, Six Feet Under, Scandal, Homeland, House of Cards, Game of Thrones, Unbelievable, Watchmen*) have attempted to promote similarly beautiful heroines: women of action (from Sydney Bristow to Michonne), women of power (from C.J. Cregg to Olivia Pope), proud lesbians (from, well, the women of *The L Word* to many of the heroines of *Orange Is the New Black*), fearsome and fearless mature women (from Ruth Fisher to Catelyn Stark), vulnerable twisted women (from Carrie Mathison to Claire Underwood), feminist cops—the list of female characters who require no male counterpart to become part of our experience goes on and on. The television series of the twenty-first century, ahead of the cinema, is a privileged place for the emergence of women's speech, expressiveness... and heroism.

Buffy, Whedon's masterpiece, has a very special place in this history as the first major illustration of this kind of female presence, and thus a stage in the development of feminism—even a theoretical moment in this history. Whedon had conceived the series as a work intended to morally transform a wide audience from the start: by putting an ordinary young woman capable of fighting vampires to the death on-screen. At first glance, Buffy looks like the pretty blonde girl who is killed in the fifth minute of a horror film; the series reverses this stereotype by having *her* kill vampires.

This proclaimed educational dimension inscribes within the series an ethical and aesthetic ambition to represent the passage to adulthood, and the heroism that consists in surviving it, in all its complexity. *Buffy* undertakes to fully represent these difficulties (introduced metaphorically as demons or supernatural adversaries), and thus give the spectators the tools to recognize and confront them: in other words, *Buffy* asks/allows its viewers to engage in their own moral construction (*Bildung*). Part of this everyday heroism embodied by Buffy is the affirmation of an ethic based on caring for others and protecting those close to us: unlike most superheroines, Buffy has an inner circle, a private life. Emotional ties, vulnerability, friendship, love (Angel! Spike!) are essential to the dynamic of the series, and it is this connection to others that makes Buffy an exception among Slayers. In the mythology of the Buffyverse, the Slayer is chosen by mysterious forces. There is only one in the world: as soon as one Slayer dies, another one is activated. The

---

* This article first appeared in *Libération*, 16 March 2017.

Slayer thus lives by violence and dies alone, her only social bond being a hierarchical submission to her Watcher, a patriarchal figure who supervises, trains, and assigns her missions. This power, initially viewed by Buffy as a curse that prevents her from leading a normal teenage life, will subsequently lead her to regularly sacrifice herself in order to save the world.

What allows Buffy to come to a conclusion and break the prophecy is her transgression of the pattern—she is not alone: she has friends. This, according to Whedon, is 'What really makes her the best Slayer ever.' This teamwork, now called ensemble, is the basis of the dynamic of many of the most beautiful episodes, such as the musical episode of season six, which expresses both the harmony of the group, and Buffy's attempts to make her dissonance heard. Buffy is a formidable Slayer, but she is also in the business of caring for others—not only for the humanity she saves 'many times', but for each and every individual through the special attention accorded to each human. Care is a strength, a 'vocation' of justice, which makes heroism available to all.

Buffy, at the end of the final season, is, for once, in real trouble against an invincible enemy, and takes her fate, and that of the series, into her own hands. The final episode addresses the changing of the rules of the Buffyverse, and rewrites the myth: to win, you have to change the rules of a radically unfair social game: 'In every generation a Slayer is born because a bunch of guys who lived thousands of years ago invented this rule. They were powerful men. So I say we change the rules. I say my power should be our power. From now on, every girl in the world who could be a Slayer will be a Slayer. Every girl who could have power will have power. Every one of us. Take your pick.'

This democratization of heroism makes *Buffy* a particularly powerful and current series—not only because of the feminist lesson, but also because of the confidence it gives to each of us today, in our ability to change the world. Our attachment to the show remains. 'I designed Buffy to be an icon, an emotional experience, to be loved in a way that other shows can't be loved. I wanted it to be a phenomenon in the culture', Whedon said in 2001. This is a prophecy that may undoubtedly be considered fulfilled.

Buffy, Take 2. *Buffy the Vampire Slayer* as Philosophy

Several books have attempted to demonstrate the philosophical interest of *Buffy the Vampire Slayer* series (most notably James B. South, 2011) as a feminist series that not only changed our lives, but also philosophy itself. It is not a collection of examples, nor is it a series that can be used for a philosophy lesson (even if we do so regularly), nor is it a series that can be viewed with a philosophical 'eye' to discover treasures—rather it is a work of philosophy, with its own system, its own universe (the Buffyverse), and its own principles and theories that produce knowledge and education for its viewers. Evoking *Buffy* is never a simple nostalgic and kitschy trip: the series is a lesson in writing, production, and direction, and although it is a commercial series (written, as they all are, for the public), it is also a perfect example of what it means to have to negotiate with constraints... and to magnify them. *Buffy* is a textbook case of the successful marriage between economic rigour and artistic demand, and the ability to improve its audience, while also seeking to please and excite them. Each year, *Buffy* continues to bring in new fans of all ages (even now, a particular new generation of teenagers and young adults are taking to the show), which are the new eyes that keep it alive. As such, *Buffy* is not an object of the past, but remains eternally topical owing to the richness of its discourse and, above all, to its 'kitsch' side, which places it outside any temporality or any fashion effect.

Buffy is the most studied series on an academic level, having given rise to hundreds of journal publications and flourishing American studies (which would also be the case in France if the series were considered as a subject of study equal to the theoretical questions it raises). As such, it continues to be a writing model for a large number of illustrious showrunners in its raising of many philosophically central issues: adolescence and adulthood, death, scepticism, sexuality, language, identity, love, and passion. Though all of these themes can be addressed here, each is intimately intertwined in the series, the story, and the construction of the characters. Here I would particularly emphasize *Buffy*'s work of moral formation. At the time of *Buffy*, TV series were often seen, especially in France, at best as a nice form of entertainment for teenagers and at worst as a dumbing down of the masses; they are now taken more seriously, but often with a dimension of snobbery or elitism. Of course, the turn of our century saw the birth of many powerful and ambitious series (such as *Twin Peaks, Six Feet Under, The Wire, Mad Men, Lost*), but we can rediscover a radically feminist series that is both popular and profound, and that has a real ambition for social and moral transformation with a similar aesthetic and intellectual ambition.

For *Buffy* is not only a masterpiece of structure, with its seven perfectly completed seasons, it is also a work of transformation that speaks of life and

---

* First published as 'Buffy, toutes les fables de ta vie', Isabelle-Rachel Casta dir., Revue Pardaillan n°8, October 2020.

the world, and whose message has lost none of its force. Since the turn of the century, TV series that manage to solve the difficult equation of quality and popular success have multiplied to the point that we can now undoubtedly speak of a golden age or *Cinquecento* of the format, which still does not yet seem to be complete. Their secret lies in the specifically American capacity to produce and transmit values while being concerned with reception, or even education, and avoiding all moralism. If the United States appears today as the leader of this revolution that has made the series format, if not a major art form, then at least an important cultural production, other countries have also been able to invest, sometimes with a certain lead, in quality production: this is the case of Great Britain, which already had a fine tradition in the field, Israel, Denmark (*The Kingdom*, Lars von Trier, DR, 1994–), France (*Engrenages* [retitled *Spiral* for English-speaking markets], *Baron Noir*, *The Bureau*), Spain, and Japan, the latter particularly in the field of manga. While there are many courses on these issues in the United States, and in several European countries, France still seems to be reluctant to consider television series as 'real' works, hence the hesitation to include them in the field of cinema. Progress in this field can only be made when we take seriously the intelligence that is brought to the making of these productions, and when curricula commit to study them systematically in their aesthetics, writing, social effects, and reception, as well as in their ethical and political stakes. *Buffy* is indeed a series that is emblematic, in its quality of writing and philosophical power, of the ambitions of the medium 'series'—it is the most impressive of those remarkable works that are the great television series, which, in five, seven, or even more seasons, have marked generations of viewers.

The value of culture does not lie in the 'great arts', but in its transformative capacity—which is well at work in the series that mark us (viewers of *Buffy*, but also of *Lost* or *Game of Thrones* know this, having seen their lives transformed by them). The educational value of popular culture is not anecdotal; it seems to us to define today what is meant by 'popular' as well as by the word 'culture' (in the sense of *Bildung*) in the expression 'popular culture'. The philosophical relevance of a film, especially a commercial one, is in what it says and how it shows itself—not in what the critics will discover in or elaborate on it; that is to say, it is in the intelligence already applied to its making. This perspective, which Cavell introduced in relation to film, equally applies to television series, and to everything that has to do with the exploration and mixing of genres—art forms that not only keep in touch with the public, but also produce education by creating a specific universe based on, and producing, its own culture. *Buffy* is a perfect example of this, as it refers to the whole of pop culture (music, films, comics), as well as to its own world. Whedon's feminist educational project, which involves not only a role model, but also philosophical and ethical questions that are explored in the analyses presented here, is at the heart of *Buffy*'s intellectual, aesthetic, and moral enterprise.

But what exactly is at stake in *Buffy*'s ability for 'mythmaking'? The key is certainly in the accuracy with which adolescence is represented as a time of transition from one age to another. *Buffy* thus reveals, through the creative syncretism with which it operates in popular culture, to be capable of expressing in a whole (if not perfectly coherent, then at least tangible) living, organic being what is primordially at stake in the sort of rite of passage that, without ritual and without end, constitutes adolescence in developed societies. For behind this age, there is a reality of violence that modern culture imposes on people and their bodies, at the intersection of biological and social data. Many authors insist that (see Allouche and Laugier, 2014) what makes *Buffy* so effective is the way in which it highlights this violence, and even the cruelty, that is expressed in this time of passage, which is at once spectacularized, and yet unformed. The series challenges everyone to find an 'arrangement', whatever it may be, with this primordial Evil—this first of the last season, so foundational to all our existences, and which constantly threatens to cause them to overflow from the outside, the inside, and from below.

Finally, we should recall one of the salient characteristics of this series: among the aspects that most commend *Buffy* to the viewer's attention, is a quality of humour, a virtuosity of dialogue, a sensitivity to language and its uses, and a characteristic mixture of the sublime and the grotesque—all of which play an equally decisive role in the loyalty of its audience to this day. It is indeed the art of conversation, perfectly mastered by *Buffy*'s creators, scriptwriters, and actors at the height of their genius (some of whom we have had the pleasure of seeing again in other flagship series, such as *How I Met Your Mother*, whose conversational art is inherited from *Buffy* as much as from *Friends*). Conversation is at the heart of the series, giving it its particular tone (expressed in a remarkable way in the two emblematic episodes of seasons four and six—the silent episode and the musical episode). This talent for situational speech—the finesse and relevance of its words—is the most important thing left to describe about *Buffy*, alongside Whedon's other series (*Angel*, *Firefly*, *Dollhouse*) that are unrivalled as sites of the culture of ordinary language.

Sensitive Impartiality

In an episode of the first season (1999) of *The West Wing*, White House Chief of Staff Leo McGarry reminds his colleagues (not without eliciting the usual sarcasm) of the origin of the Big Block of Cheese Day that they are about to celebrate—a custom, he claims, which was inherited from President Jackson: a 2-ton piece of cheese is placed at the entrance of the White House where anyone may enter and take a bite, symbolizing the openness of democracy to all. Here, once a year, ordinary citizens may come and present grievances to the president. It is on this day that C.J. Cregg, the White House spokeswoman, learns about environmental demands and the injustice done to animals. The Big Block of Cheese Day returned a year later in the second season of *The West Wing*, this time with the 'social equality cartographers' introducing C.J. (and Josh Lyman) to the inequity of the Mercator projection—a pure expression of spatial inequality through its over-representation of Western countries. In 2014, the Big Block of Cheese Day was, as a tribute to the TV series more than to a fictional tradition, celebrated by the real White House under Obama.

The question that interests me is not (only) that of a cheese that is now available worldwide and yet so little shared; but it is also that of the understanding that emerges in the mind of our dear C.J. owing to the feeling of radical injustice aroused through the description of the situations. It is this emotion that has learning value, both for her and for us. Revisiting scenes from the fifth (and underrated) season of the series *The Wire* (which describes the social situation in Baltimore) with my students in a Master's-level course on moral philosophy, I noticed that the (disgusted) reactions that regularly seize us (when confronted with the lies of a rotten journalist, the renunciations of a politician, and the avoidable death of a young person) are a means of understanding: emotion is not blind but enlightening in the moral distancing that it provokes. In an apparently secondary scene, an Iraq war veteran explodes when reading an article in the Baltimore newspaper that takes liberties with his testimony. The character's emotion, and that of the viewer, who is in turn engaged and enraged, are pathways to the truth; this is what Terry, the raging veteran, is looking for (namely, accuracy and precision: no, the assault did not take place like that; no, 'we did not have coffee, but hot chocolate'). Indignation is not a valorizing feeling that supplements a neutral knowledge or a colouring of reality; it is reality that is revolting, right down to its details.

It is as if the human being (or the researcher) were divided between emotion and analysis,ollaps the activist and the scientist. Yet there is no need to be nobly 'indignant' in the expression of emotion in order for it to move us: Erwing Goffman's anger is cold when he analyses male domination or

---

* This article first appeared in *Libération*, 5 December 2014.

the treatment of the mentally ill or the disabled in *Stigma*; Lincoln's (the character in Spielberg's film) anger is equally icy when he evokes the scandal of slavery. Nor is there any need to stand at a distance, indifferent, in order to understand and to make known 'what is happening'; that emotions and ordinary sensitivity are resources and objects for knowledge is obvious, even banal, but that they are a condition for impartiality and accuracy is still to be discovered—at least for social sciences seeking scientific legitimacy in a false neutrality that only attests to the unjust.

In her article 'The Contribution of Emotions to Impartiality of Decisions', the sociologist Patricia Paperman highlights the role of feelings in the constitution of informed judgements in legal contexts: commitment, attention to the situation, and the voices of each person are not obstacles, but the means to true impartiality. Social and moral reality requires improvisational skills that are not narrowly intellectual, nor a matter of 'pure' feeling. It is this conformist division that blocks a real response—to self-satisfied and guiltless state violence, or to the global injustice revealed by 'occupiers' everywhere.

Valls Undercut by Underwood

No matter how much we criticize *House of Cards* for its increasing implausibility, which makes it more metaphysical than political, we continue to be addicted to it thanks to the incredibly beautiful credits, the top actors—especially the return of Neve Campbell in great form—and of Frank Underwood's (Kevin Spacey) address to the camera, a pleasant form of complicity that gives us the fleeting impression of being as cynical as he is. These transgressive moments of direct address of the spectator, where the 'fourth wall' is broken down, have passed naturally from the theatre to the cinema—I am thinking of the cult scenes, for example, of *Pierrot le fou* (Jean-Luc Godard, 1965), *Ferris Bueller's Day Off* (John Hughes, 1986), or *High Fidelity* (Stephen Frears, 2000)—and then to television series. Yet it would not occur to us to answer Underwood.

It is this form of transgression that is found in the interventions of the *House of Cards* Twitter account regarding global politics: there was the quote from the British prime minister David Cameron at the time of the Panama Papers; then there was the attack on Manuel Valls for using Article 49.3 to pass his government's labour law, accompanied by the quote from Frank Underwood (*House of Cards*, s2e2), 'Democracy is so overrated.' Of course, Netflix, the only broadcaster of the series, has to do its advertising, but Underwood's tweet hit the nail on the head in its ironic collusion with Valls on the vanity of democracy: let's recall that, in the quoted scene, Underwood rejoices in being a hair's breadth away from the presidency of the United States without ever having had any electoral mandate. Valls' response—'Dear Frank, democracy is the worst regime, except for all the others'—is fortunately ten times less retweeted, largely for its pitifulness: first, for having replied ('Dear Frank'), and then its politeness (although not without embarrassment, as the emoticon ☺ betrays), to a fictional character who has nothing to recommend him (let's remember that at the beginning of season two, in addition to his schemes to become vice-president, Underwood has just pushed a young woman under the metro train); for its praise of the merits of democracy, when the point of Underwood's tweet was evidently not to mock democracy, but rather to denounce, through irony, the non-respect of its principles; then to give himself lessons in democracy by quoting Churchill, recycling in warmongering style the ultra-used reference to 'the exception of all others'; and finally, to have no other conception of democracy than as institutional regime, and failing to imagine for a moment—unlike Churchill and even Underwood—a different definition of democracy as respect, or even expression, of the will of citizens through a form of common life.

On this occasion we may detect a new positioning of *House of Cards*— initially a sort of grating and disillusioned negative of *The West Wing*, and henceforth a ruthless watchdog of the denials of democracy of which its

---

* This article first appeared in *Libération*, 26 May 2016.

hero has become the specialist. The rise of Claire Underwood's character (and Robin Wright's) has a pedagogical value, familiarizing the public with a woman in power, similar to the way in which the first seasons of *24* unintentionally accustomed the audience to a black president.

House of Cards is gradually bringing the previously unserious Claire Underwood onto the presidential ticket and into fictional equality—by the end of the season, she too breaks through the fourth wall, and it's rather chilling. The number of strong women in this fourth season (the men are often, let's face it, clowns) is impressive, from the appearance of Claire's mother (Ellen Burstyn) and her advisor Leann Harvey, to the characters of Cathy Durant, Heather Dunbar, Jackie Sharp, Kate Baldwin. The alliance of all these formidable women signals the emergence of the soft power of TV series.

In a more parodic vein, in a recent episode of *Scandal*, the heroine and campaign manager for former First Lady Mellie Grant, Olivia Pope (black icon Kerry Washington), retorts to a candidate who says, 'It's time for a black president': 'It's time for a woman president!' This intervention of series' characters and creators in political life—of which Manuel Valls was a victim—reveals the educational, social, and political ambition of these works, which faithfully prolongs those of the classics *The West Wing*, *ER*, and *The Wire*. It joins the realistic ambition of *Homeland*, which modified the dialogues of its fifth season after the November attacks, and that of the excellent *The Bureau*—TV series that, with remarkable political accuracy and through its endearing characters and highly talented actors, manage to captivate and educate the citizen, now considered capable of understanding and judging the stakes of geopolitics and terrorism. This is another lesson in *real* democracy.

Fiction Overcomes Politics

Just like *House of Cards*, the series *Baron Noir* depicts a political world from which ideals have disappeared; unlike the American series, however, there is still a will that resists even when everything goes wrong. It is not because of the name of the president (his name is Laugier) that I want to mention *Baron Noir*, which doesn't need any more praise—rather, it is for the taste and tone that it gives to politics. Here I am talking about politics as a form of human life, not just as institutions and powers (presidential, legislative, etc.) or its elections, parties, and intrigues.

It is interesting that it is thanks to a real political series that European series as a whole are moving up a gear to finally enter into real competition—if not commercial, then at least political and moral—with American productions. Already, *Borgen*, a modest Danish opus, has succeeded (in an unpredictable way) in raising the stakes of a political life driven by a form of individual moral requirement. Nevertheless, *Borgen* remains anchored in the life of central power, in a constant back and forth between the intimate (the personal and family life of a woman who claims to be ordinary), and governance. With *Baron Noir*, we have a constant back and forth between the presidential or ministerial palaces, and the terrain of local struggles—crises and misery in the north of France; that is, between institutional and daily political life. It is in this back and forth that democratic life is invented and deepened. A literal representation of the return journey is the constant car journeys made between the two locations of the series by its hero, Philippe Rickwaert (Kad Merad), a member of parliament and mayor of Dunkirk who was dropped in the first episode by the future president, his mentor Laugier (Niels Arestrup), who (temporarily) regains a foothold in both his fiefdom, and (strangely enough) in his party, in order to return to the action.

A story of personal vengeance and political revenge, *Baron Noir* appears, at first glance, to follow the plotline of *House of Cards* in season one (where we saw the calculating Francis Underwood (Kevin Spacey) betrayed by the president he helped to get elected, subsequently regain power, and become vice-president, only to then finally oust the president himself), but this is not really what *Baron Noir* is about; the real point of reference is not *House of Cards* and its cynicism of politics in the style of 'all is rotten'. Despite (or because of) its great acuity, *Baron Noir* is instead a manifesto for political life. In this sense, it is a direct descendant of Sorkin's series *The West Wing* in its serialization of what really drives the characters and what attaches us to them and that life (which one would almost dare to call bio-political)— which is something quite different from the purely calculating and ultimately abstract ambition of *House of Cards*: the desire to move towards a slightly better world and towards a more evolved version of oneself.

---

* This article first appeared in *Libération*, 1 February 2018.

The universe of *The West Wing* was protected neither from cynicism nor betrayal, but was driven by an ethical ambition, at a time (the turn of the century and the gloomy Bush years) when the Bartlet presidency presented an alternative political reality (fictional, democratic) to a reactionary state. *House of Cards*—also set among the Democrats—signalled the end of this utopia once Obama was elected to the White House. This was not because of any disappointment, but simply because there was no longer room for an alternative world. *Baron Noir*, too, represents politics as it is, here and now, real and imperfect, in a world where the ideal has disappeared, but where, unlike in *House of Cards*, political will survives. The naïve belief in progress is replaced by the question of what anyone may do in situations of real threat, or even catastrophe.

Baron Noir proposes a vision of politics anchored in ordinary and local life—whereas *House of Cards* remains an icy game of intrigue between the House of Representatives, parties, and the White House—not as a subject for a series, but as a tool for confronting reality. 'We wanted to talk about France and the best vehicle for this is politics,' says Eric Benzekri, one of the authors.

The West Wing, which is certainly more concerned with societal issues (the death penalty, poverty, abortion, terrorism, etc.), only confronts its heroes with this terrain exceptionally. The ambition of *Baron Noir*, beyond the anecdote, is in its desire to ask concrete questions (for instance, of the euro and unemployment) at the level of the city; to place politics elsewhere than in its institutional structures; and to pay attention to the details (the series is written, as was *The West Wing*, with input from experts). None of the characters is nice (this is a modern TV series), and even those who wish to embody goodness or greatness are deluding themselves; all of them, however, live from politics (for instance, the hero, the impressive Kad Merad, who manages to embody a form of charisma of the average man). The artfulness of *Baron Noir* is in using the potential of the series medium by investing it in ordinary politics, and vice versa: the genre of political series has thus perhaps crossed the Atlantic.

The second season of *Baron Noir* succeeds, despite the real political situation being turned upside down in 2017, in depicting the stakes of power in France. One is surprised by a twinge of sadness when one sees the historic headquarters of the Socialist Party on the screen (which is not a carefully designed reconstruction, but the private mansion on the Rue de Solférino, rented to the production last July—after the apocalypse of the presidential and legislative elections, and before it was put up for sale). This effect of combined reality and nostalgia sums up the principle of *Baron Noir*. How can a series rooted in the life of the Socialist Party, and which even describes its degeneration, find renewed strength? Beyond its remarkable actors and the deepening of its characters—in particular Rickwaert, a politician who finds his resilience in the strength of his ideas and in the strategies he uses to orchestrate them, the power of the series lies in its communicative taste for politics and in its reflexivity. Like its hero, it maintains and strengthens itself in spite of and in the face of adversity, adapting to new situations, however impossible they may appear to be.

The events of 2017 could, and should, have rendered *Baron Noir* and its political ambition irrelevant (a series about the Socialist Party, a fictional character based on a generation of socialists—Dray, Cambadélis, Aubry—swept aside by the Macronist wave, and a second season premised on a socialist presidency seemed implausible). One might therefore wonder how the series could survive this 'new world', where reality had 'surpassed fiction': a scriptwriter could never have imagined Trump or Macron, one might have said. In fact, they could—and, indeed, *Baron Noir* is further proof of the power of fiction when it is ahead of reality. We can recall that the series *24*, which featured an anti-terrorism hero and the first black president on-screen, was pitched, and its first season produced, just before the attacks of September 11, 2001. There is also *House of Cards*, which we now like to decry as cruelly describing, already in 2014, the abuse of power by a president perverting the political system. Similarly, *The West Wing*, as early as 2004, imagined the campaign of President Bartlet's successor, a Hispanic congressman, Matt Santos, whose biographical profile, positioning, and slogan ('Hope is real') were inspired by a young and brilliant politician from Illinois, Obama, who was not even in the Senate at the time.

The first season of *Baron Noir* presented us with the rise of Amélie Dorendeu (Anna Mouglalis), a former student of the École nationale d'administration never confronted with universal suffrage, who passed through the European Commission, from advisor to the redoubtable President Laugier, to the position of first secretary of the Socialist Party, and on the track to the presidency of the Republic. Dorendeu was elected at the beginning of season two, which puts the Macron surprise into perspective: his victory, far from being a success story, is the logical conclusion of a slow cultural process towards right-wing politics. History is organized differently in *Baron Noir*'s season two than in reality, and the union of the socialists with the right is achieved under jihadist and Front National pressure—but this is the fiction that, here, trivializes reality that falls far short of the ideals that give *Baron Noir* its innovative vitality: France is still far from the possibility of a woman president. One cannot help but compare Dorendeu's stature, reigning alone at the Elysée, to the current situation of the Socialist Party, where four men are fighting for the leadership of the party. Female figures are often strong in *Baron Noir*, which, following on from *Borgen*, takes on the educational task of representing and empowering a female president.

This desire to do better than reality highlights the theoretical ambition of the series. *Baron Noir* shows that politics still exists: even if the series takes place for the most part at 'Solfé' and the Elysée, real democratic life is woven into the actions on the ground, such as in the citizens' assemblies in the suburbs or in Dunkirk. As such, *Baron Noir*, like its hero, tries to imagine what a left-wing policy would be in this new world, which is hard on the underprivileged under the hypocritical domination of benevolent speeches. The political series is not only a genre, but a tool for confronting reality.

A curious feature of the characters in *Baron Noir* is that they all make their living from politics—literally: it is the fight for ideas that gives life and revives new hope. The year 2017 saw the discrediting of a political class, which was ready to do whatever it took to cling to its power, to the benefit of movements from civil society; in 2018, however, things are changing again: civil society is becoming the horizontal world of the immanent mobilization of society against inequalities, for rights for all—not the verticality of power and the conformism of elected officials and governors recruited on the basis of CVs. Between the two, citizens, politicians, and women still have a new role to imagine.

Serial Patriarchy

In the third season of *Baron Noir*, which follows the journey of Philippe Rickwaert (Merad), the brilliant and calculating socialist MP and mayor of Dunkirk who is destined for national success, the most fascinating character is perhaps not the main one. Rather, the series is unique in that it also tells the story of the meteoric rise of a woman, Amélie Dorendeu (Mouglalis), who in the first season struggles to become the first secretary of the Socialist Party, and in the second, in a surprising turn of events, is elected following a duel with the extreme right. As a result, she becomes the first woman president of the Republic at the age of 39.

Fiction has often been used in American or Scandinavian series to explore political hypotheses, such as the first black president of the United States elected in 2002 on *24*. *Baron Noir* similarly foreshadowed Macron's election by putting Dorendeu into orbit in season one, but also went further into political realism in season two, where Dorendeu is elected by bringing together the centre and by exploding a Socialist Party undermined by internal conflicts, hatreds, and the sclerosis of old elected officials clinging to their seats. The Macronian profile is recognizable in a young president who has never known the local political terrain, promotes a liberal policy, and works to bring elected representatives from civil society into the Assembly. Mouglalis admitted that she immediately signed up because 'Scriptwriters who, even before Macron was elected, decided to put a 39-year-old woman at the head of the state are on to a good thing.' Nevertheless, Dorendeu is going to pay a high price for being a woman: in this third season, she attracts the hatred of the political milieu, which is united against her, as well as that of many of her fellow citizens, who find her distant and snobbish. She will be much less easily forgiven than her male counterpart.

Dorendeu is beautiful and intelligent, with the oddity of a deep, unfeminine voice. It is particularly interesting that the writers did not try to make her sympathetic (like Birgitte Nyborg in *Borgen*)—she is much less sympathetic than Rickwaert, which is indicative of a moral progress in the political TV series of our century: they do not necessarily show us nice women. What characterizes Dorendeu in particular is also her feminism, which is made especially clear in the last episode, when she revisits her intellectual training (Beauvoir, whom Mouglalis also embodied), while putting away her books (just like *The West Wing*'s President Bartlet on his departure, emptying his library in which we see Foucault's *Society Must be Defended*). We recall a scene in season two when, freshly elected, she pays her respects at the tomb of the great feminist Hubertine Auclert, a moment that serves to educate the audience of the series by evoking a feminist heroine who fought for women to have the right to vote and to stand for election (breaking a ballot

---

* This article first appeared in *Libération*, 5 March 2020.

box at a polling station in 1908 during the municipal elections in Paris, where, in 2020, there are three women competing for the mayor's seat).

Dorendeu's feminism is emphasized throughout the entire season, for instance in scenes such as her explanation to her new lover and advisor that she cannot afford to have a public relationship because, as a woman, she would be reduced to her relationships and her politics would no longer be discussed. The strength of her character is in her lucidity and ability to analyse the patriarchal structure that her election threatens to undermine. Indeed, her fate—the hatred she arouses, and the final humiliation in which she is forced to declare herself unfit for re-election in order to prevent a worrying demagogue from coming to power, and, in doing so, deny all feminist ambitions—illustrates the power of the patriarchy that Carol Gilligan talks about in her recent book *Why Does Patriarchy Persist?* For Gilligan, inventor of the ethic of care, patriarchy is not a system of domination but a force—a culture—of the taking down of women who are subjected to violence as soon as they attack traditional hierarchy.

This patriarchy in the world of cinema has recently been denounced—whether it be in the form of the predominance of male heroes and subjects, or the monopoly of men on symbolically valued functions, such as that of director. The rage over Polanski being honoured at the César Awards is entirely justified, not because a film by an artist with a troubled past was being rewarded, but because the dominant male community was rewarding a man for that past, and thereby seizing the opportunity to humiliate women who encroached on its territory. This reveals a patriarchal culture rooted in the rhetoric of the 'author' that is often maintained by critics, and thus a form of violence that must be fought with new weapons.

TV series, like women, are historically a devalued format. Undoubtedly owing to a reception that was built not in cinemas but in the domestic universe, they have developed a culture that has fought or deflected the patriarchy, from such classics as *Buffy* and *Sex and the City* to today's *Homeland*, *The Handmaid's Tale*, and *Killing Eve*. *Baron Noir*, a series almost as masculine as the political universe it describes, illustrates this discreet counter-power of series in putting women forward: Dorendeu's trajectory is part of the ability of *Baron Noir* to give meaning to political speeches and battles.

Ethics and Politics of *The Walking Dead*

If the mythical series *The Walking Dead* is running out of steam at the end (actually, at the beginning) of its eighth season, it's not just because we've lost too many characters or because Andrew Lincoln, the main actor, can't take any more transatlantic travel: it's that it has gone through the cycle of the loss of the human life form, destroyed in stages in every episode of the series that sees a small group of humans attempting to survive and organize themselves in a world populated by the undead. After telling his group in one of the very first episodes of the first season, 'We don't kill the living', Rick gradually gives up, swept away by the violence of this universe, and turns on his fellow humans (enemies and friends alike) with or without reason. An invisible line is crossed again in the last season during a shoot-out in which he coldly shoots an ally from an opposing group, despite the same man previously saving his life: the ethical question, or rather the radicality of his loss, thus runs through the entire season, at the close of which Rick will (spoiler alert) end up sparing his enemy, the cruel Negan—a terrifying character who at times comes to embody the small remnant of humanity preserved in the war between humans.

The spin-off, *Fear the Walking Dead* (Kirkman & Erickson, AMC, 2015–), reflexively addresses this evolution of characters and viewers by taking us back, in its excellent first season, to a pre-zombie period when common moral sensibilities still existed: in the striking pilot pre-credits, we see one of the heroes, Nick, being stalked by an early Walker, being hit by a car, and, to our astonishment, eliciting collective reactions of 'normal' compassion and help—thereby making us realize not only that the scene is 'before' the outbreak, but also that we ourselves are desensitized. Thus, *FeIthe Walking Dead* was less a prequel than an empirical revelation of the moral transformation wrought by our sharing of Rick's gang's journey. Nevertheless, it followed the same inevitable trajectory too soon: its new season segues directly into *The Walking Dead* season eight by picking up a central character, Morgan, who joins the small group fro*lar the Walking Dead* and effectively merges the two series. A clue to the loss of the life form that haunts bollapsethe collapse of conversation, loss of the common language of the groups scattered across post-apocalyptic America, the gradual end of any common cultural reference, and the absence of a stable term, from Georgia to California, to designate these Walkers (Rangers, Rottens, Biters, Eaters, Infected…).

As a result, we are particularly sensitive to the survival of humanity in the equally violent, but this time closed, universe of the phenomenon series of the moment, *La Casa de Papel*. In what looks like a banal robbery story, albeit politicized by its stakes (the massive manufacture of currency), what is touching about the series is the way in which, through the construction

---

* This article first appeared in *Libération*, 26 April 2018.

of the characters and the relationships that are woven into the ephemeral community of the hostage-taking, both life and humanity 'grow' on the smooth and sterile floor of a palace of the Mint, which is cut off from the rest of the world. Somewhat like *Lost*, another series that elaborates on a society in a state of confinement, in *La Casa de Papel* we witness the creation of a vital fragility, a network of new relationships that recall various occupy movements of our century; inventing all over the world forms of democratic life that exemplify the demand for a less unequal world. But it also reminds us—and this is the constantly nostalgic dimension of both utopian and dystopian series—that we are no longer in the time of the Puerta del Sol, or even of the Paris Nuit Debout (which some had already tried to disqualify by accusations of violence and disorder), and the utopian society is no longer available to everyone. The decade, opened by the various democratic springs, will end with 'zones to defend', organized occupations against attacks from the outside world, like the temporary citadels of *The Walking Dead*.

Occupy Wall Street was approved (verbally) by Barack Obama, and indeed Syriza was largely used as a political model (for a while), but today's occupiers are systematically discredited (agitators, zoners, anarchists...), in a moral manner above all (filthy addicts to drugs and sex, destroyers of public property). It is easy to forget that the disobedients of the last century, such as King or Mandela, or (less nobly, but in the same spirit) the rebellious students of 1968, were already denounced as cowards and scum in the face of the moral order of the conformism to a majority's 'common sense'. To overlook this is to deny or legitimize the unprecedented harshness of a national repression in this century that, even if it managed to avoid the worst, aims at eradicating new forms of social and environmental organization; forms that are not costly for the state and are in line with the autonomy often complacently claimed by politicians for 'their' good citizens. It is now a matter of criminalizing forms of life and the behaviour of citizens who want to exemplify them—a good sequel to *The Walking Dead*.

The End of Innocence

It is rather surreal at the moment to follow (still addicted to Claire Danes) season five of the series *Homeland*, which introduces us to a gang of bearded terrorists plotting a mass attack... in Berlin. *Homeland*, since its excellent debut in 2011, has focused on post-9/11 espionage, and from the outset has concentrated on the fight against terrorism *within* American borders—with the primarily thread being the infiltration of Nicholas Brody (Damian Lewis), a sergeant in the US Marine Corps and a former prisoner of war who has been 'turned' by an Islamist leader (on his release, he is welcomed as a hero on American soil, though subsequently unmasked by a slightly nutty CIA officer).

For two seasons (four and five, so much better than two and three), *Homeland* has had its theatre of action in the Middle East and in Europe, and though, like *24*, of which it is the worthy heir, it claims to be fiction, it also uses attachment to its characters, preferably twisted, to involve us in real political issues. Its role goes further than simply this, however. Where we would have spoken, until recently, of manipulation, today, more aware of the limits of our expertise in the effects of propaganda, we would say that *Homeland* is part of an American strategy of creating a fictional universe specific to the fight against terrorism. The series is known and criticized for its caricatured approach to both the logic and work of intelligence, and to Arab countries and cultures: we remember the street artists, commissioned by the production of *Homeland* to 'decorate' a street scene with graffiti, producing the beautiful Arabic inscriptions ('*Homeland* is racist') that we see in the background of the episode. Alex Gansa, creator of the series, claimed that he would have preferred to have spotted the images before broadcast, but that since *Homeland* was meant to be subversive and open to discussion, he could only 'admire this act of artistic sabotage'.

In doing so, the producer recognized the role of political fiction—the heuristic role of forming a community, capable, even in the face of surprise, of resisting, not through armed mobilization, but through a better understanding of the causes. *Homeland* has not only endeavoured to raise awareness of the terrorist threat and the fact that the worst is always to come, but also to make us attentive and alert to the invisible threat, as opposed to simply visible signals: Carrie Mathison, entranced in front of her surveillance screen while scrutinizing Nicholas Brody's intimate life in the first episodes, is the most disturbing and striking image of the whole series—because it transforms the viewer by making us all spies, and putting us all in charge of surveillance, to be on the alert, or 'on the lookout', in the words of the heroine of *The Fighters* (Thomas Calley, 2014) in the final image of the film.

---

* This article first appeared in *Libération*, November 2015.

Homeland has thus set itself the task of making the public see and understand the causes, not the consequences, of terror; of highlighting, season after season, the role and responsibility of the United States in the attacks on its soil; and of showing the dangers for democratic life and the ideals of the nation that come with reinforced, and not necessarily effective, surveillance. Fiction thus plays a crucial role in the constitution of a new post-attack culture, and in the fight against violence—which must employ the very same weapons that have since been borrowed by the Islamic State in its propaganda techniques.

It is interesting to see how the series has impacted political reality by giving the public a reading of events that followed, such as the wiretapping of Chancellor Merkel or the return of Private Bergdahl. Where *24* was a product of terror, *Homeland* redefines the nation (hence its title, which is increasingly meaningful) by showing its effects and causes. It reflects the end of innocence and, above all, of a mistaken, even selfish, sense of security, especially in regard to the limits of a political ideal confronted by catastrophe.

This moment is that of a disaster or threat—with the recent attacks in France,[1] and then, to a lesser extent, with the political division of the country and the isolation of its most vulnerable communities. At this time, what is important is to utilize and disseminate *all* means of understanding, so as to rely on public education as the foundation of democracy. This is the task of culture, whether popular or 'high' (and we must not hesitate to pursue it here as elsewhere); it is also the task of knowledge—of the causes, effects, and vulnerabilities of our societies, as well as of the risks we can really take, for ourselves and for democracy—which is our primary resource.

Hence the need for concrete commitment to and the implementation in society—particularly in France—of the immense knowledge that already exists around the issues of terrorism, war, and geopolitics. I am not talking about self-proclaimed intellectuals who, a few hours after the killings, before the victims had even been buried, nobly took the floor in order to occupy a (well-secured) stage with their more or less adjusted moralizing interventions. I am talking about the researchers and specialists who, for several weeks now, have been offering us analyses and ways of understanding, preventing, and, in short, defending society with our weapons of democracy, education, and knowledge.

---

1 This column was published after the Friday 13 November 2015 Paris and Saint Denis attacks including a mass shooting at a concert in the Bataclan theatre.

Human Security

Those faithful to the series have noticed that *Homeland*, which, following a breathless and innovative first season, subsequently degenerated, having dragged the character of Brody (the US marine now plotting against the government) through two additional painful seasons, has since become excellent again (while you weren't watching). The storyline of the heroine, Carrie Mathison (Claire Danes), a CIA agent who is constantly on the edge, has adjusted, and consequently become both believable and exciting.

It must be said that things have changed in recent years, and 'security' series have established themselves as a genre that, beyond suspense and personal intrigue, expresses a real vision of national and human security as something that presents a shared challenge for democracies. Like the remarkable *The Bureau* in France, *Homeland* is a realistic production that, aimed at the general public, represents and expresses both the multiform threats and risks that make up the current security environment and the work that must be done to describe and anticipate these threats. The fifth season of *Homeland*, written in 2014 and broadcast during the November 2015 attacks in Paris, initially featured European jihadist cells, though the crew changed the dialogue in post-production and, some months after the shooting, added the voice of a character in the background. This ADR (Additional Dialogue Recording) sums up the ambition of *Homeland*, differentiating it from its glorious predecessor *24* that was primarily aimed at expressing the threat in the aftermath of 9/11: in contrast to *24*, *Homeland* is committed to adhering to reality, and thereby to informing, educating, and preventing—indeed, the showrunners, Howard Gordon and Alex Gansa, worked in cooperation with real intelligence experts. The originality of the series has thus been the redefinition of the contemporary terrorist threat through the figure of the homegrown terrorist, which, as recent horrors attest, has become a French speciality.

It is exciting to see how the show, which features a (strong) female president (a character also written and programmed well in advance) was, in the wake of Trump's election, taking into account the new political reality to transform the character into a megalomaniac dictator who decided to silence the opposition and imprison most of the independent officials in her administration. One of the most lucid educational aspects of this new season concerns the fatal and targeted circulation of fake news in a moment of crisis (a fabricated image, 'revealing' that the FBI was responsible for the death of a child). While 'fake news' is a term that has become a trademark of Trump's communication, *Homeland* demonstrates its relevance and manipulative power to cast suspicion on communities and governments and destroy national solidarity: the real enemy within is the divisions and tensions that fake news stirs up, weakening the social fabric.

---

* This article first appeared in *Libération*, 29 March 2018.

President by Accident

Jack Bauer is back, this time as an accidental president, in *Designated Survivor*, an ABC series that has been airing since September. Here, Kiefer Sutherland plays Tom Kirkman, an obscure Secretary of Housing and Urban Affairs, who is thrust into the Oval Office after an explosion wipes out nearly every member of Congress and government, including the president and the vice-president, who were assembled for the symbolic State of the Union address. As a result, Kirkman finds himself managing both the investigation of the attack and his position as president, being the 'designated survivor'—by virtue of his very obscurity—in the event of a catastrophe. This reversal is the success of the series' pilot, which is exemplary.

With its release in dribs and drabs by Netflix, *Designated Survivor* can be taken as anti-binge-watching therapy (reversing the effects of spending weekends or nights watching all the episodes of a season, or even an entire series), or perhaps as a loyalty strategy. Its cheapness has aroused mixed interest among critics, and yet, like most American viewers, we anxiously await the arrival of new episodes. As such, the series-loving public has recently been rediscovering the joys of the weekly rhythm, that twentieth-century antique.

The primary assets of *Designated Survivor* are *24* and Sutherland. Of course it's Jack Bauer we find in the character, even if in a hollow way: it is amusing to see the actor laboriously give in to the role of the model family man, as a president who panics and runs to vomit in the toilet—proof that the background of the past and future roles that actors and actresses play determines the perception we have of them and their characters. Jack Bauer has been around presidents long enough to make his promotion visually believable, and we find Jack's same masochism, that pathological tendency to sacrifice for America, in Kirkman. The president of *Designated Survivor*, however, suffers a series of humiliations—from surviving political rivals who call him a loser, to journalists who raise the issue of his scheduled ouster from office.

The role of President of the United States is a tired and worn-out mantra: after *The West Wing* and the brilliant Bartlet, the Nobel Prize winner in economics and exemplary liberal, we had *House of Cards* and Frank Underwood, a cunning yet fascinating scoundrel, via David Palmer or Fitzgerald Grant, the sentimental president of *Scandal*. Kirkman, by contrast, is the ordinary, accidental (I didn't say 'normal') president, the 'anybody', whose good will and attention to the lives of his fellow citizens, can, as the series shows, reinstate the Union with the help of a spokesman, Kal Penn, an actor who has also worked in the Obama administration.

24 began, by chance, in the aftermath of the September 11 attacks, and marked the first of the 'security' series that have remained emblematic of the Bush years, and of a revelation of the vulnerability of the dominant. *Designated Survivor*, which opens on the smoking ruins of the Capitol, will remain,

---

* This article first appeared in *Libération*, 22 December 2016.

equally by accident, the series emblematic of another disaster: the election of Trump, with the revelation of the deep division of a nation and the fragility of its institutions. With its cheapness and genre-mixing plot—the *Homeland*-like anti-terrorist investigation, family chronicle, and political series—*Designated Survivor* improvises, like its hero, a new form of power to suggest that real democracy is not to be found in electoral devices or institutions, but in the moral capacities of ordinary citizens.

Legendary Realism

It is funny that it is when a series is appreciated by official critics—not merely by the fans and amateur or informal critics by whom it has been revered since its inception—that we hear the inevitable phrase 'lettres de noblesse'.[2] Does this still mean anything? It seems to imply that some form of validation is needed for mainstream productions to rise above pure entertainment or average taste, or for television series to be considered as an essential place of aesthetic and political creativity. One such example that has been so appreciated by the critics, is the return of *The Bureau* (*Le Bureau des Légendes*, *LBDL*) for an excellent fourth season; it is true that Eric Rochant's series is the best example of the security genre, which has flourished since the beginning of the twenty-first century with cult series such as *24*, *Homeland*, and *Fauda*, all devoted to the fight against terrorism. *LBDL* is also further proof that the United States has lost its domination on serial creativity; this was first evident with *Borgen* and *Hatufim*, but now all of Europe, from England to Italy, Germany, Spain, and Israel, which produce excellent political series; American series, by contrast, are exhausted by niche internet formatting.

The strength of *LBDL* lies in its ambition—the quality of the narrative, the writing of the characters, and its actors—which allows it to escape the usual analyses of security series. For this reason, it is not a 'mirror of society', nor an ideological support; but a concrete and realistic tool for democratic action, through its educational value and its political and moral training of a public that is, for once, genuinely taken seriously. From the opening episode, the series teaches the viewer how the Directorate General for External Security (DGSE) works step by step, and presents, from the first season, the main geopolitical crises in the Arab-Muslim world in a clear and competent manner. The stakes of the war in Syria, but also of the departures of young Frenchmen, are carefully explained (a form of 'care' of the public) without ever being pedagogical, transmitted in the form of dialogues, in pairs or in meetings, or comments around large maps and computer screens. Season four added an extra level of complexity to this depiction, with the presentation of cyber-attacks and digital espionage, where the viewer emerges enlightened (and frightened), and more competent.

It is also the aesthetic and pedagogical ambition of *LBDL* to anchor the political analysis in the human ('human is better', Sylvain Ellenstein, a character who will be at the heart of the fourth season in many ways, explicitly claims in front of his geeky acolytes): the primary resource of intelligence, beyond the technologies described (there again, the law of the genre), are the infiltrated agents, contacts, and informants, with their interactions and

---

* This article first appeared in *Libération*, 1 November 2018.

---

2 Lettres de noblesse were documents establishing that a person was noble. The phrase is used figuratively to denote recognition of competence from a person's peers.

ways of being. This human material provides the series with its particular moral density, as well as the best vector for the difficult issues—especially its magnificent and endearing characters, 'Malotru' (Mathieu Kassovitz), but also the seemingly supporting ones, above all Marie-Jeanne (Florence Loiret-Caille), Marina (Sara Giraudeau), Raymond (Jonathan Zaccaï), and other seemingly secondary characters, such as Sylvain or, more recently, Jonas, to whom we become attached over the course of the seasons. These human connections allow moral conflicts to be expressed, such as the one that emerges in this fourth season between Marie-Jeanne and Raymond over their supposed indulgence of Malotru, but they are also the electric bearers of the tension that runs through *LBDL*: between personal affects and professional duty, between loyalty to imperatives and to loved ones—in other words between justice and care. Malotru takes this tension to its highest degree, precisely because of his perfectionist will to be loyal from and in his very betrayal; he is the most imperfect and the most sincere of all.

This final season adds a more radical element of reflexivity for the viewer who has already had the opportunity to ponder the effect on themselves of the loss of Duflot (J.P. Darroussin)—and learning to live without such a guide. Duflot is led to question, under the merciless eye of a new character, JJA (Mathieu Amalric), his own attachment to Malotru… and to *The Bureau*. JJA (a nickname taken from James Jesus Angleton, a dangerous paranoid US counter-intelligence man of the 1950s) considers Malotru, the traitor, to have been toxic to the entire service ('He's a virus and you're giving him away'), and therefore his actions have been driven by a constant obsession to 'get Malotru back'—recovery meaning redemption. Interestingly, this thesis of JJA, which really describes the driving force of the series since season two, positions him as the 'villain' in the viewer's eyes, who is able to see that he too is affected, irreparably. The way in which the series reflects (on) its effect, opening the viewer's eyes to their own blindness, but also allowing them to understand how and why they hold on to it, is not the smallest of the feats and surprises of season four: among them is the analyst Jonas' passage on the ground—similar to that of the heroine of *Zero Dark Thirty* (Kathryn Bigelow, 2012) or, more cheaply, the new *Jack Ryan* (Carlton Cuse & Graham Roland, Amazon Prime, 2018–)—which shows the entanglement of abstract geopolitics and the bloody reality of sacrificed or heroic lives (such as the encounter with the battalion of female Yezidi fighters; the constantly astonishing courage of the frail Marina). The resistance of women, in a world where misogyny, East and West, is on full display, depicts feminism in all its shades of legendary realism.

A Paper House

For those who like to devote their weekends to serious binge-watching, *La Casa de Papel*, a Spanish series directed by Álex Pina that aired in 2017 on the Antena 3 channel in Spain, is an excellent choice. It has even been re-cut by Netflix, which has globalized it into the addictive standard format episodes (around fifty minutes), and, like the mythical *24* in its time, it seamlessly sequences episodes by restarting each episode with the final images of the previous one. *La Casa de Papel* allows us to see the transformations that are at work in the world of television series, which are no longer restricted to the English-speaking world—even if American series continue to dominate. Old Hollywood domination has been internalized, it seems, to the point that Europe continues to underestimate its own production, despite the fact that, in the recent years, following the rise of the Scandinavian countries (*Borgen*, *The Killing*, *Broen*), Israel (*Hatufim*, *Fauda*, *BeTipul*), France (with, among others, *The Bureau*), and Italy (with *Gomorrah* and *Suburra*) have also entered the international competition for top-level series. One can imagine that (like *Hatufim* or *Broen* or *The Killing*) the Spanish series will also be adapted into English; but as it stands, its success is already remarkably broad and international, despite the irony of certain French critics, who have suddenly become demanding in terms of sexism or script construction. *La Casa de Papel*—anchored, like the best French productions, in the reality of the time and of Europe—is an event: aesthetic and political.

The series draws its tension and strength from its topicality. If the Spanish series is addictive, it is not only because of its narrative device worthy of *24*, where we follow the occupation of the palace and the escape of the group almost in real time (the action of the twenty-three episodes takes place over less than five days), but it is also for the originality of its set-up, the power of its characters, and the strength of its message. It is a classic heist story, with the usual elements (team recruitment, meticulous preparation, invasion, hostage-taking, negotiation, violence, release), but it is less in the tradition of *Ocean's Eleven* (Ted Griffin, 2001), *Inside Man* (Spike Lee, 2006), and *The Town* (Ben Affleck, 2010) -style heist films—to name but a few in which we experience sympathy for the thugs—though it is clear from its first images that the series will play in this category. The contrast comes from the usual constraints of the robbery—speed, stealth, escape—being reversed; rather, it is about the group of robbers *lasting*. This need to settle down and 'hold on' places them less in the tradition of armed robbery than of occupation, and their inspiration is drawn less from popular culture than political culture: it is to the occupations of squares—and to the most central of them all, La Puerta del Sol in 2011—that the action refers.

---

* This article first appeared at https://aoc.media/critique/2018/05/03/casa-de-papel-braquage-politique/, 3 May 2018.

The success of the operation depends on the number of days spent in the Mint Palace printing brand new and unidentifiable 50-euro notes, but this ephemeral durability also makes it possible to send a message to the Spanish public (gradually won over to the robbers), and to the spectator, who becomes attached to the characters and gradually takes the side of the robbers. Here the political meets the subjective, and the bonds of attachment that characterize the company of well-written series characters are combined with a gradual understanding of the nature and meaning of their actions. In one of the many touching scenes that bring together one of the young robbers, Denver, with one of the hostages, Monica (which develops into a torrid love affair despite the tense setting), there is talk of the dilation of time—we return to the *24* aesthetic that turned Jack Bauer's, and so many other characters', lives upside down in a day. The couple here jokes about a relationship where they would fall in love in an hour, argue, make up, get married an hour later, have a child, and grow old together just afterwards. What is presented as a joke, or as a cinematic narrative system, is reality itself. It is indeed as a united couple that these two leave the Mint. The whole series reflects this relationship, with its ability to create a bond between the characters and thus between them and the audience—an attachment that is built up through their individual expressions and ways of being, both in the preparation and 'training' scenes (which aim at both the moral and political education of the audience and the gang), and during the occupation. One of the strengths of *La Casa de Papel* is that it has such powerful, complex, well-defined, and diverse characters, which it uses to confront two generations: young people—all rather 'hothead', including Tokyo, a central female character—and the more mature, experienced, and fatalistic protagonists, such as the Nordic Helsinki or Moscow, Denver's father. The latter's beautiful father-son relationship that also structures the whole story sums up the current enigma of transmission. It is also able, unlike many series today that make us fantasize about the powerful or psychopaths, to cause us to attach ourselves to ordinary people such as the bank staff and to highlight their moral capacities, which are far superior to those of politicians or law enforcement officers.

This is where the first revolution in *La Casa de Papel* lies: it is able to express the political spirit of the time remarkably well, with its call for occupation and rebellion, which is politically justified by the Professor, the gang's master thinker, and with the sympathy it arouses for non-violent action in the explicit refusal of austerity and the power of finance. This call is neither superior nor abstract, however—rather, it is rooted in the humanity of individuals, the relationships they build, and the new society they invent. *La Casa de Papel* thus proposes a utopia: a utopia of agency, where people can take charge and act against political and economic powers, as well as conformity. This is a utopia that is also democratic—the robbers are equal, linked by horizontal relationships where the women regularly take power. Together with the hostages, they gradually form a society, albeit a demented one, of equals, as shown by the common outfit of scarlet overalls (which leads to the hostages and the robbers being mixed up, to the point that the police, among other calamitous actions, shoot a hostage 'by accident', or 'by mistake' as the philosopher J.L. Austin would say).

The audacity of *La Casa de Papel* is to refuse the classic device of unhealthy fascination or distant sympathy for the 'bad guys', and instead to show, in a more radical way, the justification of their approach. The Professor's role is paradigmatic and reflexive: it amounts to a pedagogy, in the same way as the training offered to militants by civil rights associations that prepares them for commando actions and disobedience. The Professor's strict instructions to avoid violence and to work with the media to attract public sympathy, by highlighting the ever-increasing violence of the forces of law and order, are evidence of this, substantiated by the many 'tutorials' on how to react and protect the defenders of the institutions. Like a classic civil disobedience action, the attack on the Mint Palace is intended to show the injustice of a financial order that creates domination out of nothing. The Professor's last lesson, of the last episode, to Raquel Murrillo, the inspector in charge of negotiating with the robbers, will have the effect of convincing her of the validity of their action, which she ends up supporting deliberately, after having supported it involuntarily, seduced by the Professor… a grain of sand in the machine of the heist, as well as the roles assigned by society.

Like Raquel, we all end the series as students of the Professor. This is probably because he is not an authority figure and his vulnerability is apparent on many occasions, whether in his twisted love story (this is Almodóvar country) or in the various grotesque situations in which the scriptwriter likes to place him, such as his entrapment within a car destined for the scrap heap.

Yes, *La Casa de Papel* misses almost none of the clichés of cinematic storytelling and builds its suspense with banal references rooted in pop culture and the mixing of genres (gangster versus cop movie, political saga, soap, teen movies, etc.), but these clichés are an opportunity for subversion. The thick Scandinavian bully is gay. The women are sexy, but strong and domineering (time for matriarchy, Nairobi proclaims). The nice, victimizing boss is a scumbag. The psychopath (Berlin) turns out to be heroic (and hilarious). The robbers turn out to be harmless, even if they do not lack brutality in their behaviour: they are careful, on the Professor's orders, not to break any lives, not to kill—even if they ritually threaten each other with death, a gesture that is the only wearying element of all these episodes.

This is the most important reversal achieved by the series: we no longer know, as Raquel says, where the good and the bad are; in any case we wish to judge for ourselves, without preconceptions. The robbers, each in their own way, demonstrate moral sense and affectivity that the chief of police, the financiers, and politicians (who do not hesitate to pass on the burden of their mistakes to regular account holders) lack. Here too the concept of robbery is turned upside down: attacking a bank would (to varying degrees) be tantamount to harming its clients, but the Professor's gang technically does not steal, it manufactures. The moral principle of non-negligence is their guide, as they cruelly demonstrate, in each of their trajectories, the nuisance and injustice of capitalist society, subsequently dismantling it by producing a mountain of paper that becomes their wealth, no more absurdly or uselessly than, as the Professor shows us at the end, the insane sums produced by and for the financial institutions. Like disobedient people—or rebels in the style of Anonymous (as the masks worn by the occupiers and hostages also remind us)—they break the law by occupying the Palace, so as to reveal the more radical injustice of an inegalitarian and violent system that constantly tries to produce its own moral justification.

It is the strength of the political demonstration that carries the series, by energizing and dynamizing relations between people that use all the resources of popular series to bring about a transformation: the great political series up to now (the legendary *The West Wing* and *Borgen*, for example) had a strong social and democratic dimension with the same pedagogical power, but were explicitly opposed to any radical approach (*The West Wing* does not miss an opportunity to ironize the anti-globalization movements…). The aim is to immerse the viewer in political life, so as to make them understand workings and decision-making processes; often to reveal injustices; or, as in the security series (*24*, *Homeland*, *The Bureau*), to reinforce collective security. Other series produce a pathology rather than a critique (*House of Cards*, *Mr. Robot*), or choose dystopia as a back door to critique. But never before has a television series taken on the mission (over the exceptional duration of this medium) of giving voice and action to the underprivileged, of offering them revenge. A bit like *Lost*, another long-running series about the development of a society in a situation of confinement, we witness in *La Casa de Papel* the creation of a network of totally new relationships and the invention of a form of life that, here too, runs on the model of the occupations, which have wanted, all over the world, to create paradigms of democracy here and now. But this life is fragile and temporary, a precarious construction. Like the heroes of *Lost* who wish to return to the island, Tokyo, extracted from the trap of the Mint Palace, then finally freed, prefers, in a reverse escape, to return spectacularly to the fold in one of the most shocking scenes of the series.

We regularly wonder why the Springs and other revolts such as Occupy have not given rise to more fictional creations—beyond the films devoted to computer hacking, and some beautiful chase scenes in Athens in the latest *Jason Bourne* (Paul Greengrass, 2016). With *La Casa de Papel*, we have the first post-Occupy fiction, which plays on the ephemeral and democratic structure of Occupy collectives, on the political stakes of our time, and on the sharing power of television series.

La Casa de Papel also reminds us, through the nostalgic dimension of utopian series, that we are no longer in the time of the Puerta del Sol, Occupy, or even Nuit Debout. The utopian horizontal society is no longer open to all: we have moved from squares and the extensive occupation of public space to the 'zone to defend', and to the organized and privatizing occupation, temporary citadels, and paper houses against the attacks of the outside world. It is therefore particularly touching that the heroes of the series are named after mythological places of globalization—capitalist and political—Berlin, Moscow, Tokyo… which also draw a cartography of places of globalized mobilization. It is also this ambivalence that makes the series melancholy and powerful; the Netflix subscriber is caught, as are the protagonists, between his or her accepted way of life, and the growing feeling of belonging to an unjust world that must be changed. The series urges us to face this difficulty, and, in this sense, calls for new forms of courage.

Bad Trip to Chernobyl

If there is one thing that the survivors of the zombie apocalypse in AMC's *The Walking Dead* (*TWD*) and its little sister series, *Fear the Walking Dead* (*FTWD*), *do* not have to worry about, it is the quality of the environment. Industry and infrastructure are out of commission, and few vehicles run on the meagre remains of fuel. Yet in the eerily titled episode 'The Hurt That Will Happen' from the fifth season of *FTWD*—as if things could be worse than the transformation of the bulk of the population into the decerebrate, flesh-eating undead—the group of survivors land in Austin, Texas. In this super-hazardous area, where the reactor core of a nuclear power plant has exploded following the massacre of its personnel, the level of radioactivity is through the roof—as evidenced by the dosimeters around the necks of the irradiated and mutated walkers who used to be the plant's engineers and technicians.

FTWD, *the* uneven spin-off of the cult *TWD*, has become an original work with its own style, even though it recovers former characters from *TWD*, such as the historical Morgan. In *FTWD*, Morgan meets Grace, a former plant manager, who has made it her mission to eliminate her infected colleagues and then bury them so as to prevent the radioactivity from spreading. The obsession with radioactivity in bodies and people—as if it were a transmissible virus—has also been noted in recent productions of the nuclear genre. *FTWD* reminds us of the vulnerability of political infrastructures and institutions, and therefore of the forms of social life, illustrated by the disappearance of a common language, and even of a unified term to designate the new reality—the dead, the walkers, the prowlers, the biters, the infected... the vulnerability of the living. It is the destruction of the political that is at the origin of the nuclear catastrophe, which one logically assumes is not the only one in the post-apocalyptic universe of *TWD*.

Nuclear power is now a central object of popular culture. This signals its late arrival at the forefront of environmental health concerns, and the discovery of the risks to forms of life created by toxic elements in their environment: chemical pollution, radioactivity, and so on. *Silent Spring*, Rachel Carson's 1962 book published in instalments in the *New Yorker* drew public attention to the effects of pesticides on the environment (birds in particular), as well as reflecting on the 'constructed ignorance' and misinformation produced by the industry, and contributed to the banning of DDT in the United States in 1972. In a similar fashion, the disaster film genre, such as Roland Emmerich's *The Day After Tomorrow* (2004) and *2012* (2009) has been a vehicle for knowledge of climate risk in the twenty-first century. *Chernobyl*, the miniseries that HBO launched to divert the frustrations of *Game of Thrones*' viewers, is part of this genre—or the nuclear subgenre of the disaster film, already represented in the cinema by *Godzilla* (Gareth Edwards, 2014)—and highlights both its success and its limitation.

---

* This article first appeared in *Libération*, 20 June 2019.

Chernobyl has become a phenomenon—a bit like *Game of Thrones* but for the shorter time span of digital binge-watching—and is much better received critically than the successful disaster films or series. But why so much love? HBO fiction provides valuable education and information to the public almost seventy-five years after Hiroshima, thirty-three years after Chernobyl, and eight years after Fukushima, when the human consequences of nuclear development were beginning to be forgotten in the face of focus on climate change. In the depiction of *Chernobyl*, we appreciate the precise description of the direct effects of the explosion on the technical staff of the power station, on the firemen who came to their rescue (irradiated with high doses to the point of dying in the following weeks in a hospital in Moscow), on the population of the region, affected in the long term despite their relocation, and on the thousands of workers sacrificed to repairing the disaster. The pedagogical way in which all the stages are retraced during a fictional trial, with the choice casting of Jared Harris—seen in *The Crown* as George VI and subsequently employed playing characters with serious health problems—in the role of the scientist Valery Legasov, who is in charge of the salvage operations and becomes the main critic of the mismanagement of the nuclear plant by its authorities, engenders a relative historical seriousness and impeccable narration to keep the spectator invested until the end (despite them knowing, more or less, the course of events and their outcome). *Chernobyl* informs the viewer remarkably well about the very real effects of a major nuclear accident, and should send a chill down the spine of all inhabitants and neighbours of countries that, by hosting nuclear power plants—even if supposedly under the control of competent technicians—expose their populations to a potential disaster.

This public impact of HBO's fiction, and its relentless and precise demonstration of a true and present risk, effectively links *Chernobyl* to the genre of security fiction, such as those works that describe contemporary terrorist threats. But this 'human security' effect is not assumed by the series' authors, Craig Mazin and Johan Renck, who present the catastrophe as the result of human errors and lies comparable with the chain of calamities that befall the characters in *The Hangover* (Todd Phillips, 2009; titled *Very Bad Trip* in French), of which Mazin directed the second and third sequels. *Chernobyl* presents the root cause of the disaster as the opaque operation of the Soviet regime, suggesting repeatedly that the better-managed and better-designed power plants of the capitalist world would not have allowed such a disaster to occur. Regardless of its obvious criticism of the East, the uncanniness of *Chernobyl is* the general denial of the present insecurity that the series exposes.

2

The Second Wave: Gender, Race, and Class

Gender Theory with *The Simpsons*

A cult episode (ranked among the top ten) of the animated series *The Simpsons* (Matt Groening, Fox, 1989–) directly confronts the question of what a theory is. In 'The Monkey Suit', The Simpsons' devout neighbour, Ned Flanders, outraged by an exhibition on Darwin and evolution, lobbies Principal Skinner, with the help of Reverend Lovejoy, to have creationism taught in Springfield schools and the theory of evolution banned. The young Lisa Simpson, who has already shown her scepticism towards religion (see 'Lisa the Skeptic'), rebels and founds an underground club to study *On the Origin of Species*. She is immediately arrested, and finds herself in trouble at her trial when facing the formidable lawyer of the creationist lobby. She is only saved by the intervention of her mother, Marge, who gives Homer a can of beer he is unable to uncap during the hearing: his simian gesticulations remove all doubt from the audience as to the kinship between apes and humans.

This episode sets the stakes for debates around theory: for years, American creationists have been calling the science of evolution a 'theory', in an attempt to prevent the unholy knowledge from spreading in schools. 'The Monkey Suit', even though the title evokes a trial from the beginning of the twentieth century, refers to recent actions by the creationist lobby—for instance, the decision by the Cobb County Board of Education in 2002 to affix a sticker to the biology textbooks used in Atlanta schools: 'Evolution is a Theory, Not a Fact: a theory of the origin of living things that must be approached with an open mind, with caution and with a critical eye.' The authors of the offending textbooks and other experts objected that this was a misuse of the word theory, as the term refers specifically to a system of explaining phenomena based on facts.

---

* This article first appeared in *Libération*, 28 February 2014.

This twisted and anti-scientific use of the notion of theory is being taken up against the concept of gender by French activists who are employing the strategies of the far right, Tea-Party style, as more effective than the traditional rantings of national conservatism—hence the circulation of the term or language element 'gender theory'. It is legitimate to respond to the attack, in the first instance, by attacking this language element; that is, to repeat that there is no gender theory in the sense given to the expression by the anti-gender clique. However, in a second step, we may reflect, with Lisa Simpson, on what a theory is.

Calling knowledge a theory, with a devaluing tone to cast doubt on acquired knowledge (while all science proposes theories), is a tried and tested strategy of militant obscurantism. What does evolution teach us, if not that humans are part of the animal kingdom and have no privilege within nature other than the place they have made for themselves? This is what horrifies Ned at the evolution exhibition. Similarly, what does gender tell us, if not that the difference between the sexes (one difference among many) should make no difference to the social destiny of individuals, and yet continues to lead to considerable inequalities? This is what bothers the denouncers of gender theory.

Because gender is science, and all science works on the basis of theories and concepts. By pointing out the risk of error in not taking the gender variable into account (by showing that work is not reduced to professional or productive work, but includes domestic work; that the so-called universalist vision of human rights excludes women; that heart disease is under-diagnosed in women, etc.), research has highlighted the androcentric point of view that ignores itself as such and generalizes based on the particular case of men. Taking gender into account is a scientific matter—of theories and of facts—and is thus the subject of studies in all major international programmes and by many researchers throughout the world.

Though questions of gender may be scientific, they raise (as they often and fortunately do) political questions, and make visible unpleasant realities of unjustifiable inequalities among groups of so-called equal citizens. This is the real cause of the attacks on gender theory. Gender research, and the facts it establishes, questions the traditional organization of the family, male domination, and heteronormativity, as well as the gender inequalities that run through our society. The gesticulations of anti-gender people, such as Homer Simpson, are the best evidence of the theoretical significance of gender.

Can't Believe It

The Netflix series *Unbelievable*, which is undoubtedly one of the greatest of the decade, denounces police negligence with regard to rape victims. The seventy-first Emmy Awards ceremony in Los Angeles was a strange one, given that *Veep*, *The Big Bang Theory*, and *Game of Thrones* were saying goodbye. Luckily, HBO proves that classic series still exist: *Game of Thrones*, which was part of our lives for nine years, predictably took home a bunch of trophies—including Best Drama Series and the mandatory award for Peter Dinklage (Tyrion Lannister). Not a single award was won, however, by one of the women in the 'secondary' category—Lena Headey (Cersei), Sophie Turner (Sansa), Maisie Williams (Arya), Gwendoline Christie (Brienne)—all of whom lost out on a vote scattering. Indeed, these rituals are no longer appropriate for such ensembles of actresses and actors who should be more properly rewarded as a single entity, as has sometimes been the case in film. The same goes for the group of young black actors in the miniseries *When They See Us*, the snubbing of whom represented a disappointment and latent racism, which was at least somewhat offset by the triumph of Jharrel Jerome as Korey Wise, the eldest of the Central Park '5' who were imprisoned for years for a crime they did not commit.

What *When They See Us* and *Chernobyl*, which won in the miniseries category, have in common is the ambition to make known the truth of events in the history of the twentieth century, and, in both cases, to educate and rehabilitate. The miniseries format allows for these political successes—from *Seven Seconds* and *When They See Us*, *both* illustrations of Black Lives Matter, to *Unbelievable*, which denounces, #MeToo style, the negligence and even brutal incompetence of police officers towards rape victims, whom they immediately dismissed as lacking credibility.

This is the double meaning of the title: no one wants to believe Mary, the first victim of the rapist, and we can't believe our eyes at the inequity of the system she faces. The focus, not on the rapist but on his various victims, engenders the incredible quality of this work and its place as one of the great works of the decade. *Unbelievable* is based on a Pulitzer Prize-winning investigation and report by ProPublica. Its radicalism is in its exposure of the difference in treatment of rape victims by male police officers—who refuse to hear and take seriously Marie (Kaitlyn Dever), a vulnerable young woman living in a community for 'at-risk' youth, and go so far as to charge her with a false complaint in order to close the case—and by female officers, who treat the rapist's next victims with respect, not only believing them, but also taking care of them over the months it takes to meticulously hunt down the perpetrator.

---

* This article first appeared in *Libération*, 3 October 2019.

The miniseries format allows for a consistently non-linear narrative that shifts back and forth between Lynnwood, Washington, where the first attack takes place in 2008, and Colorado in 2011, where Detective Karen Duvall (Merritt Wever) investigates a rape that took place in an identical scenario (a masked gunman breaks into a lonely woman's home at night, tortures her for hours, and then carefully erases all traces of DNA). She teams up with an impressive detective Grace Rasmussen (Toni Collette), who has discovered similar acts in another area. Their shared investigation is documented step by step by the series.

It's hard to describe the pleasure of watching these two remarkable actresses interact, as the first embodiment of the professionalism and friendship of a 'cop couple'—a female *True Detective*—especially in the way they manage their teams to pursue every lead, no matter how messy, right to the end. The originality of *Unbelievable* is that it doesn't value these women for their sexy, twisted, or 'badass' side, as is often the case in the police genre, but for their obsession with 'a job well done' (the expression comes up again and again), which is the best way to take care of the victims, as well as the public.

This expression also applies, reflexively, to the work of the directors and scriptwriters. *Unbelievable* is distinguished by its sense of detail, unexpectedly funny dialogue, moral depth, and the absence of any self-indulgent or sadistic representation. Avoiding rape porn requires care, and it is this care that carries all the characters—particularly Marie, who is able to regain her confidence, her voice, and her life, through the care of the psychologist who gently leads her to reveal (to herself) the truth. The masterful moment at the end of the penultimate episode, where this life-saving conversation alternates with the detectives' discovery, three years later, of the evidence of the truth in the culprit's computer, is an example of the best and most feminist presentation that TV series can offer today.

Oscars Race

The upcoming Oscars are always a great opportunity to see our favourite actresses and actors in stunning outfits, and though I would not usually miss the event, on this occasion I am morally obliged to snub the evening. Chris Rock, scheduled as last year's Master of Ceremonies, may well—if he doesn't drop out—be almost the only black person in the cast. Spike Lee, Steve McQueen (the director of the 2014 Oscar-winning *12 Years a Slave*), Lupita Nyong'o (who won the Supporting Actor Award for the same film), and Jada Pinkett Smith (with her husband) are calling for a boycott, or have at least expressed their bitterness, at the total indifference of the members of the Hollywood academy towards the talent of African American actors and directors. The list of 'nominations' of actors, actresses, and directors for the top award is staggering: the Academy, with its uniformly white nominations, has ensured that it is impossible for a black individual to walk away with an Oscar. In the categories of Best Actor, Best Actress, and Best Supporting Actor (Female and Male), there are twenty whites out of twenty nominations.

Though one might think that this is a false issue, this is not the case for three reasons. Of course, we know that Oscars awarded to representatives of minorities (blacks, Hispanics, etc.) are rare, especially when it comes to the top awards for lead role or best director; equally, those awarded to women of colour are systematically for supporting actress (only Halle Berry has been awarded for a lead role)—the supporting actress Oscar went to Hattie McDaniel, the Mammy from *Gone with the Wind* (Victor Fleming, 1939) in 1940; and, in the 2000s, to Queen Latifah, Sophie Okonedo, Octavia Spencer, Viola Davis, and Jennifer Hudson, among others.

Black men are more likely to win the lead role statuette: after Sidney Poitier in 1964, we have seen Denzel Washington, but also Jamie Foxx, Forest Whitaker, and Morgan Freeman win Oscars, while Will Smith, Eddie Murphy, Djimon Hounsou, Samuel L. Jackson, and Don Cheadle were all at least nominated in the 2000s. A year like 2004, with Foxx and Freeman winning two Oscars a few years before Obama came along, seems a long way off. Two years ago, the triumph of *12 Years*, which told the story of a young black man kidnapped and sold into slavery, might have seemed an irreversible shift towards recognition of African American talent and the history that had crushed it—however, the choices of 2015 and 2016 are a political regression. Of course, the blame is laid upon the demographics of the Academy, with the voting pool being 94 per cent white and 76 per cent male: no wonder black women don't stand a chance at the top. If there weren't two categories, actor/actress, one wonders if a woman would ever manage to win a lead Oscar—a great argument for quotas!

Those who vote for the Oscars are not representative of the public, nor of their society, though the objection is that the production has the same

---

* This article first appeared in *Libération*, 4 February 2016.

kind of bias and that black actors are not offered interesting films or roles. Last year, *Selma* (Ava DuVernay, 2014), the film about Martin Luther King and his fight for the right to vote in 1965, allowed rappers Common and John Legend, who won the Oscar for best song, *Glory*, to give a moving performance, and to proclaim their sense of radical injustice, which is still relevant—a raw visualization of injustice that makes racist nominations intolerable.

Of course, there is sometimes a feeling that the generation of great male black actors is aging and has not been replaced: where are the new Denzel Washington, Laurence Fishburne, Samuel L. Jackson, and Will Smith? Furthermore, we hear that there were no great black films this year. But what about *Creed* (Ryan Coogler, 2015), *Straight Outta Compton* (F. Gary Gray, 2015), and *Beasts of No Nation* (Cary Joji Fukunaga, 2015)? All could have earned their actors nominations. Indeed, the argument about the lack of good films or actors is reminiscent of the argument about the lack of 'qualified' black people or women to explain their absence in politics. Everyone expected an award (well-deserved) for Stallone: he may get it thanks to a black director and a black actor—the wonderful Michael B. Jordan—who are not even nominated.

One can compare the upcoming outcome of the Oscars to the equally capitalistic, but cooler, Golden Globes ceremony. This year, Globes hailed the performances of Will Smith and Idris Elba in the movies, but, above all, the prize list (which mixes different genres) demonstrates that TV series have overtaken Hollywood cinema in their ability to discover the actors of tomorrow, and to showcase their diversity: Idris Elba as John Luther; David Oyelowo; Regina King, extraordinary in the role of Aliyah in *American Crime*; Uzo Aduba, the brilliant 'Crazy Eyes' in *Orange is the New Black*, are all nominated for the Globes because the studios and writers have been able to give them roles and stories that suit them. It is no coincidence that the series *The Wire*, where we recall seeing for the first time Michael B. Jordan and Idris Elba, is the model for this visibility. It seems that the series has taken over from the cinema's capacity to represent the world in all its variety and differences, and thus to transform it.

Sleepless in Paris

I confess, I did watch the 100 per cent white nominees of the Oscar ceremony anyway, relying on the Hollywood genius of 'second chances'—and frankly (despite the 2–6 am time frame). I don't regret it: Chris Rock unleashed his opinion, in his introductory monologue about the 'White People's Choice Awards', of the real problem, which goes beyond or ahead of the nominations and awards: that of the small number of great roles and relevant films for black actors—an inequality of opportunity. But it wasn't over: just as one might have feared that the matter would be settled in the intro and then swept under the carpet, the evening went on to see a proliferation of further pro-diversity statements (including from the Academy's president), including ferocious parody numbers—Whoopi Goldberg mopping up after Jennifer Lawrence in *Joy* (David O. Russell, 2015); NASA brass hesitating to charge the taxpayer to bring a black astronaut back from Mars; and Chris Rock interviewing residents of the Los Angeles suburb of Compton about their favourite films that had nothing to do with the selected ones.

And what a pleasure it was to see *Mad Max* (George Miller), the greatest film of 2015, scoop up all sorts of awards, including the costume award to a baba-cool woman in a perfecto, who traumatized the audience; though, I might add, not even nominating Charlize Theron for best actress as the one-armed Furiosa, was a shame too, even if not race-related.

What is touching in the glamorous parade of the Oscar stage is contemplation of the trajectory of these stars, such as Mark Ruffalo (excellent in *Spotlight*, Tom McCarthy, 2015, but also in *30 Going on 13*, Gary Winick, 2004); Jennifer Garner from J.J. Abrams' *Alias* series and *Dallas Buyers Club*, Jean-Marc Vallée, 2013; or Christian Bale, from Batman to Malick, and *The Big Short* (Adam McKay, 2015). For all these actors, from Lawrence—already graced with roles of incredible variety—to Tom Hanks (magnificent once again in Spielberg's *Bridge of Spies*, 2015), the sum of their characters, first or second roles, creates a specific entity, a persona made up of the whole of these past and future incarnations, in addition to their voice, their way of being, and their expressiveness. Cavell notes that: 'In film, the actor is the subject of the camera, emphasizing that this actor could become other characters (highlighting the potentiality of human existence, the journeys of the self), unlike theatre, which focuses on the possibility that a character will (accept) other actors.'[1]

It is this entity, which we will call moral, that attaches us to actors—that constitutes their work, which is at least as important as that of directors and authors, with the key difference that women have always been able to excel in it. Great black actors do not often have this opportunity, with the exception

---

* This article first appeared in *Libération*, March 2016.

---

1 Stanley Cavell, *A Pitch of Philosophy*. Cambridge, MA: Harvard University Press, 2004.

of Laurence Fishburne, and of course Morgan Freeman, who was symbolically elected to conclude Sunday's ceremony.

Of course, we respect Leonardo DiCaprio's Oscar for his fifth nomination, but fortunately it is for this trajectory, this Leo entity—a mysterious union of ease and opacity, from *Romeo + Juliet* (Baz Luhrmann, 1997) and *Titanic* (James Cameron, 1997), to Scorsese's *Gangs of New York* (2002) and *The Departed* (2006), and *Gatsby* (Luhrmann, 2013)—and not for his latest performance in Alejandro González Iñárritu's *The Revenant*. This creativity in the circulation of stars and their ability to 'wear' different characters, which is visible on such occasions, includes the series that explore, quite systematically, this quality of the actor to figure on-screen his past and future roles: *Dexter* would not be the same without *Six Feet Under*, nor *How I Met Your Mother* without *Buffy*, or even *The Affair* without *The Wire*. *American Crime*, a particularly remarkable series by John Ridley uses this power in a radical way: an anthology series, like *True Detective*—that is to say, with a new story, a new setting, and new characters each season—*American Crime* follows a similar principle to that of the teen show *American Horror Story* by taking the same actors and placing them in new situations and characters. Felicity Huffman, Regina King, Timothy Hutton, and Richard Cabral find themselves, in season two, in socially distinct positions from those they occupied in season one. This device creates reflexivity in each character and makes it possible to explore the relations of class and race in all their harshness; in doing so, it solicits the spectator, making him or her increasingly sensitive to the plurality of points of view, as well as to the intolerable arbitrariness of the racial segregation. This underlies the polemics about Hollywood: 'Black Lives Matter', something that Chris Rock ironically reminded the audience, not for the last time, at the end of the Oscars.

Friends of My Friends

A particularly instructive moment in *Star Wars VIII: The Last Jedi* (Rian Johnson, 2017; too bad we can't keep the ambivalence of the English original title in French) is when the handsome elite pilot Poe Dameron (Oscar Isaac) gets excited (and the audience with him) at the idea of taking the lead in the fight against the First Order. All command was lost in the last attack on the rebel ship, and General Leia Organa (Carrie Fisher) is in a coma—subsequently replaced by Vice Admiral Holdo (Laura Dern), Leia's sister-in-arms and head of the Resistance's naval forces. Poe discovers a mature, gangly woman with lavender-dyed hair and a strangely fitting mauve dress, and wonders if he wouldn't be better off in her place—especially since Holdo, who is rather abrupt, welcomes his advice with the utmost contempt.

Doubt persists until the film reveals to the audience, who share the pilot's spite and distrust, that this old woman is a hero of the resistance and a better strategist than Poe—if only because she wishes to preserve the lives of others first, even if it is at the cost of her own. In this sense, it is as if the character of Holdo was created to teach the viewer this lesson, and thus educate them in a new universe.

This is just one example of the moral ambition of the *Star Wars* episode, which closes with the words of Leia (in the historic Millennium Falcon where the rebels are holed up) to Rey (Daisy Ridley), who doubts they can get away with it ('We have everything we need'), for that leaves her, Leia, and Rey. This young Rey also symbolizes this new era of *Star Wars*, a chosen one who (for the moment, of course) sidesteps all those questions of origin and descent that would amount to asking: 'Which man, Skywalker or Kenobi, is she descended from?' in order to find, quite simply, herself.

It is Dern, a legendary star discovered by Lynch in 1986, who plays Holdo, and this ephemeral *Star Wars* figure is one of those who mark us, like the ordinary and tragic heroes of *Rogue One* (Gareth Edwards, 2016) a year ago, in the same way as her appearance in 2002 in *The West Wing* (s3e22, the episode of Toby Ziegler's meeting with the poet and activist Tabitha Fortis), *Big Little Lies*, and, this year, *Twin Peaks: The Return*. This sums up the capacity of series—and sometimes films—to value all the ages of women's lives by following their transformations over the years and taking pleasure in seeing them age (like Henry Fonda, Marlon Brando, or Harrison Ford), by featuring splendid or worrying matriarchs such as GJ (Holly Hunter) in the first season of *Top of the Lake*.

Big Little Lies, with its remarkable writing and equally impressive actresses, showcases a group of women who are different, but all ultimately united in helping two of them get revenge on a criminal husband. Long before the Weinstein creepiness and the beautiful #MeToo wave, *Big Little Lies* proposed that women stand together against the enemy—including throwing him

---

* This article first appeared in *Libération*, 4 January 2018.

down the stairs. A much-needed reminder that victims of violence are not just white Hollywood movie actresses, three major television series of 2017 explored this theme: *American Crime*, whose season three evokes the systematic rape on farms in North Carolina; *The Deuce*, presenting, with David Simon's characteristic lucidity, the beatings and murders of prostitutes; and *Top of the Lake*, whose season two denounces, like the first, the impunity and indifference enjoyed by gender-based violence.

One might wonder about the moral and political edge of these American series over their own society and our national productions. By highlighting women in the diversity of life's phases, they highlight the importance of gender solidarity, which was so lacking in the US presidential election, but it is also friendship between women that emerges as a central moral issue in *Big Little Lies* and in Zabou Breitman's series *Paris, etc.*, which is catching up with the French backlog of women's group shows, and which, for this very reason, has provoked the sexist sneers of local critics. There is also the example of the friendship between Michèle (Isabelle Huppert) and Anna (Anne Consigny) in *Elle* (Paul Verhoeven, 2016), and, in *The Last Jedi*, in the farewell between Leia and Holdo.

Manly friendship has long been the driving force behind cinematic aesthetics and ethics through the privileged genres of the war film, the Western, the historical biopic, and the thriller. A first conquest was the friendship between men and women, born in the soil of classic Hollywood comedies and romantic films, such as *When Harry Met Sally…* (Rob Reiner, 1989), and of the feminism of the first wave. A second conquest, which is specific to the twenty-first century, is this friendship between women, a transforming force of a future of realized equality. Françoise Héritier thus listed the subversive possibility of two women being friends as that which is in 'the salt of life'.

More *Better Things*

Since the end of the year is a time for catching up on TV (and since binge-watching is sometimes the best cure for a hangover), I recommend the second season of *Better Things*, a comedy that received notice in 2016 for the originality of the profile of its heroine, Sam Fox, an actress from Los Angeles who runs through castings and multiple small, seedy roles, while raising her three daughters alone. The unique, husky, and seductive voice of its lead actress, Pamela Adlon—who specializes in dubbing cartoons, voicing, for example, Bobby in *King of the Hill* (Mike Judge & Greg Daniels, Fox, 1997–) and collaborations with Louis C.K. (who was hit this year in the #MeToo wave)—established the educational value of the series with its constant accuracy. Sam Fox has nothing to learn, and *Better Things* is not, unlike other series centred on a singular personality, a journey of self-exploration or transformation. Rather, she knows exactly what she is, what she can expect, and what she has to convey. The event of the emergence of a different voice (to use the title of Carol Gilligan's classic book on care), which is the real subject of this series: self-sufficient, and at the same time totally realistic.

Better Things consistently asserts an ordinary point of view through its presentation in the first person of the daily life of a fifty-year-old woman with no illusions about the sexism of her society. A particularly striking episode in the first season is one entitled 'Woman Is the Something of the Something', a transparent allusion to a 1972 song by John Lennon and Yoko Ono, which, with its controversial title, encapsulates the inequalities of the contemporary world that compound social injustice: race, gender, age: 'Woman is the Nigger of the World.' This is the subject of the episode—from the demoralizing visit to a plastic surgeon (Sam discovers the exorbitant price of a 'refreshed' face), to the recording of a commercial where she is asked to express her joy in the description of the side effects of an erectile pill, and subsequently the meeting of a homeless woman abandoned by her children to whom she has 'given everything', the whole specificity of the female experience is expressed over the course of a few minutes—above all, the ageist doubling of sexism. How are we not to think of French Minister Ségolène Royal's beautiful, refreshed face being a condition for her return to politics? Or Hillary Clinton, who deplored the 600 hours of make-up she had to put on to make her look 'younger' during her presidential campaign, a waste of time that was out of all proportion to the constraints on her male opponents, who were not required to be the freshest?

In the face of these multiple pressures on women, the theme of female solidarity omnipresent in the episode and in the series is shown to truly exist only when rooted in the recognition of these inequalities. In the terrific episode 'Woman Is the Something of the Something', we are initially puzzled by the behaviour of Sam's agent and friend Tressa (Rebecca Metz), who carefully hides from her the possibility of a lead role in a hip new comedy

---

* This article first appeared in *Libération*, 4 January 2019.

series. The episode introduces the show's two young, male creators, Danny and Zach, who have the exciting idea of giving Sam the role, but allow another woman, their colleague Jen, to do all the negotiating with the network executives (while she herself is sceptical of Sam's chances, knowing the standards of the business). They remain silent when Jen comes out of the woodwork and explains to the boss that Sam is 'like real people', not so young, but funny, which is exactly what the show needs; but Tressa herself doesn't say anything to Sam—she is under no illusions and does not wish her friend to get flamed and disappointed. This was the correct call: after a lengthy negotiation conducted entirely without Sam's knowledge—and thus demonstrating that the show is, contrary to its apparent positioning, made from the point of view of women as a group, not an individual—as intended by Tressa and Jen, it doesn't work. A further subtlety of the episode is how the two young creators, the first to get excited about Sam on their show, call Jen (who was hesitant from the beginning) a 'gender traitor'—only to instantly give up on Sam when their boss tells them he has a 'fresher' actress, Rachel McAdams, lined up for the part. At each stage, we see how clear-eyed all these women are about Sam's real chances, despite appearances, of getting a great role, which is where they stand together.

This allows the episode to conclude on a radical feminist note. At a meeting to which Sam accompanies her youngest daughter, Frankie, and against the backdrop of a speaker's words ('We're not misandrists, but we've got to get rid of the patriarchy'), Frankie informs her mother that 'Woman is the nigger of the world.' Here Sam replies that certain words should not be used, nor should struggles be confused, and that the phrase in question is by Zora Neale Hurston (forgetting Yoko Ono in passing) in reference to the situation of black women. This doesn't change the accuracy of the title by Lennon and Ono (who also wrote 'Mother', the hard-won theme song)—in any case, even if the phrase doesn't fit, women are still 'the something of the something'. Indeed, one learns as much about intersectionality in this episode (or any season of *American Crime* for that matter) as in the works of Kimberlé Crenshaw, who initially coined the term.

If the 2010s were the years of the emergence of female talent in series, the year 2018 has seen a flowering of beautiful female couples, a direct product of #MeToo, which began under the patronage of the friendship between Leia and Holdo in *Star Wars: The Last Jedi* (see 'My Friends' Friends'). The other revelation of the year, *Killing Eve*, features an MI5 agent, Eve Polastri (the formidable Sandra Oh), in pursuit of a psychopathic killer, Villanelle (Jodie Comer), who is employed in the service of a mysterious Russian network. Soon brought together by a mutual obsession, both characters are equally fascinating, though Comer in particular is simultaneously both terrifying and strangely hilarious. Once again, it is a unique writer, Phoebe Waller-Bridge (*Fleabag*), who is at the helm, and through whom we appreciate the obvious ease of the feminist tone of the series.

If we assume that modern series were born with the transition, in the 1980s and 1990s, from the single hero to male duos—*The Persuaders!* (Robert S. Baker, ITV, 1971–1972), *Starsky and Hutch*, *Miami Vice*, *NYPD Blue*—today, after a generation of M/F couples pulling the genre towards romantic comedy, F/F duos signal the importance of female bonding in the face of male heroes who are often fragile or pushy (see the idiot in *Bodyguard*). Here I am thinking particularly of Claire Danes (Carrie Mathison) and Elizabeth Marvel (President Keane) in the seventh season of *Homeland;* Elizabeth Moss (June) and Yvonne Strahovski (Serena) in *The Handmaid's Tale*; the excellent Rachel Brosnahan and Alex Borstein in the feminist and marvellous *Mrs. Maisel*, which portrays the struggle of a woman to find her own way in the world of stand-up comedy; to *Dollhouse* cult actress Olivia Williams as two women in *Counterpart*; the two amazing cops in *Unbelievable*. Similarly, men continue to go in pairs: Bill Hader and Henry Winkler in *Barry*, or doppelgängers in *The Deuce* (James Franco playing the twins) or *Counterpart*, where the two Howard Silks played, with a subtle difference we learn to perceive (in two different worlds), by J.K. Simmons, maintain a strangely friendly relationship. Friendship remains the fundamental value of the series (often a family genre), as what allows them to link everyone together, and what constitutes their indefectible romanticism. Male friendship may have been the core theme in film, together with heterosexual love. TV series have offered a space and a grammar for female friendship.

American Crime Enters the Resistance

At a time when cable, especially HBO, is losing ground to the Internet giants, such as Netflix, Amazon, Hulu and so on, who have become series producers and are vying for ingenuity in the form of *House of Cards*, *Orange Is the New Black*, and *Transparent*, it is remarkable that the best American series of the moment can be seen (in the United States) in *Post*. John Ridley's *American Crime*—not to be confused with *American Crime Story* (Alexander, Karaszewski, Smith & Burgess, FX, 2016–) and its excellent first season, *The People v. O.J. Simpson*—is rooted, not in America's great traumas, but in 'miscellaneous events' located in ordinary reality.

Aimed at a wide audience and broadcast on ABC (like the excellent but less realistic *Designated Survivor* and *Scandal*), it has an educational and transformative ambition. *American Crime* presents and analyses the mechanisms of racism and social inequality in the United States in a ruthless yet sensitive way, dealing, in the first season, with the murder of an Iraq war veteran turned drug dealer, and, in the second, with the rape of a high school student by other students. This third season radicalizes the series' anthology device, putting the emphasis on its Hispanic and black actors to directly attack the fate of migrants, in other words contemporary slavery, which is made up of violence, racism, and sordid exploitation. John Ridley, who won an Oscar for *12 Years a Slave*, uses the same cast of exceptional actors in all three seasons: Felicity Huffman, Regina King, Lili Taylor, Timothy Hutton, Richard Cabral, Benito Martinez, Connor Jessup... which has the effect of creating a sharpness of vision and ethical depth through watching the changes in their social position, look, and character from one season to the next. Felicity Huffman, in her role as Jeanette, a submissive woman who gradually becomes aware of the indignity of her relatives (employers of illegal immigrants), contrasts her role with that of season one—where she played the racist white girl—and of season two (the farting high school principal), and even Lynette from *Desperate Housewives*. Regina King, discovered twenty years ago (!) in *Jerry Maguire* (Cameron Crowe, 1996) alongside Tom Cruise, Cuba Gooding Jr., and Zellweger, plays a Muslim American woman in a headscarf in season one; a black woman revealing her class contempt in season two; and a social worker facing the impasses of the justice system in season three. Regina King is one of the greatest actresses of the moment, and the fact that this remains unclear to most says a lot about the American situation.

The double meaning of the title indicates that the crime of crimes is the 'crime of America', a situation of radical injustice that transects race, gender, and class, which Ridley manages to bring to the small screen, not in an ensemble series, but through the loss of voice: Gabrielle, the Haitian nanny who only speaks French and is thus rendered ultra-vulnerable to her cynical

---

* This article first appeared in *Libération*, 13 April 2017.

employers; Jeanette, who discovers the inhumanity of those for whom the lives of farm workers count for nothing; Shae, a young prostitute treated more horrifically by the system than by her pimp. This particular polyphony is both political and ethical. It is not a matter of alternating messages or points of view à la Rashomon; rather, it is the construction of the characters in each new context that creates understanding and a deep sense of disruption—'Bringing the viewer to an inner displacement', as Ridley summarizes. It echoes Barack Obama's cry: 'Thirty-five years ago, I could have been Trayvon Martin', after the 17-year-old's death; Obama dreamed of leaving a more equal society to the generations after him—he did not, however, find the key to ending either racism or neoliberalism, the effects of which on society have led to Trump.

The originality of *American Crime*, and what makes its presentation a fight for justice in the defence of society, is that it expresses on-screen the weight and violence of social determinisms, with all the hypocrisy of the 'equality of opportunity' that some continue to tout. This is the first series of the Trump era, which confronts us with the horrible alternation of dehumanizing neoliberalism and hateful nationalism; indeed, it is a time of global resistance to this choice. The utopian realist series of the twentieth century, such as *The West Wing*, *ER*, or *The Wire*, romanticized an unjust world with their narrative of power—even *The Wire*, to which *American Crime* is sometimes compared for its sociological ambition, had this seduction (the humour, the charm of the heroes, the police suspense). It is rather *The Leftovers*, which does not yield any pleasure to its audience, that is evoked by this third season, as if the world today were such that one cannot decently combine realism and pleasure. Though in France we were able to deal with terrorism with *The Bureau*, when will we see a series on inequality and poverty? On migrants, sex workers, and care workers? *American Crime* educates us about the risks of criminal indifference—rather like season seven of *Homeland*, which recently ended with the inscription of a face on the screen—that of fascism.

A Better World—Except for Women

It has been frequently noted the extent to which the subject of women's menstruation is repressed in TV series, despite their propensity for breaking taboos. Incest and anthropophagi actually appear more frequently than this seemingly banal event, a taboo that strangely concerns less the mention of menstruation than the physical presence of menstrual blood on-screen—an odd qualm if we think of the litres of blood spilt in some of our favourite series.

We had to wait for *Orange Is the New Black*, and now for *The Handmaid's Tale* (which has just started airing in France), to see a sanitary towel and red-stained panties on-screen. The colour of blood is present in Bruce Miller's series, right down to the letters in the credits, and keeps returning through the obsessive visual of women under surveillance walking in tight rows while wearing scarlet dresses and cloaks topped with a white coif that narrows their field of vision.

These handmaids are women detected as fertile in a world where the birth rate has dropped dramatically owing to environmental changes. Assigned to households, they are confined and ritually raped by the master of the house in order to produce a child for the obviously heterosexual couple. Though this is a dystopia, it remains a fictional but profoundly realistic story—as Margaret Atwood, the author of the 1985 novel that inspired the series, reminds us: nothing is invented, and every sadistic or repressive practice is attested to. The first effect of reality is induced by the flashbacks to a 'normal' life brutally interrupted by the reactionary revolution: the women we see enslaved and brutalized are us—the audience of the series—that is to say, women who work, have fun, have friends, and who, from one minute to the next, find themselves deprived of their jobs, their bank accounts, and all rights to vote, to abort, to read, to drive; to raise their voices.

The world of Gilead, a patriarchal dictatorship recently established in the United States, serves as a reminder that women's freedoms are fragile: the threat of terrorism and the environment can lead to their suppression—for it is for the survival of the planet that handmaids are put at the service of the regime. All women, including those of the dominant class, are reduced to domestic life.

The lead role of June is played by Elizabeth Moss, whose powerful character in *Mad Men* embodied the female emancipation of the last century. In the role of her rebellious friend, Moira, is Samira Wiley, the admirable Poussey who, in *Orange Is the New Black*, represented intellectual emancipation in prison. There is little to compare between the 'minimum security' confinement of the turbulent heroines of *Orange Is the New Black* and the cruel imprisonment of the women of Gilead, who are dispossessed of a body that

---

* This article first appeared in *Libération*, 6 July 2017.

has become the property of their master (even the colour of the maids' dresses displays the biological destiny to which women are reduced).

It is the state's control of the procreative function, and thus over the bodies of all women, that makes *The Handmaid's Tale* a biopolitical/ feminist work of fiction. As the pedagogical matron, Aunt Lydia, announces from the outset—what was ordinary is no longer ordinary, and what is not ordinary will become ordinary; it is the fragility of our present life forms, inseparably social and biological, that is exposed here.

On a further level, *The Handmaid's Tale* makes us see, even more tortuously, elements of the present. The strongest reality effect isn't the coming-to-power of Trump (and the threat he poses to the dignity of women in the United States and beyond) that occurred just as the series was being produced; rather, it's that we're already in Gilead. In a striking exchange, Commander Frederick Waterford, with whom June has established some form of conversation, speaks of the 'better world' brought about by the new power, pointing out, 'Better doesn't mean better for everyone'; it is, in fact, worse for some.

The feminism of the series is thus double-edged. In the Gilead organization, a class of subjugated, selfish, and sometimes sadistic women dominate other women who are put at their service: the name 'handmaid' merely refers to 'women with hands'—today, similar forms of service and servitude keep Western societies alive at the expense of an invisible army of laborers. Indeed, June uses the term 'army' because an army may also mobilize and act: 'When they massacred the Congress, we didn't wake up, when they blamed everything on terrorists and suspended the Constitution, we didn't wake up either.'

The spaces of freedom defended so much today are thanks to all women—a necessary condition for a vision of true feminism that is not reserved only for the winners. *The Handmaid's Tale*, by articulating feminism and biology, does not only aim at arousing nostalgia for the present, which is characteristic of post-apocalyptic aesthetics, but also cruelly questions this present, with its inequalities between women, threats to reproductive rights, and forms of contemporary slavery. It carries the hopes of the solidarity of women who, wear red dresses and coifs in demonstrations to try to preserve the right to abortion.

Class of Hate

TV series now allow the public to revisit certain histories from the end of the twentieth century, thus creating a new genre. The Emmy Awards rewarded *The Assassination of Gianni Versace*, the second part of the *American Crime Story* series, after the first season (which had already won an award), devoted to the O.J. Simpson case, *The People v. O.J. Simpson*. After the 1960s was reinvented by *Mad Men*, the 1980s and 1990s have become a new subject, carrying a common ethos and aesthetic of clothes, hairstyles, and technologies belonging to a time that is close, yet strangely distant. *The Deuce*, a new series by David Simon, describes the development of the porn industries around 42nd Street in 1990s New York. At the same time, *The Americans* has finally been rewarded, albeit insufficiently (after being ignored for six years), with an Emmy for the excellent Matthew Rhys.

The same year as *The People v. O. J. Simpson*, a TV movie, *Confirmation* (Rick Famuyiwa, HBO, 2016), was dedicated to the Senate hearings for the nomination of Justice Clarence Thomas to the US Supreme Court in 1991. Suspenseful only in principle (we see Justice Thomas still sitting on the Court today), the movie nonetheless makes us feel extreme tension in the scenes describing the long hours of hearings of Anita Hill (played by Kerry Washington, star of the series *Scandal*), an academic who denounced the harassment (verbal, unsubtle invitations, pornographic obsession) that Thomas had subjected her to when he was her colleague years before. We are chilled by the situation in which a 100 per cent male and white committee, led by Joe Biden (at the time a Democratic senator and a confoundingly cowardly character in the film) and pushed around by conservative Republicans, brutally and ironically interrogates a black, isolated, and vulnerable woman without giving the slightest credence to her assertions, and subsequently refuses to allow other women who were also victims of the same treatment by Thomas to testify. On the other hand, we are impressed by the scene in which Justice Thomas (the very convincing Wendell Pierce, a fan favourite from *The Wire*) defends himself with sincere anger at the questioning of his nomination, as the man who was to be the first black justice on the Supreme Court. Speaking of 'high-tech lynching', he invokes the (very real) racism of the political world (which was perfectly content with the stereotypical accusation of a black man), an argument that was also at the heart of OJ's defence (as if racism was all about him). The film is nonetheless a true rehabilitation of Anita Hill: it is true that today no one doubts the veracity of her testimony—if only because we realize that she had no personal interest in offering it, but also because, since then, the evidence of harassment has accumulated—without calling into question the presence of Justice Clarence Thomas in the highest court in the United States. The fact remains, however, that he lied at his Senate hearing—though his behaviour has undoubtedly become

---

* This article first appeared in *Libération*, 8 October 2018.

commonplace—not to mention the many decisions against women's rights that he has consistently approved since 1991.

When the film was released, it seemed decidedly retro—rather like the Cold War of the *Americans*, and some critics even had the finesse to point out how outdated these issues were. Today, we cannot help but return to this moment, with the questioning of the nomination of a judge to the same Supreme Court. Anita Hill herself intervened in the debate surrounding the confirmation of Brett Kavanaugh—the ultra-conservative judge proposed by Donald Trump to replace the rather moderate Anthony Kennedy and thus to give the conservatives control over the decisions of the Supreme Court, which we know are crucial for the rights of women, workers, and migrants, among others. Kavanaugh's first accuser, Christine Blasey Ford, also a woman, an academic, someone with little other reason to put herself forward than concern for the truth and the anguish of seeing her abuser reach the highest court in the land, can only remind us of Hill's situation. By contrast to Hill, however, either because Ford is white or because of the public restraint engendered by #MeToo, she was treated with respect by the Senate committee, spoke before Kavanaugh (the film *Confirmation* recalls that the order of the hearings was reversed at the last minute to have Clarence Thomas speak first), and was not, unlike Hill, deemed a slut or a liar in the press and political circles (it is true that this time we are talking about an attempted rape with physical coercion by a drunken and brutal Kavanaugh).

Only President Trump allowed himself to mock Christine Ford by mimicking her hesitations last Tuesday at a rally in support of a Republican candidate, which elicited laughter from his audience. In fact, it is these uncertainties that make her testimony credible—her sincerity, that right tone, has its effect: the power of truth in the female voice. Kavanaugh, in response, no doubt thought of the outraged (and ultimately effective) defence of Clarence Thomas, but his rage, including his hateful sneer (see Matt Damon's excellent impersonation of him on *Saturday Night Live*), had little to do with the former's defending himself in the name of race. Rather, Kavanaugh's response was calculated and bullying, a retort against the scandal of accusing someone so respectable (his argument has been that the accusation is incompatible with who he is, his background, and his character). We are flabbergasted by the multiple lies in his statement: admittedly, no one knows for sure what happened in that Bethesda house on a drunken night in 1982 (although we have some idea after Christine Ford's testimony), but no one is likely to buy the story of Brett Kavanaugh as a model student, exemplary friend, bookworm, altar boy, and dedicated soup kitchen volunteer—when multiple testimonies, including those from his friends, and his now famous yearbook, which lists his exploits, tell a different story of gilded youth, beer kegs, bullying, and crude sexism. This was evidenced by Renate Dolphin, who signed a collective letter of support for Kavanaugh, only to find that she had been collectively portrayed as an easy lay in the yearbook... and that Kavanaugh had 'Renate Alumnius' (*sic*, Latin is not his forte) on his yearbook.

Of course, one can change as one grows older, but why lie about the past? Drinking in itself is not a crime, but what matters is that the behaviour of the young Kavanaugh is incompatible with the character and the status of the good family man and ideal judge that he was attempting to cultivate in order to get his hands on a role on the Supreme Court. In any case, his conspiratorial and hateful speech, far from the impartiality expected of a candidate for the office, repulsed many—and confirmed the image of the Republican party as a party of 'Angry White Men'. These vindictive white men are not, as Trump's election suggested, frustrated working-class and poor victims of globalization—rather, they are also members of the elite. What Krugman calls their 'high-end' resentment is driven by the fear of losing their privileges, or their unbridled desire to cultivate even more. It does not matter what the outcome is of the White House-led FBI investigation—an investigation designed to rally the remaining undecideds to the confirmation of a judge with a proven track record of reactionary activism against workers, gays, the poor, and women.

The Courage of Truth on the Big Screen

Those who can't wait for the new (and alas final) season of *The Americans* can console themselves by going to see *The Post* by Steven Spielberg (2017), where, from the very first shots, we find Matthew Rhys—the main actor with Keri Russell in the cult series—as Daniel Ellsberg, a military analyst who goes to Vietnam. In 1965 he goes to the front line with the Secretary of Defense, Robert McNamara, and upon returning to the Rand Corporation a few years later, decides to secretly photocopy the thousands of pages that will become the *Pentagon Papers*—ultra-compromising reports revealing the lies of the various American administrations on the chances of victory for the United States in Vietnam. Beyond the story of the *New York Times* scoop, which was picked up after the *Washington Post* banned it, the film tells the story of old-fashioned journalism; that is, the real, not the fake (that of copy-and-paste circulation). Spielberg is keen to show us journalists such as Ben Bradlee (Tom Hanks) and Ben Bagdikian (extraordinary Bob Odenkirk), who go out into the field, and, through research and cunning, *make* the articles—from the investigation, to the writing and typography, production and distribution. The materiality of the production of information sums up the realism of the film, which accumulates details (the seat to be reserved on the plane to put down the precious package of documents, the typed article, the black metal of the press, for instance), not to create cheap nostalgia à la *Stranger Things*, but to counter, there and now, what a presidency at war with the press really is.

For once, completely in tune with current events—but far from the conventional discourse on the danger of 'fake news' or 'alternative facts' perversely taken up by Donald Trump himself, who does not hesitate to describe the truth as 'fake' when it displeases him—Spielberg manages to dismantle the political denial of the truth by describing the real process of information. Ten years ago, David Simon devoted the final season of *The Wire to* the evolution of investigative journalism, confronting fake news with serious social investigation; now *The Post*, which closes with the image and recorded voice of a hateful president holed up in his White House office, is a wonderful prequel—and not just to *Watergate*.

The film, which reunites for the first time the giants of the cinema Meryl Streep and Tom Hanks, is also the breathless story of the empowerment of Kay Graham, a wealthy heiress and newspaper owner, who is at first frightened and mute, and finally finds her voice (in the strongest sense), during a Dantean telephone conversation in which she resists the pressure of an army of men who want to make her give up. Truth and feminism are indeed the narrative forces of the film, and Spielberg accurately portrays the reality of domination—100 per cent tie-dye meetings, women at the door of serious discussion—as well as the courage of Graham, who is greeted by the hurrah

---

* This article first appeared in *Libération*, 1 March 2018.

of young women as she exits the courtroom, as a white middle-class woman who has become an icon of feminism.

At the same time as film critics were praising *The Post*, they were missing *Black Panther* (Ryan Coogler, 2018)—an equally feminist revolution, even if the plot is based on the struggle between two men. As the first superhero film aimed at a wide audience in which all the main characters are black Africans—including several beautiful, and very different, strong black women, including Nakia, the beautiful human rights activist; Shuri, Q's bonkers super-techno little sister; and Okoye, the imposing general-in-chief—who are entirely at ease with their power. *Wonder Woman* (Patty Jenkins, 2017) had taken a step forward on this issue, as the first film based entirely on a superheroine who went back to men, but Diana still remained exceptional, alone in her genre even afterwards in *Justice League* (Zack Snyder, 2017). *Black Panther* thus goes further than this by presenting a plurality of women on-screen (each linked to King T'Challa but never defined by the link), and by taking up the Hollywood theme of remarriage, which since the 1940s has given the white elite the task of representing the nation and the reiteration of 'staying together'; that is, of representing the Union.

'All women are white, all blacks are men, but there are a few of us who are brave...' was the first slogan of black feminism that this film unabashedly embraces, presenting us with the utopia of a mixed egalitarian society. To snub *Black Panther* because it is a Marvel film (and therefore simplistic), and because it is a popular success, is to miss out—not only on the blockbuster event (complacently hailed), but also on the cultural and artistic event that it constitutes—both for black people who go en masse even if they don't adhere to everything, and for the others who have the chance to get attached to these magnificent characters, while also educating themselves on mining in Africa or the history of slavery.

The casting choices of *Black Panther* are not insignificant, thanks to the talent of Chadwick Boseman, Lupita Nyong'o, Daniel Kaluuya, Letitia Wright, and others. As such, we are moved to see Danai Gurira, the mythical Michonne from *The Walking Dead*; Michael B. Jordan, young Wallace from the first season of *The Wire* and Sterling K. Brown, the powerful prosecutor of *The People v. O.J. Simpson*, who has since starred in *This Is Us, as* if it were also a question of proudly aligning all those who have allowed the TV series to prepare the revolution of cinema.

The L Word: **The Return**

For the 2004–2009 fans, the cult series *The L Word* is back on Canal+ with a 100 per cent lesbian cast, and with its main heroines accompanied by an entirely new generation. Since 9 December, we have been reacquainted, almost a decade after we said goodbye to them, with the super-classy Bette (Jennifer Beals), the media-savvy and zany Alice (Leisha Hailey), and the tomboy Shane (Katherine Moennig)—whose return to Los Angeles after ten years of absence is the narrative excuse for the reunion. The new series makes us see how much things have changed—or not—in addition to the pleasure of seeing characters we were all (male, female, LGBTQ, and straight viewers alike) formerly attached to: I particularly remember talking about it regularly with the late Ruwen Ogien, who loved it, even if, like me, he had his doubts about the last few seasons. Only by watching the first few episodes of *The L Word: Generation Q* does one understand how necessary this return was: the series once again imposes the lesbian monopoly and, as a second trademark, raw sex—the first scene of the first episode, featuring both cunnilingus and menstrual blood, displays both heritage (this is *The L Word*) and the additional progress that has been made since the series first aired: things can be shown today that were not shown in 2009. The show also needed new, more diverse characters for these new generations: Finley, Micah (Leo Sheng, a real transgender person of Chinese origin); Sophie, a Dominican woman from New York—in other words, representation of the whole LGBTQ spectrum.

Before *The L Word*, there had been a few kisses and cult scenes on *Buffy*, *Friends*, *Ally McBeal*, but it wasn't until *The Wire* and the character of Kima Greggs that there was a solid lesbian heroine—lesbian and black. Even after that, despite progress in the representation of gays on-screen, this was essentially limited to the token lesbian(s), adrift in a straight cast or story. One must remember the shock, mixed with admiration, attachment, and annoyance, that initially met *The L Word* when it arrived, marking a fundamental shift in the representation of lesbians: by a group of insolently intelligent, beautiful, wealthy women whose image unashamedly fought against the stereotypes of the suffering or marginalized lesbian. These women had hilarious conversations, went out and had fun, had lots of sex, broke up with and cheated on each other, and lived one-night stands, long-lasting affairs, and intense friendships. They introduced us, through their form of life on the screen (for it was our television screen that put it under our noses every week) to this collective life of formidable force, imposing both its normality and its reality by multiplying the profiles and styles of the characters, all more or less gay.

The L Word was not the first group show (*Friends* and *Sex and the City* came before it), but it was the first to utilize to this degree the potential of a large group of women (nearly thirty in total, connected by strong and weak

---

* This article first appeared in *Libération*, 26 December 2019.

ties of work, friendship, cohabitation, and encounters), whose extension in concentric circles around the core of the heroines covered the surface of an iconic city, Los Angeles, as their playground and, soon after, the backdrop for their political activism.

The virtue of *The L Word* was to be both an eye-opener and an education for a wide audience, which extended well beyond its 'target'. Of course, it is a series of reference for lesbians, as, far from any identity discourse, *The L Word* has thus been able to depict different and individual experiences within a lesbian and multiracial (although not enough, despite Pam Grier's superb presence) community. In this way, fiction not only represented the lesbian community, but also constructed it. Ilene Chaiken, creator of the original series and executive producer of the reboot, spoke of her surprise and disappointment that the void left by the departure of *The L Word* in 2009 had not been filled in ten years. She imagined that the drama would have all sorts of successors. But no. The lesbian series is not a genre, like the vampire series, which has been proliferated through all sorts of versions in the twenty-first century—instead, *The L Word* was a pioneer without successor or imitator. There was the excellent *Orange Is the New Black* on Netflix, which, with its strong female characters and network of gay relationships, was certainly the closest to it. But for the audience, life in a women's prison is not exactly the ordinary world—at least not with the glamour of *The L Word's* Los Angeles.

The L Word is unique and cult-like for all generations of lesbians (especially younger ones, who grew up alongside it): the new director, 34-year-old Marja-Lewis Ryan, is a lifelong fan, as are the young actresses in this new *Generation Q*. Jacqueline Toboni, who plays the young lesbian Sarah Finley ('Finley' to her friends), says she was stunned to see on set the stars of her high school days, who she was binge-watching on the first season's DVD box set: it seems that at any given moment, someone is rewatching *The L Word*: 'Because there's nothing else.'

The original series predated gay marriage, but *Generation Q*, in contrast, will feature storylines of engagement, marriage, and divorce, like so many other series. But it will also have to face, with its renewed diversity, the repressed issues of *The L Word*: the awkwardness of lesbian powerhouse Bette running to become LA's first gay mayor, the financial affluence of almost all the heroines... Since 2009, things have changed in the genre, and what is new is not just expanding the 'L' to 'LGBTQIA'—it is intersectionality and the transection of social and racial critique with gender inequality and the defence of sexualities. The imagination, moral ambition, and radicalism of the series can be counted on to stop sweeping these issues under the rug.

Best Enemies

The Queen's Gambit has been remarkably enjoyable amid the assorted horrors of this year. The plot of the miniseries (an unexpected success, reaching number 1 on Netflix), is set in the midst of the Cold War United States, and is tenuous and contrived: Beth Harmon, orphaned at the age of nine after a car accident, is sent to the grim Methuen Home for Girls in Kentucky. Escaping to the home's dingy basement, Beth meets a gruff yet caring employee, Mr Shaibel (Bill Camp), who introduces her to chess, at which she turns out to be a true genius. From episode two onwards, Beth is played by Anya Taylor-Joy, who carries the series with a talent just as impressive as the heroine's, transforming Beth from an ungrateful, odd teenager into a magnetic and singular protagonist: it is this mysterious metamorphosis of the actress that evokes the genius of the character, and is what gives *The Queen's Gambit* its bewitching appeal. It is also the chess, with its masculine image, as well as the pedagogy of the series, which is irresistible; even if one knows little about it, one is taken in by the game. The story, which follows Beth's victorious trajectory at her competitions, her openings and defences, makes chess look sexy—since the series aired, sales of chessboards have increased by more than 500 per cent in the United States. Beth's superhuman talent gives her an undeniable feminine power: neither her vulnerabilities (her melancholic search for a mother figure, addictions to just about everything), nor any glass ceiling will get the better of her.

Beth is undeniably a fictional character—no woman has yet reached this level in chess, for reasons that are hardly analysed in *The Queen's Gambit*, and it is precisely this that is her strength: for once, her genius overcomes everything, and nothing can stand in the way of a woman's rise—she benefits from the solidarity of women (Jolene, Alma) and the kindness of almost all the men, who give her support and advice, provide occasional sexual services, and accept her domination without complaint. A fiction, I tell you.

All the previous films devoted to prodigies (usually men), such as *Good Will Hunting* (Gus Van Sant, 1997), *A Beautiful Mind* (Ron Howard, 2001), and *Moneyball* (Bennett Miller, 2011), come up against the difficulty of portraying intellectual exceptionalism on film by 'normal' actors who can only exhibit it in a limited way (e.g., by hypnotic visualization of numbers). *The Queen's Gambit* achieves this over the course of a miniseries through the addictive multiplication of the chess games, and through the perfectionist demand that drives Beth—revealed in her manic elegance and the beauty of the sets. It is by positing Beth as an ideal to be reached that this series conveys a feminist ambition, by proposing a role model that reality cannot yet offer.

The Queen's Gambit confirms the impression that, since #MeToo, it is women's turn in series ('My turn', says Robin Wright's Claire Underwood at the end of the fifth season of *House of Cards*). They take centre stage in

---

* This article first appeared in *Libération*, 3 December 2020.

Game of Thrones, Big Little Lies, The Handmaid's Tale, Killing Eve, Unbelievable, and others. However, the question of gender is no longer merely statistical—it is also the question that has been raised over the last decades: the issue of visibility. Series offer us cultural tools for analysing women's situations and histories, including through figures who have nothing feminist about them.

The Second Wave of Feminist Series

Ruth Bader Ginsburg, the great progressive and feminist American Supreme Court Justice, who, having died last September, has just been 'replaced', by the Republican Senate with indecent speed, by the judge and anti-abortion activist, Amy Coney Barrett. Ginsburg was also, however, an icon of popular culture: '*The Notorious RBG*' (a nickname taken from the great rapper Notorious B.I.G.), was mentioned on the series *Big Bang Theory* (s12e6), and even impersonated by Kate McKinnon on *Saturday Night Live*. She was the subject of two films in 2018: the landmark documentary *RBG* (by Betsy West and Julie Cohen) and the biopic *On the Basis of Sex* (by Mimi Leder, a well-known director of series from *ER* to *The Leftovers*). In the latter, RBG is played by star Felicity Jones (who we saw as the heroine of *Rogue One*, Gareth Edwards, 2016) in a film that depicts her education, her relationship with her husband (Armie Hammer, whom we remember from *The Social Network*, David Fincher, 2010, and recently *Call Me by Your Name*, Luca Guadagnino, 2017, who is excellent as a resolutely feminist husband), her difficulties in finding a job after law school, and her first big case.

RBG's character also makes a micro-appearance in the brilliant miniseries *Mrs. America*, in the episode 'Phyllis & Fred & Brenda & Marc' (the title being a homage to Mazursky's 1969 film, *Bob & Carol & Ted & Alice*), which is centred on a beautiful feminist lawyer character, Brenda Feigen (Ari Graynor), another pioneering student at Harvard Law, and also evokes the LGBT struggles within the feminist movements of the 1970s. The fictional fate of RBG is an example of the interplay of popular culture and politics.

This is the era of feminist series, which have grown explosively since #MeToo, a development that, perhaps irreversibly, has brought women to the forefront of the small screen. Already, over the past decade, female characters have come to dominate where male heroes have not survived: whether in the series phenomenon *Game of Thrones*, where female heroines are in the majority in the final seasons, or in *House of Cards*, where it is the president's wife (the chilling Claire Underwood, played by Robin Wright) who ends up wielding power. *Orange Is the New Black* has brought an extraordinarily diverse cast of women to the screen in a prison series, a hugely popular genre traditionally dominated by men. Kerry Washington has long played a sexy black female politician in *Scandal*, before playing Anita Hill in *Confirmation* (Rick Famuyiwa, 2016) a film about the scandal surrounding the appointment of Clarence Thomas as a Supreme Court justice in 1991.

It is no longer just about women gaining visibility, however. After a 'first wave' in which women advanced towards equal presence in popular series, with sexual rights at stake (with the classic and emblematic *Sex and the City* and *The*

---

* This article first appeared in *AOC (Analyse Opinion Critique)*, at https://aoc.media/critique/2020/11/02/sur-la-deuxieme-vague-des-series-americaines-feministes/, 3 November 2020.

L Word), we are now in the middle of a 'second wave' that offers the public tools for cultural analysis of women's situation, confirming that the right to vote is not the same as political equality. The series *Unbelievable*, based on an investigation by the media outlet ProPublica, introduces us to two female detectives engaged in an investigation that leads them to confront a serial rapist—and a police force that is negligent, grossly incompetent, and brutal towards the victims, who are immediately deemed lacking in credibility. The feminist power of the series lies in the double meaning of the title: no one wants to believe Marie (Kaitlyn Dever), the rapist's first victim, a vulnerable young woman living in a community for at-risk youth; equally, the viewer can't believe their eyes at the inequity of the system. The originality of *Unbelievable* is that it focuses not on the rapist but on the victims, mistreated by an inconsistent and uncaring judicial system; on highlighting the difference in victims' treatment by the male police officers (who refuse to believe Marie, force her to retract her testimony, and even go so far as to violently charge her with making a false statement) and by the two female police officers who take care of them, not only treating them properly, but also caring for them by listening and meticulously hunting down the culprit. Finally, *Unbelievable* holds its own with its actresses, Collette and Wever, who are not regularly seen in the role of the strong female character, but who become the first credible incarnation of a female 'cop couple'—*True Detective* reincarnated in the feminine—and who refuse to value themselves on the grounds of being sexy, twisted, or 'badass', but instead for a job well done.

In this context, one wonders whether the feminine and feminist power of recent series is not simply brought about by the arrival in force of a whole generation of actresses ready to take this female genre to the next level, much as the Hollywood comedies and melodramas of the 1930s–1940s did.[2] Collette and Wever; Reese Witherspoon, Nicole Kidman, and Shailene Woodley in *Big Little Lies*; Regina King in *Seven Seconds* and *Watchmen*; Sandra Oh and Jodie Comer in *Killing Eve*; Cate Blanchett and Uzo Aduba in *Mrs. America*; not to mention Elizabeth Moss in *Top of the Lake* and *The Handmaid's Tale*, or even Claire Danes in *Homeland*. These are actresses who, like Hepburn, Dunne, and Barbara Stanwyck in the last century, do not have the profile of young debutantes—nor the desire to be subjected to any kind of male gaze—but rather resolutely embody self-confidence and female solidarity. In doing so, they build on the previous generation, and therefore on the first wave: Holly Hunter in *Top of the Lake*, *Succession*, and *The Comey Rule*; Pam Grier in *The L Word*; Meryl Streep joining *Big Little Lies* for the second season (in which she is the only really stand-out element).

This is not to forget the new generation: another Netflix miniseries, *Unorthodox*, describes the liberation journey of a young woman from an Orthodox Jewish community in Brooklyn; another, *Stateless*, depicts that of

---

2   See Stanley Cavell, *Pursuits of Happiness* (Cambridge, MA: Harvard University Press, 1981).

a woman accidentally trapped in a migrant camp in New Zealand; while the most radical of contemporary series is certainly *I May Destroy You*, which explores the facets of the post-#MeToo era and the question of consent. All explore the diversity of female oppressions today.

For those who wish to understand this second-wave serial feminism, however, *Mrs. America* is certainly the richest resource. The series celebrates both the diversity of feminists and their commitments, and the emerging and significant conflicts between white 'notables' and black and LGBT women that accompanied the rise of political feminism, as well as the figures of Gloria Steinem (Rose Byrne), Bella Abzug (Margo Martindale), Betty Friedan (Tracey Ullman), and Shirley Chisholm (Uzo Aduba), whose name has recently been revived by current vice-presidential candidate Kamala Harris.

Mrs. America thus scripts the culture wars of the last century, which, although our own, had not yet made their way into series. Unlike the civil rights or anti-war movements, which have been commemorated in numerous films and miniseries, the women's movement of the 1970s has been largely neglected by popular culture, either because series production has long been dominated by men, or because the front lines of the feminist battle, such as abortion and reproductive rights—a priority cause, as *Mrs. America* makes clear—domestic violence, and LGBT rights, remain controversial even today.

Over the course of its nine episodes, the series follows the decade-long battle over the Equal Rights Amendment, a measure that initially enjoyed broad Democratic and even bipartisan support but was ultimately blocked by conservative activists. In exploring both sides of this culture war over the period of 1971 to 1980, the series details the story of the women's movement, with each episode focusing on one of the figures from the time. The series thus offers lucid portraits of mythical and rival feminist thinkers such as Gloria Steinem and Betty Friedan, as well as less famous but politically crucial women, such as Republican feminist Jill Ruckelshaus (Elizabeth Banks) (a species that, hardly imaginable today, demonstrates the disastrous evolution of the Republican party since that time). *Mrs. America* is unique in that it centres on an influential enemy of feminism, Schlafly, the founder of the Eagle Forum, who died at the age of 92 just after endorsing Donald Trump, and represents another political outsider who channelled, quite successfully, 'white' angst in the face of contemporary cultural transformations. The series offers a timely examination of female political power, touching on some sensitive topics: the crucial political role of anti-feminist women defending the traditional family; the internal inequalities of the feminist movement, with the experiences of black feminists such as Chisholm, who made history with her 1972 candidacy, but faced the overall reluctance of white feminists to support her, preferring the white-male-ally candidate McGovern.

Aduba, who shot *Mrs. America* right after the final season of *Orange Is the New Black*, did so because the show highlighted so many accomplished yet overlooked women. Schlafly herself is one of those women forgotten by history, as suggested by her husband's constant boorishness, or the series' melancholy conclusion, which sees her returning to her kitchen after helping Reagan win the presidency by mobilizing her anti-feminist networks. Her supporters, including her close friend Alice Macray (the remarkable Sarah Paulson), are described with care and sympathy: in a key line in the series, Bella Abzug terms Schlafly 'the most liberated woman in America'.

Beyond this, *Mrs. America* highlights the emergence of the anti-feminist argument as a major political tool of ultra-conservative ideology that would soon be dominant among Republicans, and which crescendoed until the arrival of Trump, who subsequently gave the signal that women could be freely attacked, denigrated, and publicly insulted. This same historic moment for women is well depicted in the new series *The Comey Rule*, in particular by the scene where the whole family—the wife and four daughters—of James Comey, then director of the FBI, are in tears before the announcement on TV of the results of the presidential election: the series comes back, rather pedagogically, to the horrible moment in 2016 when the FBI had, a few days before the vote, reopened the investigation into Hillary Clinton (who had used her private, unsecured email while she was Secretary of State). With distance, one can wonder if Comey (unintentionally) played a role in the defeat of the Democratic candidate against Trump or if it was, quite simply, the irreducible (entrenched) sexism of American society that determined the outcome of the election—that is, the cultural rather than the political.

It is indeed the #MeToo movement that has allowed, after this terrible backlash, popular culture to take a renewed interest in second-wave feminists and their themes: a Steinem biopic is soon to be released featuring Alicia Vikander and Julianne Moore,[3] as well as one about Chisholm with Viola Davis; similarly, the Equal Rights Amendment itself was ratified in 2017, four decades after being blocked (by Nevada, Illinois, and Virginia), reviving hopes that it might one day be passed.

Today's TV series no longer confine themselves to the role of mirror of a society—rather, they claim the history of feminism by asserting their role within it as a direct factor of change. Aduba won Best Supporting Actress for her portrayal of Shirley Chisholm at a historic, albeit 'remote', Emmy night that saw the triumph of an unprecedented number of black actors and actresses: Regina King and Yahya Abdul-Mateen for *Watchmen*, voted best series 2019; as well as Zendaya, Maya Rudolph, Eddie Murphy, Ron Cephas Jones, and Laurence Fishburne. Regina King, a genius actress awarded for the fourth time, symbolizes the turning point achieved by series (far ahead of Hollywood cinema) in their focus on black women, no longer a token or gadget, but a legitimate political gesture with multiple implications.

These long-invisible women in cinema are certainly the most striking element in the transformations brought about by and in popular culture. Two major HBO works, *Watchmen* and the extraordinary *Lovecraft Country*, both

---

3 *The Glorias* (Julie Taymor, 2020).

of which revisit repressed episodes of American history (the Tulsa massacre), radically broaden, as *Black Panther* had already done, the audience for black characters, who have themselves become iconic saviours of their nation or the world, and in *Watchmen* and *Lovecraft Country*, black women are the superheroes. By exploring all the resources of popular culture—comic books, Lovecraft fantasy, horror, and superheroes—by featuring women as well as black actors (such as Michael K. Williams from *The Wire*, who featured on *The Night Of* and *When They See Us*), these series are emblematic of today's struggles for equality. They articulate them in a highly realistic way, through new and exuberant violence, using the horror genre to express the daily terror of black lives. In particular, black women, who have been terribly neglected in history, are now recognized to be at the forefront of the quest for women's rights: today—as in the last congressional elections—they are the strong arm in the fight against a Republican Party that has become synonymous with sexism and racism.

Of course, Trump supporters will never see these shows—or any current series for that matter, as their culture is Fox News and websites—so they cannot change them. The role of popular culture (culture in the strong sense, which educates and uplifts those willing to be transformed) is political. What gives us hope is not only the reassuringly unmanly figure of Democratic candidate Joe Biden, his respect for those who have died from COVID-19, the full support (this time) of Bernie Sanders (and the fact that Biden will not suffer from misogyny), but also the democratic revival symbolized by the presence of Kamala Harris. This is not about her political positions, which are quite moderate, but about the remobilization of 'civil society' that her presence on the ticket alone signifies, on two grounds: #MeToo and the fight against sexual harassment; that is, against the patriarchy so perfectly represented by Trump and the type of society defended by the Republicans. This movement sums up the feminist revival, which the second wave of feminist series is claiming, and which cuts across social classes: even middle-class housewives in the American suburbs are fed up with the crass machismo of Trump, who boasts of finding jobs for 'their husbands'. The second mobilization that occurred just before the election campaign and in the midst of the pandemic was, of course, the reawakening of the structural issue of police violence against the black community, with the spread of the Black Lives Matter movement and the protests following the terrible murder of George Floyd (which added to the disproportionately heavy toll the pandemic took on black and Hispanic communities). Again, the protests went far beyond the targeted community, extending to the whole of the United States, including many white women and men.

These two mobilizations, feminist and anti-racist, whose themes have been powerfully taken up by popular culture, should have an impact on the question of voter abstention by Democrats and young people, many of whom did not bother to vote for Clinton, seeing her as a symbol of the white establishment. What may win Biden the election is therefore, beyond his persona, this mobilization within the Democratic party, made possible by #MeToo and Black Lives Matter, both of which have broken into conformist Democratic thinking.

It is also the new generation of elected women and left-wing Democratic activists—black, Hispanic, Asian, and white—who are joyfully threatening the party's bigwigs by promising them painful local primaries: what a pleasure to watch the fantastic four of 'the Squad' (Alexandria Ocasio-Cortez, Ilhan Omar, Ayanna Pressley, and Rashida Tlaib) welcome the politically active rapper Common live on Instagram and, with him, dictate the melody of new democratic rules. They are resolutely part of popular culture, in the tradition of Barack Obama.

It is these TV series that contribute to the necessary transformation of the Democratic camp, by expressing, aestheticizing, and universalizing these mobilizations. This is the meaning of popular culture and its potential for transformation: TV series not only reveal a situation, but also the political tools for change, which involve, by definition, culture wars.

Impeachment

Throughout episode six of the new series *American Crime Story: Impeachment*, we see the character of Monica Lewinsky (Beanie Feldstein) arrested by the FBI, whose more or less patient agents take turns pressuring her to 'confess' to an illicit relationship with President Clinton and also to a false statement at the trial to which she was called as a witness. One inevitably thinks, buoyed by the wave of feminist American TV series of recent years, of the terrifying scene at the beginning of the series *Unbelievable* where, in the first episode, the heroine Marie (Kaitlyn Dever), under police pressure, gives up on pressing charges for the rape she has just suffered. Marie's extreme vulnerability and deep destabilization is not comparable with that of Monica, a privileged young girl whose impressive nerve has repeatedly appeared in earlier moments of the series, and there is a sense here of a comic version of the police exercise of male dominance. But episode six of *Impeachment*, entitled 'Manhandled', is simply mind-boggling in just how crass is the harassing and manhandling of young Monica over eleven hours by a bunch of men in suits and ties. They threaten her with twenty-eight years in prison—with the ultimate goal of destroying President Clinton. Monica herself, who has in previous episodes always appeared well dressed, is here in a tracksuit and socks, and is alone, at the mercy of the FBI's sordid manoeuvres. Nevertheless, she proves to be disconcertingly courageous, and, carried away by her fixation on the president and her erotomanic delirium, she gives in to the FBI, until her mother (the exceptional Mira Sorvino) arrives to get her out of the predicament.

This episode six is the moment when the series takes off, and is certainly the defining experience. Here Ryan Murphy is at his best, as he was in the most turbulent moments of *American Crime Story* season one, *The People v. O.J. Simpson*—indeed, the 1990s is his thing, offbeat and avant-garde with respect to the 1980s nostalgia that dominates series, as seen with *The Americans, Show Me a Hero, Stranger Things, The Deuce, Pose, Little Fires Everywhere, Mindhunter, Deutschland 83, 86, 89* and season four of *The Crown*. This is the decade, momentarily buried under the ruins of 9/11, when the political hatreds of the present moment fermented: race relations and homophobia in seasons one and two; misogyny in season three. Episode seven is entitled 'The Assassination of Monica Lewinsky', a reworking of season two's title *The Assassination of Gianni Versace*, and depicts the media lynching of all the women involved, including Monica and Hillary, but also the less sympathetic Linda Tripp and Paula Jones, victims of the same system of denigration of women. Sarah Paulson, Ryan Murphy's favourite actress, brings her genius to bear on the frightening and fascinating character of Tripp.

Impeachment is part of a series of rehabilitations in and by popular culture of women who have been dragged through the mud in the last century: Anita Hill (*Confirmation*, Rick Famuyiwa, 2016), Tonya Harding (*I, Tonya*,

---

* This article first appeared in *Libération*, 5 November 2021.

Craig Gillespie, 2017), and Lewinsky have all been humiliated in various ways, including by moral condemnation. This is not just a banal post-#MeToo revenge story, but a way for these women to right history, to take back control of their destiny, and even to find their voice; Lewinsky herself is a co-producer of *Impeachment* (which portrays her as a whining obsessive with few talents). *Impeachment*, explicitly part of the *American Crime Story* series, prompts us to ask *where* the crime is actually located: by focusing on the women around Clinton, all victims of the scandal up to Hillary Clinton's failed election in 2016, Murphy shifts the 'crime' of the title from Clinton's creepy, incontinent behaviour (even if the series forces us to look back ingloriously to the time when we in France laughed at 'American puritanism' as much as we laughed at Monica's assets). The question of consent is now posed in a different way, and, given their respective positions, it is clear to all that Lewinsky, however flirtatious she may have been (the detail of the thong shown comes from the producer herself), was in a subordinate position, whereas Bill Clinton was in a position of abuse.

We know the real crime: the refusal in the 1990s to allow a reformist, Democratic president to act (who, the character recalls, not without complacency in the series, was the first to place many women in positions of responsibility). Beyond this, continuing up to the present day, is the permanent desire of the conservative right to delegitimize any progressive action—to overturn an electoral result by manipulating the law, misinforming, or by using violence along with any other possible means of blocking it. The appearance in *Impeachment* of a particularly bad young Brett Kavanaugh (who was later appointed to the Supreme Court by Donald Trump) alongside the prosecutor Starr (author of the demented 445-page report that led the Republican House to vote for impeachment) clearly signals the challenge of the recontextualization carried out by the series: to allow new generations to rediscover the characters and stories that have shaped our century, and to denounce a crime that is still ongoing.

Women Save the World

Already in recent years, women's characters have begun to dominate, even in the phenomenon that is the series *Game of Thrones*. *Unbelievable* presents two female detectives conducting an investigation that leads them to confront a serial rapist, as well as a police milieu that is negligent, grossly incompetent, and brutal towards victims, who are immediately considered to 'lack credibility'. There is, at the moment, another wonderful miniseries, *Unorthodox*, which describes the journey to liberation of a young woman from an orthodox Jewish community in Brooklyn. *Mrs. America* traces the history of feminism through the journey of Phyllis Schlafly (the remarkable Cate Blanchett), a conservative activist who achieved glory in the 1970s by successfully blocking the adoption of the Equal Rights Amendment, which aimed to enshrine equal rights between the sexes in the American Constitution. It is two (or even three) masterful women who carry *Killing Eve*, which depicts the ambivalent war between Eve Polastri (Sandra Oh), an MI-5 agent and Villanelle (Jodie Comer), a psychopathic assassin. The genre of police or spy series, which until now has been rather male-dominated (in the tradition of James Bond) has also been taken in hand by women, in particular, Gillian Anderson from *X-Files* to *The Fall*; Helen Mirren in *Prime Suspect*; and the great Caroline Proust in *Engrenages*, who constructs the figure of a policewoman who is not in line with feminine ideals. It is not just a question of parity on the screen: these women propose new forms of work, friendship, and humour that transform the laws of the police and security genres—they are the ones who can be entrusted with the fate of a world that is dangerous for a multiplicity of reasons.

The inequality between women and men in the film world has long been denounced: whether in its representations and narratives, with the predominance of male heroes and subjects despite magnificent female characters; or in its industry, where only a handful of women have emerged in symbolically valued roles, such as that of director. Feminist protests in the United States and in France at the awards shows that constitute the profession's ritual events (this year no female film director has been nominated) reveal the meagre progress made in the twenty-first century in a field still dominated by the virile rhetoric of the author, propounded by critics and scholars alike.

TV series, however, have had a different trajectory. As a devalued medium, they withstand frequent contemptuous comments made by patent cinephiles towards series and their audiences, which is no doubt the result of their reception within the domestic universe, where the TV is a piece of furniture and the audience is often female. Series are historically a minor medium aimed at young people and women, and portray the family universe, allowing for the lasting establishment of female characters: examples in the second half of the twentieth century abound—from *Bewitched*, *The Mary Tyler Moore*

---

* This article first appeared in *Libération*, 19 July 2020.

Show, *Kate & Allie*, *Golden Girls*, to *Dr. Quinn, Medicine Woman* or *Ally McBeal*—with enduring series that are based on strong female characters, while cinema of the time offered very few equivalent films. The true feminist revolution in series took place at the turn of the century with the cult series *Buffy the Vampire Slayer*, and the arrival of the cable channel HBO. HBO gave birth to the provocative *Sex and the City* in 1998, which featured an almost all-female cast of four independent (at least in principle) women in search of the ideal sex life in New York.

HBO not only had the nerve to launch *Sex and the City*, but also a series of major works that both established series as cinematic works in their own right and positioned women in a dialogue of equals with men: *The Sopranos*, *Six Feet Under*, and *The Wire* are classic series that played a role in undermining the domination of men by exposing male fragility. In this respect, other networks competed with HBO, such as AMC with *Mad Men*, a masterpiece that dismantles the patriarchal and capitalist society of the 1960s, or *Desperate Housewives*—which, like *Sex and the City*, presents a range of women characters, this time housewives in an upscale suburb—or the cult classic *The L Word*, the first and last 100 per cent lesbian series.

Since then, deliberately feminist series, often featuring an ensemble of women as *heroes*, have almost dominated the market; see, for instance, Jane Campion's magnificent *Top of the Lake*. The most visible have been *Big Little Lies*, which brings together the biggest stars of today, *Orange Is the New Black*, a Netflix classic, and recently, *The Marvelous Mrs. Maisel*, *The Handmaid's Tale*, as well as *Killing Eve* and *Fleabag* by Phoebe Waller-Bridge (regularly rewarded at the Emmys and Golden Globes). These are series that not only feature women, but are also *feminist*, with markers such as the presence of Elizabeth Moss, who was seen in *Mad Men*, *Top of the Lake*, and *The Handmaid's Tale*. In France, the underestimated and excellent series *Engrenages* has as its heroine a female cop, an ultra-competent chief, who, single and unstable just like the standard male characters in police series, has a great deal to do with the series' success.

The aesthetic power of television series has adjusted well to the gradual physical and ethical prominence of women. The polyphonic character of series allows for a plurality of singular expressions, the staging of disputes, debates, and misunderstandings. Their extension over a temporality of several years, through the return of the seasons, allows women to better settle in the landscape, while the focus on families gives a new place to private life and brings an emphasis on professions such as health and justice. It is this methodology of series, not only their narrativity but above all their introduction and construction of the characters, that makes them relevant and morally expressive: it forces us to revise the status of morality, to see it not in rules and principles of decision, but in attention to ordinary behaviour, and in individuals' styles of expression. All these transformations of morality are linked to the inclusion of women in moral philosophy, which has too long excluded females by being excessively abstract and contemptuous of private feelings. The material of the television series allows for a contextualization, a historicity (regularity, duration), a familiarization, and an inscription in ordinary life that allows for the democratization of the 'personal' in series.

Cavell, in his classic work *Pursuits of Happiness*, asserted the importance of collective writing to film, as well as the function of the scriptwriter and actors in the elaboration of a film's meaning and value. We realize that television has inherited, in a new form, the challenge of moral education from popular cinema: a viewer who follows a series from the beginning can live with its characters for five or seven years or more—a considerable length of time given that there are few people in real life who are with us for so long. The fact that women have a lasting presence in the lives of male and female viewers is essential to the transformation of gender representation. The small screen offers a unique site of expression for these new faces, whose diversity is evident in the credits of *Orange Is the New Black*. Feminist series were the first to display intersectionality, even if *Sex and the City* was criticized for its cast of white women. The next step in the representativeness of series was the presence of women from racial minorities (Kerry Washington, star of *Scandal*) along with older women: Pam Grier on *The L Word*, Meryl Streep in *Big Little Lies*.

In an excellent episode of *The West Wing*, 'Bartlet's Third State of the Union' (2001, s2e13), one of President Bartlet's White House staffers, Sam Seaborn (Rob Lowe), learns through a chance conversation with presidential spokeswoman C.J. Cregg (Alison Janney) and her assistant Carol Fitzpatrick that the White House staff gym provides comfortable bathrobes, which are available… only in the women's locker room. Green with envy, he is indignant: 'It's an outrage. There are a thousand men working here and only 50 women, to which C.J. retorts: 'Yeah, that's right, the bathrobes are the scandal.'

This exchange illustrates how easy it is to be outraged by any apparent advantage given to women (as shown, for example, by the masculinist mobilization over child custody for divorced or separated couples, or the uproar over the unveiling of a male municipal candidate's private life). The moment also shows how mainstream TV series have regularly been the site of feminist tweaks by using the audience's attachment to 'relatable' characters—even in a mainstream series that is not particularly feminist, there are moments of public education towards a more inclusive society. TV series are thus historically the site of a democratic emancipation that today culminates in the cross-representation of class, age, race and sexuality (the presence of gay and now transgender characters, not only in the classic *Six Feet Under* or *The L Word*, but also in more 'popular' series is undoubtedly strategic).

The strongest lesson of these works that highlight the diversity of women in various life phases is the importance of gender solidarity (which was so lacking in the US presidential election). However, it is also the friendship between women (already at the heart of *Sex and the City*) that emerges as a central moral issue in *Big Little Lies*. In its two seasons, *Big Little Lies* depicts a group of women who are different but all, in the end, united to help two of them take revenge on a criminal husband. Even before the #MeToo wave, *Big Little Lies* proposed that women should all fight back together against what they acknowledge as the 'main' enemy.[4]

---

4 Christine Delphy, *L'ennemi principal* (Paris: Syllepse, 1997).

Screening Intersectionality

'Intersectionality' is a term that often provokes at best confusion and at worst aggression. This may be because the concept is not always explained, but it also has to do with the difficulty feminists themselves have in thinking about the inequalities between women and defending a 'black feminism'. To understand intersectionality, one needs to look no further than the characters on the three-season series *American Crime*, whose lives combine poverty, lack of education, and racial and sometimes religious oppression. The show, using an ingenious technique common to certain anthological series, casts the same actors throughout its three seasons, but in different roles, with variations in the characters' social positions and profiles from one season to another. By showing the same actresses—in particular, the excellent Regina King and Felicity Huffman—and actors—especially Timothy Hutton—in inverted social situations, *American Crime* explores class, gender, and race relations in all their difficulty and complexity, and renders directly perceptible the arbitrariness of racial segregation, which can lead, seemingly ineluctably, from poverty to exclusion and delinquency. It is not a matter of alternating points of view as in the film *Rashomon* (Akira Kurosawa, 1950), but rather of constructing characters in new contexts, which creates both understanding and shock, and reveals, better than any discourse, the full weight and violence of discrimination. And the show is broadcast on a major public network, ABC, making it more democratic than if it were on cable or an online platform.

Intersectionality thus viewed on-screen is a necessary, everyday concept, and it allows the viewer to understand, beyond the accumulation or combination of traits, how women's very identities are themselves intersectional, and how domination today is defined by multiple oppressions. It is a tool that renders visible extreme yet ordinary forms of discrimination and vulnerability, and in particular those of black women in the United States. Before *American Crime*, the series *Orange Is the New Black* was the first to have put on display, within a closed world of women, inequalities of race and class as well as sexual differences. To be sure, at the aesthetic level it was rather conventional, in that the two main characters were white women, but in the end the series foregrounded strong black female characters, who were portrayed by such excellent actresses (Samira Wiley, Uzo Aduba, and many others) that the political message came across naturally. This was even the case in a seemingly more standard series, *Scandal*, which focused on an iconoclastic, conquering black woman, Olivia Pope, played with authority by Kerry Washington. The series veers into caricature with its multiple improbabilities and plot twists, but it is nevertheless true that the presence of this woman at the centre of the series—gradually transcending her undeniable

---

* This article first appeared in *L'Obs*, 9 January 2019; it has been translated by Daniela Ginsburg.

quality as a sex object for powerful white men—also constitutes a small revolution, even if the class dimension is only present implicitly. It is notable that questions of intersectionality have been more easily addressed by television series than by film, and by fiction rather than by theory. In the case of television, this is thanks to the mobility and reversals of situation made possible by a narration that stretches over several years, the attachment to characters that the series format allows, and the educational aims many series harbour. In the case of theory, which was slow to develop thought around intersectionality, this has to do with the fact that feminist movements and thinking were long dominated by white women.

Kimberlé Crenshaw is one of the major figures of feminism and an authority on the theory of intersectionality, black feminism, and critical race theory.[5] She was the one to introduce the term 'intersectionality' in the late 1980s, in a now classic work entitled *Demarginalizing the Intersection of Race and Sex: A Black Feminist Critique of Antidiscrimination Doctrine, Feminist Theory, and Antiracist Politics* (1989). The first thing to understand about intersectionality is that it does not refer only to a complex system of multiple oppressions (connected to race, class, or gender). The idea of multiple oppressions is not new; it emerged at the end of the nineteenth century, and, in any case, analyses in the social sciences often consist in studying combinations of multiple factors (age, sex, geographic origin, etc.). The injunction to think about a plurality of relations of domination together may thus seem redundant, since after all, realities are already 'intersected' by definition; gender is always racial, social, and so on. So what is new here? We may think of the powerful slogan of American black feminism in the 1980s: 'All the women are white, all the blacks are men, but some of us are brave.'[6] The slogan denounced the double exclusion of black women: from white bourgeois feminism and from sexist black nationalism. Black feminists created a political movement of singular importance in the United States built on the denunciation of these oppressions. Their struggles are beginning to pay off, at least within academia, where thinkers such as Angela Davis and Crenshaw are now recognized. We may also point to the last elections, in which a significant number of women of colour emerged as political leaders and were elected. As a loyal and determined electorate, women of colour are on the front lines in the new struggles against a Trumpism that combines all forms of hatred (classism, sexism, racism, ageism, etc.). In fact, Trump provides a sort of negative illustration of intersectionality in the way he targets women of colour who are involved in grassroots activism.

---

5   Kimberlé W. Crenshaw, *On Intersectionality: Essential Writings* (New York: The New Press, 2017).
6   See Akasha Gloria Hull, Patricia Bell-Scott, and Barbara Smith (eds), *All the Women are White, All the Blacks are Men, But Some of Us are Brave* (New York: The Feminist Press at CUNY, 1982).

Black feminism is a critique of hegemonic white feminism, so-called first-wave or mainstream feminism, which masked the complexity of the forms of exclusion experienced by minority women. This brand of feminism, anchored in a denunciation of relations of domination between men and women and the need for 'womankind' to enjoy the same opportunities as men, presents the subordination of women as universal and common to all women. However, it actually expresses the demands and needs of just one specific kind of woman: white, heterosexual, Western (or Westernized), urban, and middle class. In this way, feminism reproduces and reinforces a logic of hierarchy between women—which intersectionality reveals, to the chagrin of some.

Intersectionality is obvious in the service professions analysed by theories of care; in these professions, certain women serve and care for other women, and also, thereby, ultimately men. Perhaps the most feminist series of the moment, *The Handmaid's Tale*, which also stars Samira Wiley, alongside Elizabeth Moss, is based on this structure, and exposes the hierarchical and hate-filled relations between women in a patriarchal society.

The theoretical contribution of intersectionality is to have gathered under one term various feminist critiques—of sexism, of racism, of class injustice, as well as of ageism and heteronormativity—and to have turned it into a principle of action rather than a lament about domination. It is not enough to demand gender equality; one must face up to these oppressions and their mutual imbrication, which defines women's lives and which feminism can no longer deny—or else it risks ignoring violence against women as has been publicly revealed in the wake of the #MeToo movement that began in late 2017.

It is notable that Crenshaw is also an activist, like Davis and all the major black feminist thinkers, for whom thought is a weapon, and activism, rather than being something that causes one to lose objectivity, serves to clarify and focus one's view of reality. In 1996, Crenshaw founded the think-tank The African American Policy Forum, which has supported innovative research on violence against women of colour in the United States. In February 2015, she launched the hashtag #SayHerName on Twitter, which has catalogued over a billion cases of police violence against women. She carried her work forward with the African American Policy Forum, publishing the report *Black Girls Matter: Pushed Out, Overpoliced, Underprotected* (2015), which proposes a series of recommendations for taking the specific needs of black girls into account in social policy in the United States.

There are historical roots to Crenshaw's activism. In 1991, she worked with the team that represented Anita Hill during the Supreme Court confirmation hearing of Clarence Thomas (whom Hill accused of sexual harassment, and who was nevertheless confirmed, thanks to the support of Republicans and the cowardice of Democrats).

Almost three decades after her work on Hill's legal team, Crenshaw's was one of the most important voices in the public debate over Kavanaugh's confirmation, which painfully echoed the wrongs done to Hill in 1991, an ordeal from which, according to Crenshaw, we still have not recovered. The vulnerability specific to black women was entirely denied or ignored at the time: anti-racists were incapable of understanding the role of gender in *The Affair*, and feminists were unable or unwilling to confront the various racist stereotypes at work in it. In fact, it was because of a lack of intersectional thinking—a lack of theoretical tools and political use of them—that the confrontation between Hill and Thomas devolved into such a collective humiliation, grotesquely repeated in 2018 with the contested confirmation of a new judge to the Supreme Court.

At the moment of Kavanaugh's confirmation (a judge with decades of decisions in favour of class, race, and sex discrimination to his name), Crenshaw reminded us that it was black feminist networks organized in the wake of the Hill–Thomas affair that fought for real social justice, something that theoretical frameworks limited to race or gender alone—as is often the case with critical thought in France—constantly risk missing. This is the meaning of intersectionality: it is not only a critical concept that allows us to see the imbrications of injustices both historically and today, but it is also a project for uniting struggles for justice. Today, it is a weapon in a political battle of which women of colour are the first victims as well as some of the most visible combatants.

The New Wave of French Series

I had started to neglect *Lupin* (Kav & Uzan, Netflix, 2021–) but was called to order by American friends who love it ('2021's first TV crush'). In fact, how can we not be happy with a French series that manages to outdo other Netflix products of the moment? This is primarily because of how Omar Sy carries it with both ease and a touch of provocation in the current national context, where race has become a subversive subject. As we know, Sy is not the nth incarnation of the gentleman thief, which would have been a casting trick quickly forgotten, but his heir. Lupin makes racism a theme of the series, while also paying tribute to a cultural tradition by making the transmission of works—Leblanc inherited from black father to grandson—a central theme.

More subversively, Assane constantly points out and mocks white racism, in the kind and cruel style of *He Even Has Your Eyes* (Lucien Jean-Baptiste, 2016) playing with his invisibility as part of the Louvre cleaning team (typically ignored personnel because they are racial minorities) in the first scene, and, later, with his mega-visibility when he later goes to the auction and buys the famous queen's necklace. When the seller questions him, 'I didn't expect a buyer like you', and Assane retorts aggressively: 'Like me?', the former is embarrassed: 'Er, so young.' Assane does not hesitate to attack people head-on about their racism, or the issue of colonial exploitation (the 'Belgian Congo'). He plays on the probability that the police will confuse him with other black men during the Louvre robbery and when he breaks into prison; he pretends to be a computer scientist to gain access to a crooked police commissioner, taking it in his stride when someone doubts his qualities. Lupin and Sy not only entertain us, but also educate us on the very topical issue of invisibility: 'You looked at me, but you didn't see me.' Assane is one of the invisible people (like his Senegalese father, a driver and victim of the wealthy Pellegrini), and his genius is, under Arsène's moral patronage, to take advantage of it: 'Those at the top don't look at us, and that's how we're going to get rich.'

The international circulation and adaptation of series that raise questions and highlight character profiles that were hitherto little present in French series thus generates a realistically diverse image of France. Like the beautiful family series *This Is Us*, its French adaptation *Je te promets* puts a young obese woman and an adopted black boy at the centre of the story and family. Critics had mocked *Je te promets* in advance for being unable to match the quality of the original (which is often snubbed by them anyway), yet not only does the series allow a wide audience access to the emotional force of *This Is Us* (which is little known by French audiences), but it also offers a French version in the truest sense, by integrating its singular characters into a national social story. Precisely what created the emotional power of *This Is Us* was the

---

* This article first appeared in *Libération*, 19 February 2021.

construction of the pilot, and the moment of realization that the three neurotic characters you've seen over the course of their thirty-sixth birthdays, are those three babies their father, Jack, is looking at in the hospital. While in the original series, this is at the moment when the man who found the abandoned black baby lights a cigarette in the nursery, in *Je te promets* it is after the cigarette, the moment when Mitterrand's face—it is May 1981—is seen on a TV. The weight of the past constantly determines *This Is Us*, but the French version adds a shared experience from 1981 to football and the AIDS years. *Je te promets* is thus admirable for the real work of adapting situations and dialogues, as well as the talent of the actors (especially since this version is often extremely funny)—notably the devastating performance of the great actress Marilou Berry, who manages to outshine even the excellent Chrissy Metz (thereby placing the character of Maud at the centre of the series, while the American *This Is Us* revolves around the incredible Sterling K. Brown). In this way, each version has its central subversion.

It is interesting that all these series refer to a past of the 1970s and 1980s, establishing a shared nostalgia: as such, the great cinephilic and serialistic treat of the moment is *OVNI(s)* (Canal+, 2020–2022), a series that takes us back to the end of the Giscard d'Estaing presidency years and evokes GEPAN, a (very real!) service of the CNES (the National Centre for Space Studies, the French government space agency) that investigates strange phenomena. Aesthetically rich and historically fascinating, it multiplies references to popular culture (comics, music, and cinema), as well as to science, through its comedy of remarriage that follows the conversation of an original scientist couple—Melvil Poupaud and Géraldine Pailhas—worthy of the Hollywood stars of the 1930s and 1940s, while inventing new and hilarious personalities (such as Quentin Dolmaire, like a kidnapped 1970s Arnaud Desplechin). *OVNI(s)* innovates by its poetry, its freedom, and its power to evoke an era full of futuristic and utopian ambitions (it is ten years after 1968), and so it is not surprising that a fictitious and funny Spielberg should be inspired by the sympathetic GEPAN crew, recognizing in it 'the new wave'. It does not matter then that some of us knew that era and others didn't—like the young authors of *OVNI(s)* Clémence Dargent and Martin Douaire—this new wave of series lives and enjoys this past, showing it both to be irretrievably over, but also rich in still unused possibilities and future solutions.

Lupin: From Visibility to Repair

When Assane Diop (Omar Sy) majestically leaves the Châtelet theatre where he has just trapped his mortal enemy, the great bourgeois Pellegrini, smiling and disguised as a fireman wearing a rasta wig, at the end of the first season of the series *Lupin*, one cannot help but be reminded of the opening of the series, when Assane slipped unnoticed into the team of cleaners at the Louvre to set up the theft of the queen's necklace. Indeed, *Lupin* makes invisibility the first trait of the gentleman thief, which is both a social and political theme: Assane plays on his invisibility as a black man in French society, as well as his hypervisibility when he goes to the auction of the famous necklace. When the salesman tells him that 'I wasn't expecting a buyer like you', Assane-Lupin, charming as he is, does not hesitate to point out the racism of the French—as he continues to do even more explicitly in the second part of the season.

When he emerges from the Châtelet Théâtre among an armada of law enforcement officers, he becomes, despite his stature, invisible once again in the uniform of the service professions. This invisibility refers back to his personal and family history—his father Babakar (the excellent Fargass Assandé) was a driver and victim of the Pellegrini family, who accused him of stealing the necklace, leading to his imprisonment and death—a representative of a class of expendables who are required above all to be 'discreet' (as stated in the scene showing the hiring of Babakar Diop by Pellegrini) to the point that their lives matter very little. Assane, when explaining his strategy to his accomplices, asserts that they are to take advantage of their invisibility as blacks or Arabs: 'they don't see us and that's how we'll get rich'. Netflix picked up on the same formula for its teaser in early June: if you ask when *Lupin Part 2* is coming, 'you're looking but not seeing'.

I know many fans are disappointed with this part two—slated for the end of 2021 and arriving surreptitiously, adopting the stealth style of the hero: according to Sy, 'we made it look like it's at the end of the year to be a surprise'. This second part certainly does not have the same surprise effect of the first—the story sometimes appears redundant, playing a little too much on the present-past. It accumulates, like so many current series, technological gadgets and fictional smartphone applications—though Assane remains at his best in classic micro-tricks, as when he steals the badge of the sympathetic detective Guedira (Soufiane Guerrab) and uses it to impose himself on a crime scene. But the last episode gives the new series its full meaning, with the ultimate provocation of Sy's wandering around in red (exuding a presence that grips the viewer in a new way), continuing with a boat ride on the Seine to the sound of Dutronc's song, which, anticipated from the beginning, is finally reappropriated by *Lupin*.

It is an additional dimension (almost superheroic) that Assane acquires in this second part, losing his lightness on the verge of tragedy with the

---

* This article first appeared in *Libération*, 1 July 2021.

kidnapping of his son Raoul. The few weaknesses (already present in part one) are not what motivated malicious critics—rather it is that some simply cannot stand the fact that the best-known French series abroad, a historical success for Netflix, is a series whose very French hero is a black man, and whose image is of a colourful France that is a far cry from *Emily in Paris*, or even *Midnight in Paris* (Woody Allen, 2011). *Lupin* was a provocation from the outset in the current national context, where evoking differences of origin and the injustices that they entail has become a subversive subject. The audacity of *Lupin* was well spotted by the magazine *Marianne*, which spread derogatory terms about the series ('smoke and mirrors'; 'political correctness') and its star (we miss 'the classy Georges Descrières'), which were in line with its recent editorials and opinion columns attacking anti-racist movements.

Because *Lupin* does not simply showcase Omar Sy's charm, it belongs to the same family as *La Casa de Papel*. It demonstrates once again the political strength of popular culture, the only effective tool against the cultural regressions of the moment. The first subversion of the series (part one) was to deal with invisibility, while carrying out the provocation of putting Sy on-screen as Lupin; part two, however, goes one step further by taking Assane's revenge against his father's racist killers to its conclusion—and thereby demonstrating that it is not enough simply to show black people on-screen, or to exploit their popularity. Assane-Lupin is on a quest for justice. The fight against racism is not about visibility, but redress and repair.

The Chair: War is Declared on Campus

TV series, initially confined to domestic life, took their place in our lives when they began to explore professional worlds, allowing us to discover, from the inside, worlds with which we were only familiar from the outside, the public-facing side (hospital, court, government, police, sport, etc., each profession having given rise to a genre of series); or which remained entirely mysterious (intelligence agent, psychoanalyst, businessman, undertaker). We have discovered the type of training provided by series, and the turning point achieved with those produced from the 1990s onwards (particularly *ER*): the integration of characters into viewer's ordinary lives; the initiation into unexplained forms of life and into new, and initially opaque, vocabularies. Although at the outset we find ourselves in a land whose language we do not know, we successfully learn to speak it through the educational experience of the series: five years in the Baltimore of *The Wire* with Omar as our teacher was a real education.

For this reason, it is unsurprising that a series would come to look at the world of academia—not from the familiar angle of boozy campus life on teen shows, but from the angle of university politics, and an academic department with its rivalries, promotions, and battles for office space. At this time of year—when the pleasure of being in real life is mixed with anxiety—it is wonderful to see Sandra Oh (well known since *Grey's Anatomy*, and become a star with *Killing Eve*) on the small screen as the chair of a department of literature in *The Chair*—a chair that, when she sits on it in her new office, promptly collapses, as if an advanced summary of the story. Professor Ji-Yoon Kim, the first Asian and first woman to head the English department at the moderately prestigious University of Pembroke, sets about her task with zeal while caring for her adopted daughter, Ju Ju (hilarious), and her love interest, colleague Bill Dobson (Jay Duplass). As is the case when one takes on such heavy responsibilities, one has to be able to 'make things happen'—in particular, to recruit the young and talented Yaz McKay (Nana Mensah). Here we are at the very heart of university politics: one imagines that the research programmes, the progress of the students, and the place of their university are what interest the colleagues in the department, but here we see that the priority, which mobilizes even the most indifferent, is the recruitment of new professors. This is petty but logical, insofar as what makes up universities all over the world are these colleagues—the human group that teaches, and on which *The Chair* chooses to focus.

The Chair has often been treated by critics as a highly stylized drama, but underneath its wacky exterior it remains realistic. This is exemplified by the description of the rivalries between conservatives and innovators: Elliot Rentz (Bob Balaban), whose fame is behind him, still has a lot of academic power (which he can't help but use to block the promotion of the brilliant black

---

* This article first appeared in *Libération*, 9 September 2021.

McKay, also a Melville specialist). It also comes across in the description of political changes: the elderly medievalist and feminist Joan Hambling (Holland Taylor, always legendary) believes herself to be on the side of the new militant generations, but clashes with the young head of the Title IX department (where she complains of discrimination following her exile to an office in a noisy basement), whose rather skimpy attire she takes the liberty of criticizing ('everyone can see your pussy').

The temptation would be to say that the show tries to present different points of view and reconcile them through the attachment to these characters, from both old and new generations, that it engenders. But rather it is the opposite: divisions are drawn between the young people who 'don't get it' and the elders who don't understand a thing, even when they are popular and open-minded—Bill, who as a joke imitates a Nazi salute in class, resulting in a viral video and a cascade of disasters, and Ji-Yoon, who doesn't stand a chance. Along the way, Ji-Yoon comes to understand that university is not (as she says at the beginning) 'a refuge from bullshit', but precisely the opposite.

The Chair reveals the extent to which the culture wars are present at the heart of American universities: far from being dominated by the spectre of 'cancel culture', racism, sexism, and ageism all permeate the practice of teaching. The series also shows, pedagogically, the reasons for the current demands—but also the hypocrisy and inefficiency of a system that exploits them (with Ji-Yoon in the position of a fuse). In the last century, a (male and white) chair ruled over the territory, and Ji-Yoon, like Tony Soprano, arrives at the end of an era—and yet, as *The Chair* explores, this is also the story of a woman who saw herself as a pioneer and is now part of the system… without being able to change anything.

The series is produced by the creators of *Game of Thrones*, which is a small indicator that we too are at the end of an era—the era of the major series that form part of our lives over years, as Benioff and Weiss have moved on to the current ease of miniseries (a few episodes on a niche subject). And yet the intrigue and violence, obsession with status and prestige, and the complication of personal relationships are all still present. No one is safe: the much-desired tenure does not protect. The academic world remains a place—one of the very few—where people from different backgrounds and generations coexist and learn from each other. This is why politicians, who are constantly tempted to discredit it, pay such disproportionate attention to it, and why it is therefore perpetually in danger.[7]

---

7 As witnessed by the immoral French polemic on *'islamoleftism'* launched in 2021.

A Tribute to White Trash

How sad that I couldn't cattily comment on this year's Golden Globes, spoiled by the 'revelation' of the corruption and lack of diversity of the clique that awarded them—the HFPA, eighty-seven highly courted members, not one of whom is black. Even if it is rather shameful to be awarded this year, we can rejoice at the recognition given to Kate Winslet, extraordinary in *Mare of Easttown*, one of the great series of 2021. Yet overlooked on the list, just as it was at the Emmys, is the popular series *Maid*. It's a gripping series, which one cannot help but frantically advise others to see as soon as one gets to the end—and yet it's *so* hard to watch and remarkably stressful—more so even than *Squid Game*. *Maid*, adapted from Stephanie Land's autobiographical *Maid: Hard Work, Low Pay, and a Mother's Will to Survive*, shows in realistic detail what it is like to be poor in the United States (and elsewhere), and the vulnerability of a woman with children. The series makes this pressure palpable every minute—the stress on the viewer, certainly incomparable to that of the lives *Maid* describes, makes it an experience of psychological violence, which is also its subject. This is not the same as the shock and awe of the brilliant and multi-awarded *Succession*, with its depiction of extreme wealth and power and the pathologies it generates. Certainly, *Maid* also suggests that money cannot solve everything, as the heroine, Alex, a cleaning woman, realizes when she enters the private lives of her clients, but it changes the format of the problems: the misfortune of a rich person is different from that of Alex when every day she fights for each penny, facing the harshness of the capitalist world.

Alex (Margaret Qualley) is a young mother from the state of Washington with no job or degree who decides to leave her alcoholic and abusive partner, Sean (Nick Robinson). She takes their 3-year-old daughter, Maddy, and, with the help of a cool social worker, finds work in a seedy cleaning service, Value Maids. For months, she scrubs toilets, lives with little to no money, struggles to find daycare and housing, and to get custody of Maddy. We see her living in a shelter for abused women, filling out form after form to get much-needed and paltry welfare, while also being pressured by her crazy ex. *Maid* does an exceptional job of capturing the detail of this life and the urgency that makes every mishap (an absent client, a missing car, etc.) a nuclear catastrophe and a huge setback.

Alex never knows exactly how much money she has in her pocket, and to depict this way of life, this visually genius show regularly displays on the screen, in the upper right corner, her expenses and income. As soon as she earns a few dollars, the tally reveals that Alex must immediately spend them and go back into the red, not knowing if she will be able to feed her daughter.

One can only be struck, after having experienced a few years of feminist and anti-racist series, by this presence of poor white women, 'white trash',

---

* This article first appeared in *Libération*, 14 January 2022.

who reshuffle the cards of 'white' feminism without returning to it. I'm thinking here of Ruth Langmore (the incredibly talented Julia Garner) on the series *Ozark*. Ruth, like Alex, dreams of college, but for her brother. Alex, Ruth, and even Mare, are characters developed through intersectional struggles, and these series show through them the reality and diversity of oppression while avoiding becoming misery porn. Housework (a care profession) falls to women/the poor/racial minorities/the dominated… the combinations are varied. Intersectionality reveals the difficulty of valuing jobs where you literally take care of shit: filthy toilets, devastated apartments full of garbage, hoarders' messes, which Alex ends up making her slightly more remunerative speciality because no one else wants to.

Margaret Qualley—who gained notice in *The Leftovers* and *Once Upon a Time in Hollywood* (Quentin Tarantino, 2019)—carries the series through her intense expressiveness mixed with a mysterious obstinacy. Nick Robinson makes us as vulnerable to Sean (a total loser) as Alex is, thanks to his earlier roles in *A Teacher* and *Love, Simon* (Greg Berlanti, 2018). The highlight is Andie MacDowell, Qualley's own mother, who finds a role of her own as Paula, Alex's bipolar and troublesome mother.

Like *Unbelievable*, another landmark feminist series from Netflix, *Maid* is also a story of women who are there for other women—helping them find their voice. Not everyone Alex encounters is nice, to say the least, but ultimately salvation will come from (black) women such as Denise, the wonderful house manager (BJ Harrison), Regina (Anika Noni Rose), a seemingly atrocious client who becomes a friend, Alex and Paula's ultimately strangely salvific relationship. Their interaction, and the paradoxical forms of care it invents, make *Maid* a radical experiment—and the best response to reactionary mockery of 'victimization' at a time when care, attention to others, and its corollary, the perception of inequality, is under threat.

Family Stories

In the last couple of years, we have left behind (or have been left by) *The Affair*, *Homeland*, *The Bureau*, *Ozark*, *Better Call Saul*, and *This is Us*, among some other extraordinary TV shows. This experience is always accompanied by sadness, and leaves us wondering about what would happen to our favourite heroes if we could continue our journey together. The difficulty of parting from characters is a remarkable phenomenon that reveals the strong attachment we develop towards characters we see on a regular basis: characters, plural, because nowadays there are hardly any series with a singular hero. Long narrative arcs allow for the recurrence of secondary characters. This recurrence, over the run of a series, weakens the hierarchy between main and secondary characters. Thus, it is difficult to speak of a series character in the singular, given that series' narratives are inextricably intertwined with the collective destiny of their heroes. Instead, it is more productive to speak of them as an ensemble, a cast of characters.

The causes of our attachment to characters or actors who play them are complex and not just a matter of identification, or even of complicity or admiration, and they change over the duration of the show. In some series, the very status of characters can change: in *The Wire*, the main character of the first three seasons, Jimmy McNulty, almost disappears in season four, and in *Orange is the New Black*, a 'secondary' character such as Poussey takes centre stage in numerous episodes. There are several recent shows that challenge our sense of attachment by killing off characters who have been essential to the narrative: this is, of course, the case of *Game of Thrones* and *The Walking Dead*. Thus, our attachment to a series cannot be reduced solely to the experience of attachment to a single character.

Ensemble series with numerous characters such as *Games of Thrones*, *The Walking Dead*, or *Engrenages* represent their characters as members of the same family. Whether they are part of an actual family or not, the relationships between these people become increasingly familiar to us. There is a familialization of the series' cast. This familiarity of series characters, in the double sense of what is familiar/close to us and what constitutes a family for us, helps to describe the possibility of a collective bond—and also establishes the central element of long-running series: the family. This is at the heart of recent series, replacing the individual or the couple, which were the central subjects of classic cinema (Westerns, crime thrillers, romantic comedies, etc.). It was the subject of *The Sopranos*, *Six Feet Under*, *Breaking Bad*, *The Americans*, *Modern Family*, and of course *Game of Thrones*; it is even more prominently the main subject of *Succession*, *Ozark*, and *This Is Us*—even if these families are twisted, blended, or might appear atypical. It is this ensemble or familial character that allows for an attachment to even unsympathetic or ambivalent characters, as in *Ozark*.

---

* This article first appeared in *Libération*, 3 February 2022.

The major series thus operate through familialization by establishing associations between the characters over the years; and even when we are not dealing with a family at the start, we become a part of one at the end. *Mad Men* and *The Bureau* are interesting illustrations of this, when families are formed from professional groups. By the very logic of their long-term association, the characters in the series are led to develop family-type relationships, and to integrate us into them. It is because of this aspect of the series that we find it difficult to extricate ourselves from the characters.

This is the case with the iconic family series *Ozark*—a 'white trash' series that is an unexpected choice for a 'prestige' Netflix series. The series starts with the culture shock of a city-dwelling family, the Byrdes, who move to Missouri under duress to revive a money-laundering operation for a powerful Mexican cartel. Long underrated, *Ozark* is one of Netflix's best productions; it is an example of a family series that roots itself in a family structure, while also creating an extended family beyond the nuclear Byrde family. It brings all its characters together in a 'type', a grey area between good and evil—the Byrdes, Marty and Wendy, increasingly slide towards the latter in the later seasons. The temporality of the series makes their slow moral degradation even more impactful—and this is a great asset of family series (as in *Game of Thrones* and *The Americans*)— through the moral and physical evolution of the children. This family solidarity is complete in the last seconds of the series (but no spoilers).

It is also only in a long-running series that we could discover a female character as demented and deviant as Darlene Snell or a figure as hypocritical and fascinating as Wendy Byrde, Laura Linney's great role. Ruth Langmore (the excellent Julia Garner), a character whose strength and vulnerable intelligence actually carry the series through to the final tragedy, must also be added to *Ozark*'s set of exceptional, tough, and compelling female characters who give the series its moral radicalism.

Ozark has been compared to *Succession* on the basis of the moral transgressions committed by its unlikable or, in the case of the latter, downright vile, characters. *Ozark*'s characters are indeed morally dubious and disturbing— yet not to the point of turning attachment into hatred. They remain ordinary people, sometimes likable, always capable of disappointing us, and also of reassuring us. The final season offers several points of revelation. Leaving the series is like being torn away from a family that is twisted but very much our own.

The family genre is at the heart of the recently completed beautiful series *Better Things*, starring Sam Fox, a Los Angeles-based actress who chases castings and small, seedy roles while raising three daughters alone. *Better Things* is not a journey of self-exploration or self-transformation, instead consistently asserting an ordinary point of view, presenting in the first person the daily life of a 50-year-old woman without any illusions. At the end of the series, Sam achieves a form of separation from her family, which, rather as in *The Americans*, sees parents abandoned by their children. But the tragic melancholy of *The Americans* gives way in *Better Things* to a perfectionist optimism, where leaving the family creates new possibilities for self-development.

Yet the main event of the last few weeks has been the conclusion of the beautiful series *This Is Us*, a quintessential family series whose characters have become deeply embedded in our experience, in large part thanks to outstanding acting performances, including the extraordinary Sterling K. Brown (Randall), that carry the series to its end.

The series is built entirely around the story of a family over three generations. The first two seasons are steeped in the anxious anticipation of the untimely death of the dynasty's patriarch Jack Pearson, which is hinted at in the early episodes. As a point of symmetry, the last two seasons focus on the more predictable death of the matriarch, Rebecca. This loops back to the founding episode of the series, that of the birth of the 'Big Three'. The pilot, which blended the present and the past—Kate's, Kevin's, and Randall's 36th birthday and the day they were born—displayed the series' method of looping back to past events to allow us to understand them in a variety of new ways. The pilot gradually and skilfully revealed the bond between these three very different people—a black man, a white woman, and a white man—by showing the founding events of the series: Rebecca's difficult delivery of triplets with the birth of two twins, Kate and Kevin, and the tragedy of the third baby's death, as well as the Pearson couple's adoption of an abandoned African-American baby on the same day. The following seasons tell the story of the difficulties of the adult lives, but also of the childhoods, of the Big Three, the premature death of their father, Jack, his youth, that of his brother Nick, and of William, Randall's biological father. The narrative, which moves back and forth between different periods in the characters' lives, allows—as in any long-running series—not just the characters, but also their relationships, to deepen.

Within the elements of this collective hero family, we find again what Wittgenstein calls family resemblances. The greatness of *This Is Us* lies in the fact that it projects the idea of bonding onto a real family, which is made possible by the complexity of its composition and history. The beauty of the first episode is that it brings together a seemingly broken family, while the whole series proceeds to make a family out of the various traumatic events that the protagonists have experienced. Of course, this is not the only show to use a family as a character (consider the classic *Six Feet Under* and the excellent *Modern Family*). But *This is Us* is the only one today that builds familial links through all its episodes and the narrative of the show.

In this sense, *This is Us* may be the last great classic series, simultaneously radicalizing and exhausting the subject matter of the majority of twenty-first-century series. It is the series that led us to integrate and adopt, like the Pearson family, all sorts of new members into our imaginary family, in concentric circles—right down to the missing brother, the new spouses of the ex-spouses, friends of the biological parents, and more: the definition of inclusiveness.

This Is Us has thus become more political over its run, presenting the multigenerational fate of a white, middle-class family that adopted a black child in the 1980s. Rebecca Pearson, at the beginning of the second season, recalls the moment in the first episode of the series when, in the maternity ward, having lost one of her triplets, she is persuaded by Jack, her husband, to adopt an abandoned black baby, Randall: 'This stranger became my child and this child became my life.' *This Is Us* affirms that the United States is mixed and multiple, in its history and its present, in this us that embodies the US(A) beyond the Pearsons.

The pedagogy of the show goes even further, since in the fifth, post-COVID-19 season, Randall sees the news of George Floyd's death on his phone, which deeply upsets him. From that point forward, *This Is Us* confronts head-on the question of race through a powerful return to the trajectory of Randall's life, a black child raised in a white family. Again, the series is self-reflective. As viewers, we come to realize that what we saw from the beginning as a beautiful story of integration was also a painful story of denial. This is the lesson of *This Is Us*—it teaches us not by making us love this story and these characters any less, but by making us understand some (not necessarily pleasant) things about ourselves. Throughout the series, the characters' neuroses and imperfections endear them to us, because they create the flaws and vulnerabilities where our care or concern can slip.

The finale, written by the show's creator Dan Fogelman and simply titled 'Us', could have been an unending fest of emotion and tears. Instead, it is strikingly short for a finale, humbly returning us to the ordinary life of a nondescript lazy Sunday in the Pearson family, when the little ones were 10 years old. Opening with Jake and Rebecca waking up and going through a thousand little things of family life, this 106th episode reveals what has historically been the show's strength: highlighting the little moments that crystallize the value of a family and make up the salt of life (to use the title of Françoise Héritier's wonderful book). In its final moments, *This Is Us* finds itself by the side of Jack and Randall, two exceptional characters whom the series has been able to create from totally new family ties. It should not be forgotten that this beautiful series was aired on a traditional television network, NBC, using a model that was thought to be outdated: one that makes us wait impatiently for what will happen next week, with new episodes and the return of the seasons. Are these long-running series, which carry us with them for five years or more and become part of our experience and the temporality of our lives, a disappearing format? We have now entered a different temporality, that of miniseries formatted for a long weekend, to be viewed on laptops and smartphones. These are often excellent, but their incursions into our personal history, and no doubt their position within the history of series, with a few brilliant exceptions, more limited. It remains to be seen whether TV series, a format that has managed to renew itself several times (whether at the turn of the century with HBO, and recently with the streaming platforms), will be able to surprise us again.

3

Spoilers, Stories, Stars

My Life in Series

The recent string of series is not going well: the long-awaited fifth season of *Game of Thrones* is having trouble getting off the ground, despite Cersei's evil ways; and the conclusion of *Mad Men*, which was the primary show of the 2000s, is rather depressing in how it resolves the classic difficulty of saying goodbye to our favourite characters. Could our series be at the end of their tethers? Or are we? Are we, at last, tired of this form of art and life that, at times, is so heavily organized around series? I do not believe so—just think of the discoveries of 2014, such as *The Affair*, *True Detective*, *The Leftovers*... true aesthetic and moral explorations that, each in their own way, have renewed the format. Similarly, recent developments have seen mainstream cinema becoming serialized in various ways: the *Star Wars* series, *Mission Impossible* and *X-Men*, and the films of the Marvel universe, with its superheroes, Thor, Tony Stark, becoming serialized, with each film contributing an element to a story (admittedly a little confused and caricatured) that is written over a period of years. This is largely driven by the fact that the cinema series, unlike most TV, is never entirely closed, as the return of *Mad Max* or the *Terminator* prove. This seriality allows us to find characters over the long term with a continuity that is quite different from the one that allowed us to see the young heroes of *Friends* and *Buffy* grow up over the years.

We sometimes hear television series being denigrated in comparison with the true great art of cinema: we forget—in addition to the fact that true lovers of great art denigrated, a century ago, cinema that has since become 'classic'—how close cinema has come to series. I am not only thinking of the great directors who are supposed to have given the format its 'letters of nobility' (Lynch, Scorsese, Fincher, Van Sant), but also of the serial properties of cinema that allow us to return to places and characters long after, or even long before, the first encounter. The prequel, as we know, plays on the search for origin or youth (of which *Terminator* is an example, with

---

* This article first appeared in *Libération*, 22 May 2015.

a particular reflexivity), and is part of the effect of a sequel or series by exploiting the attachment to the hero whose trajectory is being explored (Anakin, Darth Vader, Superman, Magneto), and on a sentimentality that is distinct from the attachment to the characters but is linked to our experience of the film itself.

The pleasure of seeing *Mad Max: Fury Road* (2015, George Miller, as in 1979), apart from its unbridled feminism and visual imagination in terms of repulsive creatures and devices, is linked to the memory and effects of our first viewing at the dawn of the 1980s (celebrated in this review)—that is, the post-apocalyptic atmosphere, the big trucks, and electric guitar. Thirty-five years later, there is no fetishism or regression: a film, in our experience and despite all the possibilities we have today of seeing it again, is still the memory of seeing the film. As Stanley Cavell admirably theorizes in *The World Viewed* and in his autobiography *Little Did I Know…*, our individual lives are aligned with the experience of the films we have seen, and the company of the people with whom we have seen them.[1] His conception of the cinematic experience as an 'autobiography of comrades',[2] connected to the practice of going to the cinema in a group, allows us to conceptualize a further autobiographical link between series and cinema: the way in which our lives are made up of fragments of cinema, orientated in relation to these moments of film that are part of our experience—exactly like dreams or real events—that haunt us:

> [People bear these films] in their experience as memorable public events, segments of the experiences, the memories, of a common life. So that the difficulty of assessing them is the same as the difficulty of assessing everyday experience, the difficulty of expressing oneself satisfactorily, of making oneself find the words for what one is specifically interested to say.[3]

The memories of films, on which Cavell builds his readings, are inscribed in us as strong and real as memories the events of our lives: 'They become further fragments of what happens to me, further cards in the shuffle of my memory.' I remember seeing the first *Mad Max* in the 1980s; *Terminator* in the 1980s and 1990s; watching *Twin Peaks*, *Friends*, and *ER* at home in the 1990s; *Alias*, *Buffy*, *The West Wing* in the 2000s; and *Game of Thrones* evenings with my family: these films and series are memories of my life.

I remember seeing the masterpiece *Comment je me suis disputé… (ma vie sexuelle)* (Arnaud Desplechin, 1996) at the Pantheon cinema, as well as subsequent conversations about it with friends, and with Stanley Cavell who

---

1 Cavell, *The World Viewed*, Harvard University Press, 1971.
2 Cavell, *The World Viewed*, ch. 1.
3 Cavell, *Pursuits of Happiness*, p. 41.

had loved it. Our memories of films are memories of our youth. By making a film about the lives of his characters before this film, Arnaud Desplechin is not just making a prequel—he is affirming the essentially nostalgic structure of cinema through its nature, as a memory; that is, a past that is forever gone, but an experience that is forever incredibly alive.

Masochistic Jack

All those who, with a heavy heart, had deleted their *24* ringtone four years ago during the farewell of Fox's most famous series, are now both delighted and disturbed: Jack Bauer is back for a ninth season: *Live Another Day*. The hero, rather diminished and aged after four years, is also augmented in the sense of 'human enhancement': he has been given a facelift and has buttons everywhere (under his skin), which allow him to send signals and explosions from a distance. Indeed, the transmission of information has been at the heart of *24* from the start, in the form of protocols, networks, image analysis, visual recognition, and data dissemination, and has given the series its visual identity, with the split screen simultaneously presenting both actors in a conversation. But this technological device that sustained the series has, in fact, now become the threat itself—that is, the threat to human life created by the entire surveillance network in which it is now embedded. The enemy that Jack Bauer fights—even if there is still the basic repetitive compulsion to save the President of the United States—is no longer terrorism from outside, but the global threat to human security (not just that of states) created by the technologies responsible for ensuring it.

The final image of Jack, who, four years ago, was flying away at sunset, was provided for his collaborator, Chloe O'Brian, by a drone, which ties in with the pitch for the new series: Jack, spotted via a drone sent by the CIA to a London squat; Chloe becoming, in the meantime, a mix of Edward Snowden and Lisbeth Salander (*Millennium*), and going underground to deliver thousands of confidential documents to the public. The defence of WikiLeaks—and of the spaces of democracy and freedom opened up by the circulation of information, especially the 'secret' information that is kept from the public—by a cult character from *24*, and the vulnerability of a sick president surrounded by scoundrels, show, if further proof were necessary, that *24* is *not* the reactionary and macho Bushist series (the dark counterpart to *The West Wing*) that has often been snubbed by seriphiles.

24 is the series that accustomed the public to seeing a black president on-screen (David Palmer, undoubtedly the best character of the series). In its last two seasons, it installed a woman, Allison Taylor, in the White House, and it did not hesitate either to represent the dangers of nuclear and biological weapons, to humanize terrorists, or to question the competence of the executive branch and the intelligence of diplomacy—in short to express public debates that are rather absent in France.

Though the series initially looked to have been followed by *Homeland* (with its fantasy of techno-surveillance) and *House of Cards* (with its calculated political cynicism), these series, initially praised for their realism, have not come up to scratch. *24*, as the quintessential post-9/11 series (even if it was already filmed and scheduled before the attack), never claiming to be realistic,

---

* This article first appeared in *Libération*, 23 May 2014.

was a new opus that could sign the return of political utopia in a world threatened more terrifyingly than by terrorism or war—threatened, instead, in its very humanity.

In the meantime, Kiefer Sutherland in *Melancholia* (Lars von Trier, 2011) had exhibited, not without masochism, his inability to save the world (or even to morally confront the catastrophe) in the face of Earth's inescapable destruction (by collision with another planet). Kiefer is effectively Jack. The return of *24* is proof of how important a character is in our lives as viewers: we missed Jack, and we're glad to have him back, even if it feels a little weird, in the same way as seeing the return of a friend who's gone off the grid. He is opaque, a stranger to himself, as characters always are when they come back from the dead (I'm thinking here of Buffy, recreated on a new network after her death in the fifth season). But what exactly was missing? The indestructible hero? No, we have the superhero movies for that, and Jack is not indestructible—rather, he is vulnerable, each time returning a little more destroyed; he comes back in this new series because he can't help it, and we watch because we too can't help it, a compulsive return that is referenced in the James Bondesque title of the season. The series was once accused of sadism for its ritual torture scenes, but in his repetitive tendency to save the president and the world (always to his own perdition and regular torture—as well as that of his loved ones, his darling Audrey, and even Chloe as soon as she returns in the new series), it is indeed Jack's masochism that is displayed, and that, as he claims, we share. Asking for more.

Eye of the Drone

It was under the gaze of drones that season eight, and thus the entire series of *24*, ended. This, in short, ceded the human power to give us images to the drone that transmitted the last images of our hero Jack Bauer, walking off into the sunset, under the emotional gaze of his faithful CTU sidekick, Chloe O'Brian, as well as our own. In the same way, it is a drone that spots Jack and returns him to us in the unexpected reboot of the series, four years later. Likewise, it is a drone that creates the pitch for Day 9, which, slipping out of the control of the young soldier in charge of piloting, goes and slaughters an American squad in Afghanistan. This is a drone that, taken in hand owing to the vicious cyber-attack of a terrorist network, will threaten London, where the American president is that day, by launching a series of missiles to destroy a hospital, and, in doing so, making visible both the effects and causes of these 'clean' wars to which the rulers of the contemporary world aspire.

A drone was also behind the terrorist action that, three years earlier, targeted the house of a 'notorious terrorist', killing him and part of his entourage, while arousing in his widow, Margot al-Harazi, a mortal hatred for President James Heller, politically responsible for the attack. She is played by Michelle Fairley—yes, our beloved Catelyn Stark, survivor of *Game of Thrones*' 'The Crimson Wedding'. Further proof of the influence of the show's characters on their actors, it is Catelyn who lends credibility to Margot's demented and cruel character and allows her to have a conversation of equals with President Heller, over Skype. This circulation of actors between series allows for the creation of a moral and narrative thickness as soon as the characters appear on-screen—in this case, the great Gbenga Akinnagbe from *The Wire*, Tate Donovan carrying with him the tragic gloom of *Damages*, and the great British provocateur Stephen Fry in the role of the British prime minister—and is certainly one of the primary elements of the richness of current TV series.

This gives the moral power to Margot-Catelyn, who otherwise would be a typical old villain character, to legitimately pose the problem of the responsibility of the anonymous action that killed her terrorist husband. Since the appearance of drones, much has been said about the lack of responsibility they lead to for the actions they are ordered to carry out, actions that are both targeted (on arrival) and depersonalized (at the source): there are technical advantages (the possibility of avoiding collateral victims), legal advantages (possibility of acting on any citizen, on the basis of a simple suspicion), and moral costs, which are hotly debated by American researchers. Between two techniques of warfare and assassination, the archaic and despised suicide bombing and the modern and secure remote-controlled drone (which is never exposed when it kills, and therefore, grammatically speaking, does not kill,

---

* This article first appeared in *Libération*, 20 June 2014.

but eliminates), it is difficult to decide which is more dehumanizing. The technology of the drone, combining targeting, security of the agent alone, and unaccountability, is characteristic of post-industrial societies in its negation of human commitment, as it is present in hand-to-hand combat, and in the ethics that Cora Diamond describes in 'The Case of the Naked Soldier'.[4]

For Margot-Catelyn, true inhumanity, the ultimate cowardice, would be on the side of this disengaged and clean action that limits securitization to oneself—as is suggested in *24* by President Heller's almost suicidal gesture. This asks us which side has the worst barbarism: the extreme violence, also remote-controlled, of terrorism, or the voluntary ignorance of those who deny the reality of their actions—denial shared by all citizens of the nations of the North who prefer, despite the fact they are right in front of us, to ignore the causes and effects of our domination and 'security'.

Drone warfare, with its inseparable surveillance of the governed of all countries, and the future risk of uncontrollable and unpunishable attacks on any of us, thus participates in the invisibilization of victims, in de-realizing the intolerable (global injustices, mass murders, health and industrial disasters), and finally in neglecting human life, which have characterized capitalism for the last century: it is this construction of ignorance, this radicalization of scepticism, that constitutes the true threat to humans and their 'security'. No wonder Chloe O'Brian is going to WikiLeaks!

---

4   Cora Diamond, 'Le cas du soldat nu', in *L'importance d'être humain*, translated and edited by S. Laugier, E. Halais and J.Y. Mondon (Paris: Presses Universitaires de France, 2011). Unpublished in English.

Spoiler Alert

Long gone are the days of Montaigne's belief that one should not judge before the end: 'In judging another's life, I always look at how it has ended.' The time is also long gone when one would not have allowed oneself to evaluate a work—film, book, or, in this case, a series—before having seen it to the end (at least of the season). From the very first episodes of *True Detective*'s second season, fans and critics alike expressed their disappointment as if it were a personal offence.

The series so adored last year—mainly for the bayou atmosphere and Matthew McConaughey's accent—has since been met with harsh criticism: a conformist view of Los Angeles, overly familiar mobster and loser characters, as well as plot confusion, to name but a few. Indeed, the Los Angeles of *True Detective* is confusing because it is a mix of contemporary culture, *Swingers* (Doug Liman, 1996), *24*, and *L.A. Confidential* (Curtis Hanson, 1997). Nevertheless, this second season also contains some revelations, notably the impressive performance by Vince Vaughn, an actor of underestimated genius, and we find wonderful and singular female characters (including the policewoman Rachel McAdams), unlike the first season in which the women were merely instruments for a largely male-centred plot. Here the women are the ones who bring the story to a close and give it meaning—particularly in the final moment when, exiled and combative, they express the resistance of life; the heroes are endearing in their imperfection, which goes as far as the self-destruction of men. Along with premature judgement, the terror of the spoiler is the second plague of the series: if we can still call a viewer a 'seriphile' whose primary pleasure comes from suspense, what about the pleasure we take in the show? What about the pleasure one gets from watching a film again, even ones with major 'reveals' such as *Gone Girl* (David Fincher, 2014) or *Sixth Sense* (M. Night Shyamalan, 1999)? Not to mention *Titanic* or *Lincoln* (Steven Spielberg, 2012), whose outcomes are known ahead of time, without, it seems to me, detracting from their intensity.

The worst crime series can be accused of today seems to be giving the public hints of what is to come: *Game of Thrones* is a particular example where the pressure is so great that spoilerphobia takes up most of the critical energy. The same obsession, which also extends to films, devalues series as genuine works, and thereby undermines any serious criticism of them. One should not treat the audience of series with contempt, one might say—disavowing misplaced elitism; TV series empower the viewers, who, through their experience and preferences, are capable of educating their own judgement. The populism of series must also be a perfectionism, asking that everyone go beyond their own conformities and not be satisfied with their own impressions.

---

* This article first appeared in *Libération*, 17 September 2015.

David Simon, the author of the cult series *The Wire*, does not bother with spoilers: the title of his latest work, *Show Me a Hero* (a six-part HBO series), is itself a spoiler: the Scott Fitzgerald adage to which the title refers ('Show me a hero and I'll write you a tragedy') already gives away the end of the story—even without the Wikipedia entry, since *Show Me...* tells the true story of Nick Wasicsko, a young mayor of Yonkers (a city of 200,000 inhabitants in the state of New York) who, in spite of himself, became embroiled in the fight for racial desegregation and the implementation of a law inspired by urban planner Oscar Newman, who was imposing the construction of public housing in white neighbourhoods in the 1980s and 1990s. The spoiler is the real thing.

The series, in an even more documentary-like style than *The Wire*, presents a whole democratic galaxy of characters as striking as Nick (the brilliant Oscar Isaac, a star who manages to stay on the same level as the others), which is its primary lesson—that is, democratic aesthetic without moralism: every point of view is expressed and heard. Democracy is thus presented not as a discourse (hollow and hypocritical) or political system (totally corrupt), but as a form of life and social transformation—in the fate of the poorly housed women who will slowly benefit from desegregation and leave the housing estates (Carmen, an Dominican immigrant worker and mother of three children; Norma, a medical assistant who loses her eyesight; Doreen, at first confused, but who subsequently copes magnificently), and of the white inhabitants who, like Mary (Catherine Keener), will evolve from visceral and violent opposition to the arrival of foreigners, to acceptance and subsequently support, primarily motivated by shame at the repulsively racist behaviour of their dear white neighbours.

The lessons of these experiences over the last century are obviously relevant today: tragedy (the political and individual disaster of Nick Wasicsko's trajectory) is matched by democratic and ordinary success, however fleeting and limited it may be—for democracy is not a political game, tragic or ridiculous, nor is it a set of grand moral principles. Rather, it is the slow, imperceptible, yet visible micro-change of human beings on the screen—of their sense of responsibility towards others unknown. The democratic populism that is called for today only makes sense (spoiler alert!) when it is rooted in the possibility of self-transformation.

Addicted to *Narcos*

The viewers of the best Netflix series appreciate, even if they will deny it, the vicious sequence of episodes and the display at the bottom right of the screen during the end credits ('next episode in 4…3…2 seconds') that is conducive to binge-watching—and is, in any case, highly enjoyable. On the other hand, however, I imagine that many, like me, have nothing but contempt for the display at the bottom left of the screen that suggests skipping the opening credits: 'Skip intro.' Skip the intro of *Narcos*??? It's hard enough not to play it over and over again. Netflix has had the luck—or rather made the choice, by having the music composed by artists solicited for the occasion—to create title credits so successful that they have become classics in themselves. I'm thinking, of course, of the musical ambition expressed in Jeff Beal's composition for *House of Cards*, which remained unchanged across the seasons and is all that remains of the series (which sank into total nonsense (a constitutive tendency) in its sixth and final season, despite Robin Wright's immense talent, its feminism (the beautiful revenge of the plan on its 100 per cent female government), and its realistic description of the risk to democracy posed by any strong presidential power. As if to demonstrate, through this brief and tenuous final season, that the series could not survive the departure of Kevin Spacey (present through his absence throughout the episodes), the season's inaugural crime of killing off the character of Frank Underwood to 'preserve his legacy' (threatened by 'his behaviour'), leads one to read the entire season as a desperate gesture to save our memory—and thus our love—of the series.

I'm also thinking of Regina Spektor's long, beautiful song, 'You've Got Time' that accompanies the opening of *Orange Is the New Black*, also commissioned for the occasion, with its sequence of imperfect, anonymous faces that were also an early feminist manifesto.

The credits of *Narcos* also made the series a Netflix 'signature' in its first Colombian season, thanks to the magic of the song 'Tuyo' composed by Rodrigo Amarante. This violent series, devoted to the ravages of drugs and the development of large-scale trafficking in the South to supply the infinite American market, was, it should not be forgotten, the first series to put Netflix among the greats, in competition with the cable channel HBO; and Netflix, like HBO, now also has its mythical products (who didn't know at the turn of the century that HBO meant *Sex and the City*, *The Sopranos*, *Six Feet Under*, *The Wire*?—and in the 2010s that Netflix means *House of Cards*, *Orange Is the New Black*, *Narcos*, *Stranger Things*…?). *Narcos*, however, has a special place on the list, thanks to the credits, the 'magical realism' of Pablo Escobar's demented story, and the genius of actor Wagner Moura. But Netflix also assumed its identity with *Narcos* and thus became creator, through its products, of a new form of addiction to Internet series, soon to be

---

* This article first appeared in *Libération*, 29 November 2018.

characterized by binge-watching and freedom from the obsession with spoilers (although we already know the end of Escobar's or Kiki Camarena's story, that's not what matters).

This assumed transformation of the series' audience is certainly what allows the new season *Narcos: Mexico* to follow on so naturally from the three seasons of *Narcos* despite the 'myth', so to speak, of the beginning of a new series set in Mexico in the 1980s, a little before the epic of seasons one and two. As soon as the credits roll ('Tuyo' again), we're back in the same universe, with the same confrontation of two heroes (a trafficker and a policeman) but perhaps with a rebalancing in stature. Miguel Angel Félix Gallardo, the elegant 'skinny guy' who became the 'godfather' of drugs in Guadalajara, owes his rise to his cunning, authority, and cool; but he lacks the mythical and fantastic dimension of Escobar, even if Diego Luna's performance, which we already appreciated in the magnificent *Rogue One*, is formidable. What makes *Narcos: Mexico* worth watching is first the face-off between Felix and the DEA agent who has been hunting him since the first episode and his arrival in Guadalajara, Enrique 'Kiki' Camarena (Michael Peña)—a breathless, long-distance 'face-off' that is only concretized in a final encounter in which Kiki, kidnapped by the gang, becomes the master of the script, predicting his imminent death and Felix's coming downfall; secondly, the supporting cast, largely up to the level of the previous seasons (Don Neto, the excellent Joaquín Cosío, Rafa, Mika, Jaime…); thirdly, the aesthetic and moral heritage of the Hollywood films of the 1970s–1990s (*The Godfather, Scarface, Carlito's Way*); and finally the pinnacle: the offbeat crossover with Narcos and the delightful return of Wagner Moura, equal to himself, in a sympathetic encounter between Felix and Pablo.

Narcos, with its phone tapping, moral ambivalence, obsessions, collateral victims, and political cynicism, is today's real successor to *The Wire* (not *The Deuce*, even if David Simon aspires to it—fun to watch, but not so innovative). It is not the least of the qualities of the US network's flagship series that, from the start, it has been largely narrated in Spanish and subtitled for the English-speaking public (like the recent worldwide success of the Spanish show *Casa de Papel*), which has provided some nice irony at a time when President Trump is closing his mind and his borders to the South, exercising violence equal to the inhumanity of the thugs of *Narcos*.

Valar Morghulis and after

'It's not TV. It's HBO' was the slogan of the cable channel in 1997, which offered us, in what now seems to be a golden age, series such as *Sex and the City*, *The Sopranos*, *Six Feet Under*, *Entourage*, *The Wire*), which have changed the way we see the world, as well as the social status of the works in question, which are often neglected because of their mainstream nature. After a short period during which it seemed that the network was being overtaken by other networks (AMC with *Mad Men* and *Breaking Bad*), HBO took over the reins of series culture with *Girls* and *Game of Thrones* (*GoT*)—two series unlike any others. One does not have to be a fan of medieval fantasy, bloody fights, dragons, soft porn, or even George R.R. Martin's saga to be a fan of *GoT*—it is not even necessary to like 'TV series'.

Cult HBO series such as *The Wire*, comparable to great cinematographic or literary works, have nevertheless remained TV—great TV, for the discerning viewer, exploiting to the full the expressive and narrative resources of the small screen, which have given the TV series its 'letters of nobility' as they say (as if the series were in essence of rather low extraction), making a favourite occupation an object of study, even of erudition and distinction, and an element of subjective exploration and self-identification.

'It's not Porn, it's HBO' is the title of a short YouTube video that points to a trademark of HBO, from *Sex and the City* to *Girls*. *GoT* is also the glorious originator of the neologism sexposition (i.e., sex scenes used as a backdrop to the main narrative). This generates a background of domination from which superb female characters emerge: Catelyn Stark, Brienne, Arya, Yara, all of whom illustrate the capacity of the series to invent a (sometimes modest) female heroism—in the same way as *Girls*, in which Lena Dunham creates a new and twisted figure of the bravery of being a girl. *GoT* and *Girls* are thus more in line with the cult series of the 2000s, *Buffy the Vampire Slayer*, than with the HBO classics.

For many of us, one of the most distressing personal events of the last few years was the unexpected and cruel death of Eddard Stark (Sean Bean) towards the end of the first season of *GoT*. And how many upset and indignant text messages were exchanged, across all generations, upon discovery of the traumatic moment of the massacre of the rest (well, not quite) of the Stark family in season three, episode nine? This capacity to arouse and prompt the broad sharing of moral emotions through freeing their expression is one of the original features of this series, which reworks our experience unlike any other.

---

* This is a compilation of articles first appeared in *Libération*, 27 April 2016, 29 April 2019

The main categories are listed below:

Waiting

What series would generate such an anxious expectation of the new season among an audience that goes far beyond the fans of medieval fantasy or *24*-style TV marathons? Indeed, *GoT* goes beyond series addicts, fans, and exegetes—those new specialists who were beginning to have their own little territory—and simply explodes the TV series concept with its plural and its privileged medium (television). *GoT* holds the record for most downloaded series, for fan activity, and for public citations, and has changed our vocabulary and grammar, making 'Khaleesi' a common noun and 'Hodor' an ordinary phrase. Reconnecting its fans with the weekly rhythm of a soap opera, it is this rhythm that contributes to the strength of the series, through its inscription in the life of the viewer in a human duration of the days and weeks, a form of expectation that the philosopher Wittgenstein noted as a basic element of our forms of life. This new way of inhabiting time for the usually voracious consumer of series responds to the temporal extensibility of the seasons in the series that gives *GoT* its atmosphere and sensitive texture.

Values

For it is not moral values, but capacities to act that define the heroes in a world where, from the first season, it is clear that good will not win. The quest that drives these characters is not (with a few exceptions) the Iron Throne, simple survival, or even happiness—impossible for those who have conquered power in a world that is entering winter. This a priori disconnection of good and happiness, good and morality, displaces human fulfilment in individual honour and self-realization—made explicit in the education that the master-at-arms Braavosi gives to Arya, teaching her that 'fear is sharper than the sword'. This Starkian definition of heroism opens it up to female capabilities, as in the Icelandic sagas that form a significant background to the series. The character of Ned Stark sets the scale of this moral evaluation throughout the first season, if only by the way he walks and expresses himself—including through his gaze (remember the moment when, upon his arrival at King's Landing, he is asked to change into a more appropriate outfit). The value is no longer in good and evil, nor in customs and habits: Daenerys Targaryen accepts, not without difficulty at first, the barbaric ways of the Dothraki, and later hires, in her conquest, an army of 8,000 bloodthirsty brutes (each one, their leader claims, boasting of the quality of their training, has killed a baby in front of its mother).

The meaning of the slogan 'It's not TV it's HBO' was, at the time, purely elitist and distinctive: it was indeed television, but super television for an informed public, the maximum and perfect exploitation of a format that allowed freedom of language, the association of original characters, and the treatment of political, ethical, and sexual issues. Now, television series have become a cultural element, and everyone now has their own 'best of', a (social) distinction being established between quality series, on a par with cinematographic masterpieces, and the commercial stuff; that is, the series becoming an object of specialized erudition on the one hand, and of self-identification on the other, and connivance through the sharing of tastes and genres. *GoT*, a television blockbuster, explodes the field of 'quality' series or geek erudition. By opening up to the diversity of popular cultures (literary, cinematographic, video), and by mixing genres, like the cult series *Buffy the Vampire Slayer* (probably the only one to create a comparable universe, using similar methods), *GoT* approaches the ideal of popular culture—and that of the beginnings of Hollywood cinema—of a democratic culture that can be truly appropriated by all. Unlike, for example, the *Lord of the Rings* film series, the world of *GoT* is not a coherent universe born of the medieval erudition of a Tolkien, but—like the original George R. Martin saga—it unabashedly amalgamates cultures, eras, and genres (medieval epic first of all, but also Viking, Antique, Renaissance) without ever having to fear anachronism, in a world where time and space are redeployed without losing their axes or their familiarity. Though the series has been accused of sexism (because of its deplorable pornographic tendency), what counts is that, like *Buffy*, *GoT* integrates and supports feminist demands by creating unforgettable female role models in a world that is obviously dominated by men. It is this political dynamism that foregrounds *GoT*'s democratic power.

'Tits and Dragons'

GoT expanded the concept of the TV series. It is a series that belongs to fans, and is the most downloaded and cited of all. It revived the traditional mode of consumption of the format when it was assumed that series would be consumed as box-sets or binge-watching. *GoT* swamped its viewers during the ten weeks in which it invaded their lives. With the weekly rhythm of the serial, the imagination is set in motion by that anxious, curious waiting for what comes next. It is its vital rhythm that is the strength of the series. Its mode of inhabiting time responds strangely to its rescaling of the seasons: *Winter is coming*. This temporal texture is coupled with another modality of waiting: from the first episode, the viewer is caught, enlisted in this world where anything can happen. The end of the pilot showed us the young Bran Stark, who had been followed with increasing interest from the outset, climbing a tower and surprising Cersei and Jaime Lannister, who throws him out of the window. From this foundational moment, *GoT* engages with many taboos—incest, the invulnerability of heroes, and the protection of children—that structure the hierarchies of human life. In addition, what is worse is our surprise at enjoying the dalliance of Kingslayer in season three with Brienne. The appearance of this character, a giantess with proportions more suited to the big than the small screen, is a surprise. As for Ned Stark, his character surprisingly continues to hover over the entire series so far: despite the fact that he had a hard time politically, according to Machiavellian analysis he represents a moral figure who impresses us, as in any real encounter. *GoT* surprises us, but this is because we surprise ourselves, male and female spectators alike, with our reactions. In addition, there is the diversification of characters and the subversion of dualisms (able–disabled, man–woman, old–young, even human–non-human, living–non-living). The heroism of Arya Stark, Daenerys Targaryen, and Tyrion Lannister—with Peter Dinklage's 'premiere' topping the credits—makes *GoT* a democratic series: dwarfs (Tyrion), fat slobs (Samwell), the physically and mentally disabled (Bran, Hodor), prostitutes, savages (Ygritte, Osha), hideous monsters (Clegane, etc.) all exist on the same level as more presentable heroes. *GoT* is also a feminist series, despite criticisms provoked by its scenes of sexual abuse, because it integrates feminist demands, creating unforgettable female role models in a world still obviously dominated by men. It is also this political dynamism (which liberates or reveals the ordinary heroism and power of action by women, the disabled, slaves, and populations from the South), which is the democracy of *GoT*. In this way, the series approaches the ideal popular culture since the beginning of Hollywood cinema– a culture capable of being appropriated by all, thanks to an education that teaches us heroism is within the reach of everyone.

Yes, Jon Snow is still dead. He even spent the entire first episode of the season frozen on his table, while the other characters, Sansa, Theon, Arya, and Tyrion, each made their mark (on us too) on the ever larger territory encompassed by the credits of *GoT*. There is also the annual rite of waiting for the new season of *GoT*, with its procession of hypotheses, teasers, recaps, redundant commentaries, and delirium over spoilers. The rhythm of *GoT*, whose narration is explicitly built around a structure of waiting, is now inscribed in our lives, this time creating the expectation of a possible resurrection of the hero massacred in the last episode of season five. We are aware that in *GoT* anything can happen, as seen in such traumatic scenes as episode nine, which includes the sudden beheading of Ned Stark, who had seemed to be the main hero in the first season, and the carnage of the wedding in the third season. It is this permanent threat to their lives, apart from the richness of the writing and performances, which creates our attachment to *GoT*'s characters. This feature is shared with another popular series, *The Walking Dead*, which completed its sixth season with similar suspense: who was actually crushed in the last scene? The potential loss and constant vulnerability of their heroes builds a special relationship with the public, especially in a century replete with threats to human life. Each, in a kind of excess and adapted from other works, *GoT* and *The Walking Dead* has rehabilitated two of popular culture's most underrated genres, namely fantasy and the zombie movie, giving them an epic dimension as well as a particular realism, built on our attachment to characters who are imperfect yet striking, and who become part of our own stories. So much so that their loss, possible or realized, becomes personal, yet mourning is impossible because they are still there, even if they are dead—and not just because they are fictional characters! Ned and Jon Snow, like Shane, Beth, or Tyreese, are still alive even when dead, and this makes their loss irremediable and melancholy.

They Are the Walking Dead

The fifth season (not completely successful) was a turning point, as until then there were at least two *GoT* audiences: those who had read George R.R. Martin's five volumes and were more or less forewarned, and those who discovered the story on TV and were regularly in shock ('Aargh!', 'No!'). The democratic nature of *GoT* puts an end to this ultimate segregation. The series is no longer an adaptation, having caught up with Martin. In going live, 'off the page' it has become independent of the written saga, perhaps losing in narrative as it takes off, while developing its hold as a pure TV series. As Andy Greenwald stated on ESPN's blog *Grantland*, it is possible that 'what we took for an exercise in adapting a book for television has led to making a book from television'. Furthermore, there is the question about how to continue writing novels with a new threat constantly looming and despite the protests of the followers: the series might spoil the books.

The tyranny of the spoiler ('spoilerophobia', which is nothing but the obsessive quest for spoilers) is certainly the dark side of the GoT phenomenon. Certainly, *GoT* infantilizes, achieving the paradoxical feat of taking us back to childhood by means of a very adult TV series. The terror of the spoiler, however, blocks reflexivity and introduces unbearable constraints into an area that has liberated its audience. How is knowing what will happen (which is known anyway) a problem? What conception of vision and criticism justifies such a normative delirium? One would come to appreciate the rude behaviour of the actor, Ian McShane, a magnificent Swearengen in the cult series *Deadwood*, scheduled to appear in season six of *GoT*, who spoiled a character's return from the dead, responding to the indignation of online *GoT* fans with 'get a life', adding, crassly, 'It's just tits and dragons.' Neither breasts nor dragons, however, are what captivated audiences in the first episode of season six. Rather, it is the pure pleasure of finding Brienne and hearing her once again pledge allegiance to a Stark woman. The strength of *GoT*, beyond its ability to make everything fit onto a small screen, lies in the moral aspiration and life force that carries it in such moments, and in the ability to gradually bring together the characters spread over its territory.

It is women, at least as much as men, who represent this form of perfectionist aristocracy: Catelyn, Brienne, Arya, Yara, and even Khaleesi, are the true moral successors of Ned, holding high the values of an imperfect world. Yet bravery and perseverance are not everything. Moral resources are also found among the humble, the vulnerable, and children—Samwell, the coward (a role comparable with that of Hugo in *Lost*); Bran, the cripple; and Shae, the maid. These characters create new and unprecedented formulas with regard to heroism. Given the fact that *GoT* is more realistic in doing so than historical series, it finds its realism in proximity to humans, its emotional strength in humanity, and the modest heroism of characters doomed to death ('Valar morghulis', s2e10), but who in the meantime, as the late Ygrette told Jon Snow, just like us must live.

Star Wars: Our Contemporary Mythology

Why are we waiting for 'The Force Awakens', Episode VII of *Star Wars*, which we can see in France before the rest of the world, thanks to our Wednesday movie release nights? Without always being experts in this universe, many of us are fans of the saga, as *Star Wars* is both a space opera and the great saga of our contemporary world, which has been with us since well before the *Game of Thrones* series, which has only occupied us for five years. *Star Wars* therefore has, and continues to have, a real imprint on our lives as the mythology of our present.

No Mythology without Inscription in the Long Duration of Human Lives

From the audience's point of view, more than forty years will have passed between the first film released in 1977 (first called *Star Wars*, and then renamed *A New Hope* to fit a broader narrative) and Episode IX, scheduled for 2019. Who can beat that? Even *Twin Peaks*, a cult series, will most likely have its third season only twenty-five years later. This span of time means that, for those of us who discovered it as teenagers, the *Star Wars* universe will have accompanied us for a large part of our adult lives, and thus provides the greatest example of the place of these popular works in the formation of individuals, their morals, expressions, and their ways of being – from the efficiency of R2D2 to the intellectual class of C3P0 and the magnificent expressiveness of Chewbacca; from the romantic charm of Han Solo to the torrid eroticism of Leia in a bikini in *Return of the Jedi*; from the tragic Shakespearean love story between Amidala and Anakin to the rigid fidelity of Obi-wan. How many times have we talked about the dark side not falling, or the Force being with us? That the vocabulary of *Star Wars* has even penetrated political language is evidence of one of the key characteristics of the series: its immense influence on popular culture in general, but also on our daily lives, conversations, friendships, and morals.

As far as the characters are concerned, the saga also unfolds over the long term. We know that Episode VII is set some thirty years after the end of the first trilogy and the victory of the Jedi over the dark side, and thus we meet the descendants of Darth Vader and the queen-then-senator Padmé-Amidala. This same Darth Vader whose childhood and tragic trajectory we saw in Episodes I, II, and III, all shot between 1999 and 2005—that is to say, more than twenty years after the original trilogy. The real *Star Wars* experts (of which I am not one) speak of a 'prelogy' for this 'prequel' (account of the events that precede the original film), which is a model of the genre and has since delivered many further interesting examples, including *X-Men: First Class* (Matthew Vaughn, 2011) and Desplechin's *My Golden Years* (2015).

---

* This article first appeared in CNRS Le Journal, 16 December 2015

No Mythology without Political Tragedy
If the beginning of the saga was marked by the struggle of Good (Luke and the Jedi knights) against absolute Evil (the Empire), the sequel adopts a more troubled vision: the itinerary of Anakin Skywalker—a Jedi knight who has fallen to the dark side of the Force to subsequently become Darth Vader—reveals the fragility of Good. Here his trajectory is political, moving from the Jedi ideal of his childhood to a megalomaniacal, almost fascistic, fascination with power. He declares, in a key moment of conversation with his fiancée Amidala in Episode II, that power 'must be reserved for one of worth' who deserves it. 'Who, then? You?' asks Amidala, a character who, having seamlessly moved from queen to senator, represents the values of democracy and the galactic republic that are found in his daughter, Leia. In Episodes I–III, Good only exists as a resistance to Evil, and thus it is this rebellion and resistance that *Star Wars* has portrayed since its inception, especially with the appearance of Princess Leia, fighting against the Empire.

A diverse and numerous cast fills Lucas' work: in the lead roles, actors of different generations, from Harrison Ford to Natalie Portman by way of Ewan McGregor, though somewhat known already, subsequently acquired a worldwide aura. One of the additional characteristics of *Star Wars*, however, is our equally great attachment to the supporting roles, for instance Chewbacca and the robots R2D2 and C3PO, whose actors are the only ones to have participated in all the episodes. A true laboratory of multiculturalism, *Star Wars* is the first work to have created such a strong relationship between characters (primarily human but not exclusively) and its audience over such a transgenerational period.

No Mythology without a Chosen One
From *Star Wars* to *Buffy*, *Matrix*, *Harry Potter*, *Lord of the Rings*, *Hunger Games*, it is always in a form of seriality that the figure of the Chosen One, the one who will save us, is deployed—in which respect *Star Wars* is emblematic of the quasi-religious traditions of the great sagas. The structure and sequence of the two trilogies make the question of the Chosen One an essential element of the narrative by introducing a haunting question: who is the Chosen One? Between Luke, who has all the classic characteristics (an ordinary boy of modest profession who lives with his aunt and uncle on Tatooine, and does not know what his destiny will be), and Anakin, who is more twisted, but whose sacrifice seals his destiny, who should be chosen? Such doubt and questioning about the Chosen One is certainly an original feature of *Star Wars*, and an influential element on the more recent examples cited above.

No Mythology without the Moral Education of a Wide Audience
Early on, *Star Wars* introduced us to multiculturalism and galactic multispeciesism by presenting us with a variety of worlds (from Tatooine to Naboo

to Coruscant), and even arousing our moral indignation in a scene in Episode IV, where robots ('humans only') were forbidden to enter a bar (even though it was frequented by some rather monstrous specimens), presenting us with a wide variety of life forms that were endearing, and thus making use of our ties to the characters over time. Even the subversive figure of Jar Jar Binks—the object of homophobic delusions on the part of some fans—creates continuity. In any case, *Star Wars* has always innovated, including by introducing strong women into a male universe. It is this attachment to characters that, in any great series, allows us to inscribe the moments within ourselves, a fatal attachment that is represented and sealed by the tragic scene at the end of Episode III, in which Darth Vader's mask closes and locks onto Anakin at the moment of Leia and Luke's birth.

Star Wars illustrates exactly what the star thinker of pop culture Pacôme Thiellement says about popular culture: it 'opposes the idea of an elitist culture, which would only reach an educated part of the population, but is not to be confused with mass culture, produced by this so-called "elite" with a view to keeping the population in ignorance and misery'.[5] *Star Wars* culture has been a part of my education: I am of the generation that saw the first trilogy (1977–1983) in my youth, when we still sneered at American blockbusters and the alienation produced by mass culture; I saw the second trilogy (1999–2005) more than twenty years later (with my young children), when everyone had discovered their first *Star Wars* on television or in a repeat performance at the cinema. Likewise, I'll go to see Episode VII with my now adult children, even if I can foresee the recriminations of those who will be disappointed.

It is, and will be, a very different experience to see the episodes in the chronological order of the narrative (from I to IX, in 2019), and to discover or rewatch them in the order in which we discovered them in the cinema—that is, that of our personal history. It is not the least contribution of *Star Wars*, through its genius of narration and the attachment to its characters that it engenders, to offer us the possibility of such diverse and renewable viewer experiences to inscribe in our lives.

---

5 Pacôme Thiellement, *Pop Yoga* (Paris: Sonatine Éditions, 2013).

Rogue Princess

How do we explain the grief and sense of personal loss that so many of us felt when we learned of Carrie Fisher's death? The actress and writer had been a pop culture icon since her role as Princess Leia alongside Harrison Ford (Han Solo) and Mark Hamill (Luke Skywalker)—which was 40 years ago (she was 20 at the time), in the inaugural episode of the *Star Wars* saga.

In an autobiographical sense, *Star Wars* is first and foremost, for me, the beautifully written trilogy of 1977–1983, whose charm, beyond the war against the Empire, was in large part thanks to the very romantic comedy-style relationship between Leia and Han—as well as to the particular humour of the robots C3PO and R2D2, including their non-human counterparts such as Chewbacca, and to the moral demands of 'the Force', 'the Rebel Alliance'.

We find all these characters in Episode VII. Leia is very much present; not, as she jokingly imagined in an interview before filming, 'in an intergalactic retirement home', but still a fighter leading the rebellion against 'The First Order' inherited from the Empire. She is reunited with her old companion, Han Solo, both of whom have aged but are oddly the most touching element of the narrative (the feminist Carrie Fisher did not shy away from ironizing on the different pressures put on men and women in these circumstances). It's not a spoiler to point out that Han Solo dies in Episode VII, killed by the evil son he and Leia bore, Kylo Ren. The death of the actress Carrie Fisher is also a farewell to a key character in the saga –different but as written.

Leia is an extraordinary figure who can be followed from her birth (at the terrible end of Episode III, *Revenge of the Sith*) to her maturity in Episode VII. The twins Leia and Luke, the offspring of Padmé Amidala and Anakin Skywalker, were born at the exact moment of Anakin's imprisonment— charred by his battle with his master Obi-Wan—in Darth Vader's armour, and the death of Padmé (Natalie Portman). The solemn presentation of the two babies to both the screen and to Obi-Wan (Wikipedia tells us that the same 'actor' was used for both shots), creates the transition between the "first" trilogy (I, II, III) and the second, earlier trilogy, so as to connect them by a naturalized—and emotional—link, through the viewers' familiarity with the characters of Luke and Leia.

A Role Model for Generations of Girls

We know that in the script the twins Leia and Luke are separated and, between the first two trilogies, grow up in secrecy, concealed from their father. Leia is subsequently found at the age of 20 in 'A New Hope' (played by Fisher), is present across the whole of the 'second' trilogy, and then returns forty years later in VII. Episode VIII, where she is present, has already been

---

* This article first appeared in *CNRS Le Journal*, 4 January, 2017

shot, but Episode IX will probably have to do without her. Here it is clear once again that it is the attachment to the character, reinforced by the sight of her birth, then by that of her ageing, that carries the dynamic of the saga.

Star Wars has often been criticized as being a man's game, for being dominated by its male heroes: Anakin, Luke, Obi-Wan, Han Solo. Leia was thus a role model for generations of girls in this universe: noble and a fighter, spiritual, resistant—and sexy (ah, the golden bikini of Episode VI), without being a superwoman or a Jedi. Like Buffy, she paved the way for a properly feminine heroization, in the form of a high ideal that is accessible to all. Indeed, this 'ordinary' fighter aspect is also found in the Leia of Episode VII, where the new trilogy (VII–IX) expresses the desire for diversity that Lucas has clearly had since the beginning of *Star Wars* (the main heroine of VII, for instance, is Rey, a young girl with a young black boy as a companion). Nevertheless, the character of Leia remains the emblematic female figure of the saga.

For it is again on the singular face of Fisher (reconstituted with photograms of the actress at 20 years old) that the new 'parallel' film *Rogue One* closes. Here, the action takes place just before the second trilogy, with a group of rebels getting ready to steal the plans of the Death Star, a weapon of mass destruction developed by the Empire and tested at the beginning of Episode IV in a traumatic scene. Here again, beyond the explicitness of an element of the famous credits of IV scrolling on the screen in yellow letters, the effect is to reinforce the links *in* the saga, and thus *to* the saga. I'm also thinking of the touching and anachronistic inlay of Hayden Christensen's face, the Anakin of Episodes II and III, in the final and festive scene of *Return of the Jedi*. And it is all the more upsetting, in the wake of Fisher's death, to see the princess' face at the close of *Rogue One*, pronouncing the film's last word: 'Hope.'

'No rebellion without hope', several characters in *Rogue One* repeat again and again. This film, apparently unpretentious, is more powerful than Episode VII, which has been accused of being too much of a remake of Episode IV, depicting the formation of a small group of rebels around a young woman, Jyn, who will sacrifice themselves to the end in the fight against the Empire. The film pays tribute, in a way, to the unseen sidekicks whose actions allowed the victory of the Rebel Alliance over the dark side. There are no Jedi in *Rogue One* (apparently this will be a feature of the 'parallel' film series), but rather ordinary fighters—human and robot—who are carried by a somehow democratized Force, reborn through its weak forms to the 'new hope'. The film is also distinguished by a fine array of supporting actors (including guest stars Forrest Whitaker and Mads Mikkelsen), who are not (yet) well known (although I have no doubt that Riz Ahmed, Diego Luna, and Felicity Jones will be the stars of tomorrow), though nevertheless remarkable. It is a film that, for once in the series, is finished (i.e., without any possible sequel) by the sacrifice of the characters, all of them 'secondary'.

What is a supporting character, if not the one who carries a film (hence the expression supporting actor/actress) and whose presence, even if incomplete, leaves a lasting impression on the viewer? Just think of the importance of so many secondary characters in the *Star Wars* saga, as well as the impression made on us by the heroes of *Rogue One*, even though they have no future or posterity. The supporting role is a key element of popular culture, conveying the message that the most important character is sometimes the most humble and the least visible, and thus that seemingly minor characters can be permanently inscribed in us.

And I can't help but think of Fisher's post-*Star Wars* career, often neglected in comparison to the glorious trajectory of Ford's, which was made up of supporting roles that were sometimes forgotten or failed. Of course, there have been personal vagaries, a princess who remained rebellious and quirky for life, a rogue—representative of a cheerful and still Hollywood anti-conformism, but as an actress Fisher never achieved the fame and glory of Princess Leia; she remained a legend without being a star. But this series of 'secondary' roles or moments of conversation, whether in the *Blues Brothers* (John Landis, 1980), *When Harry met Sally* (Rob Reiner, 1989), or David Cronenberg's recent *Maps to the Stars* (2014) in which she plays herself, also traces a singular trajectory deeply inscribed in each *Star Wars* fan, and in the Western popular culture of which she will remain an emblematic figure.

Last Action Hero

Top Gun: Maverick (Joseph Kosinski, 2022), the long-awaited sequel to the iconic 1980s action film, is not a masterpiece. But, unlike most blockbuster films, it is an excellent film, and a constant pleasure to watch; those who accuse it today of being a pale copy of the original are also those who were never able to appreciate the first *Top Gun* of 1986 (Tony Scott), which made Tom Cruise the popular culture icon of the 1980s and a star who is still omnipresent today, thirty-six years later—think of the recent *Mission Impossible: Fallout* (Christopher McQuarrie, 2018) and the excellent *Edge of Tomorrow* (Doug Liman, 2014). Revisiting the first *Top Gun*, one is gripped by its longevity—it's not just a brilliant debut or the revelation of an actor, but the explosion of a star, with boyish, unabashed, and devastating charm—contextualized in a military story of fighter jets, spiced with romance and 'bromance'. I had discovered Tom Cruise's genius when, by chance, I went to see *Risky Business* (Paul Brickman, 1983, the same year he appeared in Coppola's film *The Outsiders*), where he already astonished his audience in a cult scene that has become a quintessential image of solo dancing, in underwear and an Oxford shirt. The year of *Top Gun* is also the year of his most beautiful role, as Vincent Lauria, in the masterpiece *The Color of Money* (Scorsese). It is too convenient to forget that the star of blockbusters of recent years and *Mission Impossible* (with different directors, from De Palma to John Woo), has carried a series of classic films, from *Born on the Fourth of July* (Oliver Stone, 1989), *The Firm* (Sydney Pollack, 1993), *Eyes Wide Shut* (Stanley Kubrick, 1999), and *Minority Report* (Spielberg, 2002) to *Collateral* (Michael Mann, 2004). There are also his 'small' roles, as in *Magnolia* (Paul Thomas Anderson, 1999), or 'small' films, such as the beautiful *Jerry Maguire* (Cameron Crowe, 1996). To encounter the actor so long after, a little aged but still mostly as he was, is not only comforting for his generation (OK boomer); but it also gives us a vision of our history. This is not a matter of individual triumphs, but of a history of the cinema, which I will call 'popular' for the sake of convenience and which, simply put, is the great cinema of the twentieth century: both demanding and seductive—a species in danger of extinction. What happened to Ridley and Tony Scott, James Cameron, John Woo, Michael Bay...? Cruise is the last remnant of their unforgettable blockbusters.

The return of *Top Gun* is also part of the narrative return to the 1980s to films, alongside series (*Stranger Things*, *OVNI(s)*, *Show Me a Hero*, *Chernobyl*, *Deutschland 83, 86, 89*, *The Americans*, etc.),. It is interesting that in our present moment of war between East and West, we return to the time before the fall of the Berlin Wall. The first *Top Gun* was set against the backdrop of the conflict between two superpowers, with a real and ritualistic adversary (the Soviet Union) and an explicit risk of nuclear apocalypse. In the new

---

* This article first appeared in *Libération*, 3 June 2022.

Top Gun, the hero Pete Mitchell (Maverick) is faced with a generic 'rogue state'—Russia—that has in its possession high-tech aircraft and is building a weapons factory in a mysterious mountainous region. The circle is complete.

But the question is less geopolitical than aesthetic: the film reflects on the technological achievements of the last decades and is naturally in line with *Mission Impossible*. It is impossible not to think of the latter franchise when Pete is entrusted with his typical 'last mission'—training a squad of young, super-talented pilots for an extremely dangerous and urgent mission. From the very first scene, we see, as a trope of the genre, an authority figure lecturing the rebel hero: Rear Admiral Chester Cain, fittingly played by Ed Harris (of whom we never tire), tells Pete that pilots like them are obsolete in the age of drones and digital technology. This is obviously about Cruise, not Pete, and about defending the values of classic cinema in the face of the streaming age: yes, the 'old cuckoo' still flies, as in the thinly veiled metaphor of a scene where Tom Cruise and his young Padawan manage to escape in a rusty F-14. The central question posed by the film, which carries with it the history of popular cinema of the 1980s, as well as that of the twenty-first century, is less the necessity of combat pilots than the relevance of such a film star. It is the question of the 'stuff of heroes' (the title of *The Right Stuff*, 1983, a film that was a blueprint for *Top Gun*), of that specific texture of great film actors, which Cavell calls photogenesis, and we could call cinegenesis or now TV-genesis. This goes for Ed Harris, but also Jon Hamm (the Cyclone), whose perfect character echoes Don Draper's military past, as well as all the remarkable young actors on Pete's team (the excellent Glen Powell in the role of Hangman, Monica Barbaro as Phoenix, Greg Tarzan Davis in the role of Coyote)—such a strong line-up in the constitution of the group is well within the scope of the old-fashioned action film.

Top Gun is not a franchise, nor a saga, and certainly not a 'universe'; *Maverick* is not even really a sequel, but a kind of reminder. There is the California aesthetic and the bromance, echoing the dramatic story of Pete's friendship with the late Goose, whose death haunts Pete as much as the rest of us, and whose son, Bradley 'Rooster' Bradshaw (the exceptional Miles Teller), is reunited with the hero. There is also romance in the love affair with Penny Benjamin—Jennifer Connelly reprises her mysterious and allusive role as the 'Admiral's Daughter', the object of Pete's attentions in the first *Top Gun*. Experts will note that, rather than a romantic storyline, what we have here is obviously a 'remarriage'—Penny and Pete have known each other well and then parted ways, swearing that they would not see each other again; yet, in a classic manner, the film brings them back together, although certainly with less erotic passion than in 1986 (which is here reserved for the torrid scene of the volleyball game).

At the time of the first film, Connelly had already performed in *Once Upon a Time in America* (Sergio Leone, 1984). *Maverick* sends us back to a history of cinema, our own. But the real stars of *Maverick* are the action sequences—the low flying, the aerial combat, Cruise on his motorcycle wearing his original Top Gun jacket. With a concern for realism that is similar to that of spy series and films, the flight scenes were shot in real F/A-18s. Actors had to train for these action shots, and each image showcases their work generously. This taste for work well done is what opens up the space for emotions on the big screen, and what we enjoy most is the absence of digital special effects (which paradoxically abound in current series, including 'prestige series' by HBO).

Tom Cruise is an *effet de réel* of his own: he is a reminder of what cinema can be. He sends us back, in his inalterability, to the historical thickness of cinema—a secular form of life where we go to theatres to see a pilot do a hover or a couple argue. *Top Gun* is part of the fight to keep it, against the onslaught of franchises and platforms. Our late action hero is a treasured relic of classic cinema, and Cruise's commitment to it should earn him intellectual respect, rather than mockery.

A year before, the opening credits of *Annette* (Leos Carax, 2021) seemed to jubilantly, yet sombrely, relaunch cinema to the tune of a song with a meaningful title, 'So May We Start'. In a totally different genre and in its own way, *Top Gun* puts a new coin in the jukebox and gives us back our faith in cinema on the big screen. Certainly, this is more effective, and happier, than any moralizing incitements to get off the couch.

4

Metaphysics

Vampires

Some will always be puzzled by the invasion of Western culture, from *Dracula* to *Twilight*, by the figure of the vampire, at once terrifying and seductive. Both books are important because they do not aim to explore yet another mythology, but to identify an element, one might say a theme, that has become crucial to our culture, and more specifically to popular culture in its most notable contemporary forms: cinema, novels, television series, songs, comics, and video games. The figure of the vampire also shows us how contemporary culture translates, expresses, and stylizes questions and answers that are essential to help us understand the radical transformation that has taken place in the democratization and dissemination of reflections on these cultural forms across the twentieth and twenty-first centuries, through material of unimaginable richness and diversity. Two particular dates that mark radicalizations are the turn of the twentieth century, with the publication of Bram Stoker's *Dracula*—the source novel for the entire contemporary vampire *genre*, primarily in film and literary fiction—and the turn of the twenty-first century, with the *Buffy the Vampire Slayer* series, Whedon's masterpiece and the source material for a whole new metaphysical and moral development, in which the vampire shifts from being a horrific figure to a non-human alter ego that crystallizes our questions about human nature.

The vampire has appeared as the central figure of popular culture and multiple themes. Why is this so? Because today it allows, better or more effectively than any other, the figuration and democratization of essential questions that everyone must and can take up for themselves; it expresses, in a unique and radical way, contestations and conceptual transformations that have not yet found their place in school or 'classical' training; and because it allows for the education of teenagers and adults, as Stanley Cavell would say, the first, along with Robert Warshow, to have deliberately sought to study popular material (Hollywood comedies in his case) in order to show

---

* A longer version of this article first appeared as the Foreword to Marjolaine Boutet, *Vampires: au delà du mythe* (Paris: Ellipses, 2011).

its power of thought and force of moral education. Consider the importance to teenage culture of the *Buffy* series, in which Angel reverses the stereotype of the terrifying vampire, becoming a heroic and sacrificial soul-saving character who flies to the rescue of souls in distress in the night-time devastation of Los Angeles. Vampire-themed television series are sites of moral innovation: Willow and Tara's love story allows the introduction of a lesbian couple into a mainstream series; Buffy enters into a sado-masochistic relationship with Spike; and *True Blood*'s African American characters set the tone for the series.

Not all of these characters are vampires, but it is clear that the figure of the vampire allows for liberation, openness, and a transformation of the relationship with the other. This is particularly explicit in *True Blood*, a series based entirely on the vampire as a metaphor for queer so as to challenge the norms of racial and sexual domination (the luscious character of Lafayette allows for a double subversion). The series admirably poses all the problems of difference and integration (mainstreaming versus assertion of identity) through the political and moral claims of the vampires. Furthermore, the change of focus from monstrous vampire (a parasitic creature to be killed) to humanized vampire is explicit in *Buffy*, where its heroine is torn between the need to slaughter vampires, which is her calling and profession (Slayer), and her love for both Angel, and then Spike. The spin-off, *Angel*, whose hero, as we understand it, is a vampire, is also rich in its claims to the acceptance of differences and monstrosity, and whose radicality is not to be overlooked.

The vampire has one central characteristic: he or she is not human. This is one of the principles of the genre (it is an analytical proposition, as logicians would say). A vampire can have a soul (Angel, Spike) and all the characteristics of a human (refinement, culture, generosity: Bill Compton or Godric), but is not human, because human, in this universe, is not a matter of moral characteristics. And as is regularly pointed out, the vampire is dead. He or she can eventually and exceptionally become human (that's the whole story of Angel), but then is no longer a vampire. This is the fundamental point that makes the relationship between humans and vampires so rich as it develops in the universe of novels, films, series, and comics.

The figure of the vampire, in its various iterations, makes it possible to represent death in a concrete, bearable, even sympathetic form (that of a dead person who is still present and with whom one may have a human relationship), and, particularly for an adolescent public that is discovering the anguish of finitude in a new way, in the form of a choice (the vampire Godric chooses to disappear) between an eternal and a finite life. This alternative is at the heart of the vampiric problematic, which allows not only for a form of mitigation of death anxiety, but also, more interestingly, for the validation of the idea that an ordinary, limited life, however agonizing the prospect of annihilation might be, is better (or at least no more unthinkable) than an eternity of solitude. The positive (and religious) myth of eternal life gives way to the ordinary romanticism of finitude, while leaving open the aesthetic possibility of varied representations of death: the tragedy of ordinary mortality is never denied or mitigated; however, as the tragic (and cult) episode of *Buffy* season five, *The Body*, remarkably shows, it is where the raw and intolerable reality of the human corpse coexists, in a surreal finale.

A similar euphemism can be seen in the conception of sexuality that the figure of the vampire allows. It is the combination of the themes of death and sexuality, as we often hear, that gives the vampire figure its power, with the vampire's bite being depicted as both frightening (sexuality as bloody and devouring, with horrific consequences) and yet attenuated (without sexual penetration or, more often than not, the risk of pregnancy). It is understandable that the portrayal on-screen of genital sex involving a vampire (apart from the technical difficulty that might present) constituted the breaking of a taboo, but the vampire also allows for an aestheticization of phenomena that were hitherto not very visible, including in X-rated cinema. Pascale Molinier notes that in *Buffy*, for example, the revelation of the vampire is marked by physical transformations that refer to the effects of sexuality: the face wrinkles, the nose comes up, and the teeth become visible, the face takes on a repulsive and animal aspect, in the same manner as the transformations that accompany sexuality, both exciting and worrying, and the sign of an overflowing. Vampires thus embody sexuality in its demonic aspect, as a passage to another state that is no longer entirely human: what Teresa de Lauretis calls 'the inhuman in itself' is here represented by literal inhumans, whom the heroes of the series love or become. Vampires and other demons thus make it possible, far from attenuating sexuality, to take sexuality seriously by blurring the boundaries between normal and perverse, heterosexual and homosexual, in the creation of a space for the staging of sexual drives, of which (genital) sexual relationship with a vampire is the extreme expression. The character of the vampire slayer also makes it possible, like the female vampire, to subvert the male domination represented in penetration: the use of the stake to kill the vampire creates true pleasure—'When you drove the stake in, it gave me a crazy effect' (dialogue between the potential Slayers, *Buffy*, s5e12)—while reinforcing the registers of sexual equivalence. From this perspective, the figure of the vampire is also, in the world of popular culture, a resource for sexual education (and is sometimes, as is the case of *Buffy*, openly proclaimed as such), but with the surreptitious introduction of a rather poisonous vision of sexuality, on the side of the sexual death drive.

Furthermore, at the beginning of the twenty-first century, the vampire may have represented a consensual version of the darkly handsome man, a contemporary transposition of 'Prince Charming', who is an idealized figure of virility that quickly proves boring (a point that is made in *Angel*). The *Twilight* series of novels, and then films, plays on both the reassuring possibility of a non-genital sexuality and this 'handsome' dimension of the vampire. The tormented and peroxide-ridden vampire Spike, clearly out of step with the model of the virile seducer, and who is always ready to 'throw himself into evil like a party', may be preferred to Edward Cullen.[1] The vampire nevertheless also allows us to revisit the great myths of Western love: 'love at first sight', immediate connection and absolute recognition, desexualized love, love as giving meaning to life, or love as overcoming social obstacles, such as differences of class and species.

Here again, the theme of the vampire allows for a subversion of hierarchies and classifications at a time when the boundaries of love (but also of friendship and feelings) do not have to conform to definitions of the human. What criteria can be given for this, if not precisely the anxiety of desire for foreign bodies combined with the death drive? In the worlds of vampires, the contours of the self are unstable; metamorphosis is always possible and distressing; love is both eternal and transitory; and anything can happen: you die, you are reborn, you are several different people, you are transformed. But, well, that's life.

---

1 In his own words, *Angel*, season five, episode eleven.

Dollhouse – *Bildungsroman* and Counter-Fiction

A little-known work by the brilliant TV writer Joss Whedon had far too short a life (two seasons, 2009–2010), but remains intellectually and morally compelling. This is first and foremost because of the series' bold premise: human 'dolls' in the service of a house of the same name, who are given personalities according to the needs of their clients. Rossum is a lucrative company that offers 'special' services: the provision, for a limited period of time (their 'personalities' will be erased after each job), of a perfect human—that is to say, perfectly suited to the client's request, and therefore their demand for services, whether professional, emotional, or sexual. Its central character is Echo (the incredible Eliza Dushku, though the whole cast, notably Olivia Williams as Adele, Rossum's ruthless yet ambivalent boss, and Fran Kranz as Topher, the computer geek in charge of the dolls' maintenance, is impressive), who is (in the first few episodes) successively a romantic and sexy fiancée, a computer genius, a businesswoman, a dorky student in love with her college professor, a successful FBI agent, and a wife and a stay-at-home mother devoted to her child. These are not, however, role-playing games. In *Dollhouse*, 'dolls' are implanted with computer cards and 'reset' after each use through memory erasure, to return to being somewhat evanescent and minimal beings, 'stored' in the 'Dollhouse' where they live a zombie-boarding-school existence (sleeping in containers, exercising, drawing, playing) until their next mission.

Dollhouse is a distant heir to the classic movie *Blade Runner* (Ridley Scott, 1982), which remains strong and surprising after thirty years. The extra twist here is of course that we are dealing not with 'replicants' (artificial humans, who may have all the characteristics of humans), but with naturally occurring humans made artificial by stripping away their characteristics and replacing them with others as required. The dolls are recruited on a voluntary basis, with a five-year stint of work for the Dollhouse (the standard contract) being a substitute for severe punishment, or sometimes a way of escaping unbearable lives or memories. The character of Echo arose when a young terrorist, Caroline, was caught breaking into Rossum to sabotage it, and had to choose between being sentenced to death or working for the Dollhouse. In this sense, the Dollhouse is a prison (and the recurring theme is that of escape, which is obviously mythical), where actual imprisonment is presented as a path to redemption; this imprisonment corresponds to the image of the mind as enclosed in the body, an image (philosophical and moral) of which, as Wittgenstein would say, we are also imprisoned by, and from which the series sets out to free us.

Dollhouse presents itself as a contestation—and then a progressive and absolute destruction—of the apparently clear principles on which Rossum's

---

* This article was first published in *Multitudes*, n° 48, 2012 business (and a whole history of philosophy) is built: the idea of the body as the foundation for or container of spiritual characteristics and capacities for action, or of a spirit detachable from the body, imprisoned or integrated in it.

Through the radical nature of its initial premise—which allows for variations as infinite as human expectations of others are—and through the arc of the narrative, which sees the gradual emergence of Echo's self (by the end of the series she has become the leader of an anti-Rossum revolution), *Dollhouse* is a counter-fiction—an ultra-subversive counter-fiction that aims at a transformation of our reality—even more so than Whedon's seven-season masterpiece, *Buffy the Vampire Slayer*.

Buffy, as a feminist portrayal of an ordinary girl who could fight (against vampires, and then against all dangers), was the first subversion that engendered further subversive iterations (notably that of the boundary between human and non-human, and between life and death): *Angel*, the underrated Buffy spin-off, attacked the definition and generation of 'humanness' through a series of unnatural pregnancies and births. In turn, *Dollhouse* highlights the difficulty in the (adult) world of service relationships: what do we expect from others? By presenting, over the course of the episodes, the desires and fantasies of the Dollhouse's clients, the series expresses Whedon's primary interest: 'What each of us gets from the other in our most intimate relationships, whether sexual or otherwise.'

If care is understood as an appropriate response to human needs and vulnerabilities, what does it mean when humans are placed at our service (or simply are in service) in order to meet our needs? *Dollhouse* deconstructs and reinvents our classical attachment to the TV character by presenting bodies that, despite the repeated and complete erasure of their memory—which includes implanted bodily patterns—gradually sediment a personality in the form of connections to others, elective affinities, and resistance to oppression. What characterizes all these doll characters is the emergence of their self despite the repeated forcing of personalities onto them: thus Sierra, Echo, Victor, Alpha, anonymous in their names taken from the military alphabet, progressively develop a self through awareness of others.

Martin Shuster has brilliantly analysed this thesis of the show in his essay 'What It Means to Mourn'.[2] What this fiction tells us, among other things, is that we are a body, and that we make and improvise a mind (or minds) in it. The character of Echo emblematizes this counter-fiction: successively 'implanted' with multiple personalities, both male and female, which she ends up assuming all at once (including that of Paul Ballard, the love of her life, who dies in the last episode), Echo invents her person in the bodily and emotional sedimentation of her attachments and encounters.

---

2   My analysis here owes a lot to M. Shuster, 'What It Means to Mourn', in *From Alpha to Rossum: Inside Joss' Dollhouse*, pp. 233–245 (Dallas, TX: Benbella Books, 2010).

Her 'real' personality is no longer Caroline, the young woman originally 'erased' and used to create Echo; she *is* Echo, a body that builds its soul through its transformations, and from the remains of the thousand erased personalities and voices of its 'memory', of which Caroline is ultimately only a possibility. As such, Echo is not Caroline erased: Caroline herself is imprinted on Echo.

Dollhouse, which can be called a *Bildungsroman* in the radical sense of the word, is in a sense (and despite the criticisms that have been made of it) the ultimate feminist's show: a woman creating herself and constructing her subjectivity out of nothing—or nothing other than the uses to which she is put. One cannot help but think of Ibsen and Nora's claim to independence in his play of the same name.

Whedon's fans will recall that one of the reasons the series was cancelled was that the producer was uncomfortable with the direct reference to the satisfaction of sexual fantasies by Rossum's 'dolls' in the early episodes. But the problem was not so much sex, which is, after all, a central theme of most television series, as it was the subversiveness of the Dollhouse with its focus on service activities as prostitution. The Dollhouse is effectively a brothel, and the show, in its more playful episodes, deals directly with the issue of prostitution, though this is not a denunciation of prostitution as exploitation. Just as fans of *Firefly* will remember how prostitution was morally justified through the character of Inara (one of Whedon's finest) and her integration into the *Firefly* crew, similarly the set-up of *Dollhouse* integrates sexual services into a globalized human service not so as to denounce prostitution, but, more subversively, to put before our eyes a society of generalized prostitution—a service society that is fictional, but is also well and truly our own.

Once again, the question of care is raised, along with that of our expectations of others: that the human being, and the emotional demand that defines it in the most intimate sense, has become a commodity or an instrument *in the service of*. It is the reverse, a caricature, of each person's very real need for attention, and for care. In any case, *Dollhouse* is an unyielding demonstration of the danger of defining humans by criteria, performance, and capacity, and not, for example, by singularity and resilience.

Post-Apocalyptic Year

Despite our affection for *Game of Thrones*, the promising comeback of *Homeland*—now with Carrie (Claire Danes) rid of the ball and chain that was Brody—the KGB in the spotlight in *The Americans*, and the hilarious killer Billy Bob Thornton with seductive cop Allison Tolman in the series version of *Fargo*, *The Leftovers*, created by Damon Lindelof and Tom Perrotta, is the most brilliant series of 2014. Presenting us with a world where, one autumn day, with no explanation, 2 per cent of humans vanish from the face of the Earth from one second to the next, rather than chasing a mystery in the manner of Lindelof's previous work *Lost*, the series describes the invisibly destroyed lives of the remaining inhabitants: as if the disappearance without trace of a portion of humanity suddenly makes visible the weight, difficulty, and cruelty of earthly existence.

The 2010s have thus made us sensitive, in various new ways, to the fact (previously conceived as a given) of being on Earth and attached in some way to the planet, through the opposite image, that of being unattached and lost in space like the panicking Dr Ryan (Sandra Bullock) in *Gravity* (Alfonso Cuarón, 2013), with paradoxically the most spectacular images being the final ones of the heroine's return to Earth—her laborious steps on the shore after having emerged from her capsule making us experience the reality of gravity; and like Cooper (Matthew McConaughey), who in *Interstellar* (Christopher Nolan, 2014) is searching for a new planet to 'colonize' (such is the standard vocabulary in these intergalactic contexts) for the humans who are starving and suffocating on an Earth that has become uninhabitable.

The post-apocalyptic film genre that has been dominant since 2010 reflects the degradation of life forms on Earth. The promises of interstellar travel and life elsewhere are a direct response to the threat of extinction, which, once vaguely and theoretically projected into a distant or constantly deferred future ('Winter is coming'), is conceived of not only in the generationally near future, but also already in progress. What is called exobiology now inseparably explores—as does fiction, which has also become a form of enquiry—the origin and fate of life on Earth, as well as the possibility of other life forms in the universe.

The nagging ethical question in *Interstellar* is the choice between saving the humans present on Earth today and future generations. Phrased more radically: what are these future generations, if not the future of the privileged? The selfish choice is not the one we think it is, as illustrated by the excellent character of Dr Mann (Matt Damon), who, though proclaiming to be working for the future of the human race, only thinks of saving himself at the expense of his companions (which mirrors the film *2012* (Roland Emmerich, 2009), which told of a departure from Earth reserved for the elite, like the *Titanic*'s

---

* This article first appeared in *Libération*, 2 January 2015.

lifeboats). In *Interstellar*, Cooper understands that we cannot save the Earth without saving (all) the humans alive today, and that the only ones responsible for the future and the present 'are us'; the answer, once again, is in gravity (which has become a tool to transmit the solution).

The very real environmental degradation that has been occurring in Western countries for centuries is finally causing concern and mobilization since it is now being exacerbated by the involvement of other countries in resource exploitation and thus climate change. As the economist Amartya Sen has pointed out, the focus on climate change overlooks environmental inequalities—the inequalities in living conditions around the world. The year 2015 rang out with warning signals and grandiose calls for action in the run-up to COP21 (the climate conference in Paris): how can we fail to see that the stakes are vital? But when we euphemize or calculate by talking about 'risks', we are denying the reality of the losses that have either already taken place or are now under way.

The greatest series of 2014, *The Leftovers* signals nothing else: the apocalypse is not coming, it is already here, in our brutality and selfishness that only make us more vulnerable. The disappeared, the 2 per cent, are not 'elsewhere'. There is no 'Plan(et) B', and rather than failing to colonize other worlds, we should decolonize our own.

The Affair: The Art of Being Alive

It's quite strange to find Noah Solloway (Dominic West)—the hero of *The Affair*—with Sarah Treem and Hagai Levi in Paris, far from the beaches of Long Island or the streets of New York. The final episode of season three sees him wandering around a cartoonish Paris, between the quays of the Seine, small cafés, and charming hotels with his new sweetheart, a French academic, Juliette (Irène Jacob), whom he met on a campus as a resident writer after his release from prison.

Noah has been convicted of the fatal accident that was one of the main threads of seasons one and two, when responsibility for the disappearance of Scott Lockhart (a scumbag whose loss no one regrets) actually fell on (spoiler!) his first and second wives, Helen (Maura Tierney) and Alison (Ruth Wilson). To complete Noah's moral redemption, he emerges traumatized from three years in prison, having endured the abuse of a terrifying warden (it's great to see the excellent Brendan Fraser back). Does this sound far-fetched? Certainly, and many viewers complain that the series should have ended after two seasons, once the Noah–Alison case was exhausted and the Scott Lockhart death case was cleared up.

Yet the same people continue to watch, and will most likely continue to do so into the fourth season, which, against all the odds, has been scheduled by Showtime. As such, *The Affair* illustrates the strength acquired by a story, places, and characters, which, once 'unleashed' and entrusted to us, continue their trajectory, carried by the mystery each constitutes.

This is reinforced by the initial device of telling the 'same' events by alternating points of view from the different characters—first that of the heroes Alison and Noah and then, in the second season, that of their spouses, then exes, Helen and Cole—which made the originality of the series. The intensity of Maura Tierney's and Joshua Jackson's performances (the latter already brilliant in *Fringe* in this process of subjectivization, democratically dissolves the hierarchy of secondary versus main characters, for instance in the touching eighth episode of season three, which, in returning to the Alison–Cole couple, foregrounds the irreducibility and impossibility of their bond.

Season three offers a sense of reflexivity, with the show reflecting on the process that had been its charm (which was sometimes neglected in order to follow the characters in their singular trajectories through the little details that differentiate the protagonists' visions: the outfit Alison was wearing, who hit on whom, where a certain exchange took place, etc.). From now on, the process is radicalized—as in the Paris scenes where, in the Noah version, the French-language exchanges are not subtitled, and Juliette is much more charming as seen by Noah than by herself.

---

* This article first appeared in *Libération*, 7 June 2017.

We realize that Alison is much more mysterious and attractive, strange and cynical, from Cole's or Noah's point of view, whereas in her own perception she is fearful and neurotic. The story thus acquires a nostalgic dimension, as the scenes become less alternative narratives than memories soon to disappear (as in Gondry's *Eternal Sunshine of the Spotless Mind*, 2004), with a sceptical dimension created by the alternating points of view, which do not engender clear access to any of the people.

The novelty of this season is that the ignorance (the mystery) of the other extends to oneself, as Wittgenstein would say. Noah's vision (his time in prison, the persecution he suffers) turns out to be (spoiler!) purely hallucinatory. Similarly, Juliette's husband, stricken with Alzheimer's, mistakes her for his first wife; furthermore, Helen has been mistaken about her life for twenty years, as Noah's sister Nina obligingly explains to her. The revelation is therefore not in the heroes' perceptions, but in the moments of brutal expression of truth. Cole admits that he still loves Alison, but wants to be a 'good guy'. When she is asked how she survived, in a crucial conversation with a young woman she met at the hospital, Kendra, who has just lost her child, Alison replies without giving it much thought: 'I had an affair', adding that it was a way to feel something. She concludes: 'It's amazing to be alive. People take it for granted, you and I know it's not.'

The main thing is thus to be alive, which is also the theme of *The Walking Dead* whose seventh season has thankfully just resumed after a mid-season break (during which we languished waiting for Rick (Andrew Lincoln) to finally find the strength to rebel against the ruthless tyranny of the 'Saviours', their impressive leader Negan (Jeffrey Dean Morgan), and Lucille, his barbed baseball bat). The first episodes plunged us into a disarray and disorientation similar to that of the various heroes—isolated and separated by the narrative itself, which was broken up into individualized and interminable episodes. Once they finally regroup, the truth comes out of Aaron's (Ross Marquand) mouth, in a line that has already become famous: 'Either your heart's beating, or it isn't.' Like Rick's friend Michonne's (Danai Gurira) statement at the end of episode eight: 'We're the ones who have to live. That's why we have to fight.' The episode, called 'Hearts Still Beating', reminds us that *The Walking Dead* is not a story about the undead or 'zombies', a term entirely banned from the show, but, like *The Affair*, is a meditation on our form of life, as well as an exploration of the ways in which fiction can rekindle and make understandable that hard-to-define feeling of being alive.

Remarriage, Again and Again

With its innovative narrative structure offering multiple points of view, *The Affair* shows political and moral ambition until the very end. TV series are, among other things, sites of creativity and cinematographic invention. We remember the trademark of *24*, with its seasons of twenty-four one-hour episodes, which followed in real time (more or less) a busy day in the life of agent Jack Bauer. *The Affair* is another series that innovated in terms of narrative by presenting us with different points of view of a love affair. In the first season, the series juxtaposed the stories of two main protagonists, Noah (Dominic West) and Alison (Ruth Wilson), but it was less a question of confronting incommensurable visions than of multiplying points of view on a shared reality, which is constructed before our eyes over a period of years. For, in the second season, the device is extended to other protagonists, in particular to the neglected spouses, Helen (Maura Tierney) and Cole (Joshua Jackson) (who soon had nothing 'secondary' about them), though this method did not last much beyond the first two seasons. In the latest, however, it returns with full force.

The equal attention paid to the characters—including, in this final season, the multiple descendants of the four heroes—and the care the actors give them, is the greatest quality of *The Affair*, alongside the moral texture of the characters, developed over the last five years (especially Noah, played by the great Dominic West, who brings to the story the complexity of *The Wire*). There is morality without moralism, as shown by the final and, in a sense, immoral forgiveness offered by Helen to Noah (caught in the #MeToo tornado, an embarrassing opportunity for us to reflect on our own perception of his story), or, for example, the inventiveness of the relationship between Helen and Sierra, Eddie's mother (the child born of a brief affair with Vik, her companion, who disappeared at the end of the fourth season). This is also true of the general way in which the show teaches us, over the years, to accept and even love the foibles of endlessly annoying characters, while educating us on all sorts of adult subjects—PTSD, drowning, Los Angeles, insanity, sexism, climate, and, of course, the upheaval a sexual encounter can create in and around a life.

The finale (almost an hour and a half long!) of the series gives meaning to the whole story, and to the jump in time to thirty years later, where the fifth season is set. Here, in a Montauk devastated by climate change, Joanie, Alison's daughter, goes in search of the truth about her mother's story. The end-of-the-world atmosphere, and the gradual revelation of the death of the protagonists of the affair, gives the conclusion of the series a metaphysical power equal to the final minutes of *Six Feet Under*.

The series, which has had its moments of weakness and shadiness, achieves its own redemption over time, in particular as Noah dances to an 1980s

---

* This article first appeared in *Libération*, 7 November 2019.

song ('The Whole of the Moon') that he choreographed for his daughter Whitney's wedding in 2020, a wedding that became the occasion for his reunion with Helen. The Hollywood comedy model of remarriage, described by Cavell in *Pursuits of Happiness*, returns here with all its classic genre features, such as the sharing of a wilderness adventure (Helen and Noah facing the fires in Los Angeles and confronting a rattlesnake, at which point they realize how much they enjoy spending time together), the final argument, and the decision to 'change' to start over, like the heroes of *The Awful Truth* (Leo McCarey, 1937). Remarriage thus represents the acceptance of oneself, of mortality, of the passing of time, and the need to live together while preserving youthfulness and a form of immaturity. By exploring this reference, a rare occurrence in series, *The Affair* displays its philosophical and moral ambition to the end.

This is similar to *Room 212*, Christophe Honoré's beautiful film from 2019, which is the same length as this latest episode. It is also a story of separation and reunion: the film is condensed into one night, during which Maria (Chiara Mastroianni) finds herself in a hotel room across the street from her husband Richard (Benjamin Biolay), who has just discovered on his wife's mobile phone evidence of a series of infidelities of which he had no idea. In *Room 212*, Maria meets a number of characters, including a version of her own Richard (Vincent Lacoste) who is twenty-five years younger—which does not displease her: 'If you can no longer cheat on your husband with your own husband, where are we going?' After a series of adventures and unsettling encounters, Maria and Richard reunite at the end; and though one never doubts the film's melancholic conclusion, it is called for by the rule of the genre. Here the reference to remarriage is made even more explicit: Richard's last name is 'Warrimer', one letter off from the name of the couple in *The Awful Truth*, Jerry and Lucy Warriner—and, indeed, Dunne (Lucy) is mentioned in the acknowledgements, after Woody Allen, as if the inexhaustible genre of remarriage were constantly providing good reasons to pursue it further.

Blade Runner Has Lost its Scepticism

Blade Runner, directed by Ridley Scott and released in 1982, is such a cult film that we forget how coldly it was received by the public upon its release, despite the success of *Alien* (Ridley Scott, 1979) three years earlier, and that it was despised by the critics. Scott did not yet have the rebellious aura of *Thelma and Louise* (1991) or the grandiose *Gladiator* (2000), and so we are delighted that Villeneuve's film, *Blade Runner 2049*, is neither a remake (like the recent *Total Recall*, which is far inferior to the beloved original), nor even a real sequel that exploits an original thread (like the new *Star Wars*), but instead a tribute to a film that has not only influenced world cinema, but also our vision of the world—an indicator of the importance cinematographic works have in culture, just like great works of literature. *Blade Runner* is not only a cult film, but a twentieth-century classic, which contributed to the creation, along with the first episodes (IV, V, VI) of the almost contemporaneous *Star Wars* (1977–1983), of the science fiction genre, of which Harrison Ford was already the 'signature' in 1982. The actor moves from the seductive and romantic character of Han Solo to Rickard Deckard, a cynical detective character in the style of a 1940s crime novel. An average specimen of humanity, he will prove to be even more troubled in his hunt for 'replicants', those rebellious, powerful, and dangerous artificial humans whom he is responsible for eliminating. Contemporaneous but at odds with the jubilant *Star Wars* space opera, *Blade Runner* invented the aesthetics of twentieth-century terrestrial science fiction (reworked a thousand times since) with its specific texture and style mixing neo-noir special effects and gloomy, miserable, rainy urban atmospheres, with futuristic and baroque skyscraper architecture, flying cars, deformed creatures, and blurred, oozing, or flashing images. This future society, alive but also dark and devastated by poverty, violence, and demographic decline, is our own. Well before the post-apocalyptic streak that characterizes so much of twenty-first-century fiction, *Blade Runner* symbolized the pre-apocalyptic sense of threat to humanity.

Blade Runner's 2019 is our time, and the question it asks is ours: that of the definitions and limits of the human. With the pre-apocalyptic style, a metaphysical question emerges that takes the form of a sceptical question: how do I know if I am dealing with a human? The existence of android robots, improved replicants, Nexus 6 in the film, who are far superior intellectually and physically to humans, questions humanity—in the same way as other films, such as *A.I.* (Steven Spielberg, 2001), *I Robot* (Alex Proyas, 2004), *Ex Machina* (Alex Garland, 2014), and the extraordinary series *Real Humans* and *Westworld*—have also done more recently. Nevertheless, *Blade Runner* was the first to express philosophical scepticism, the notion of doubt as expressed (before being refuted) in Descartes and Hume. 'Deckard' is almost named after the former, whom Pris makes reference to: 'I think,

---

* This article first appeared in *Libération*, 5 October 2017.

Sebastian, therefore I am.' Some may recall that Hume is the name of a key character in the series *Lost*, which also centred on a sceptical questioning of the reality of experience for its characters.

Blade Runner reveals itself, to use an Stanley Cavell's expression, as 'a moving image of scepticism': no longer as a doubt about the reality of the world—a classic theme of scepticism, which can be found, for example, in films from the 1990s such as *The Matrix* (The Wachowskis, 1999), *The Truman Show* (Peter Weir, 1998), *ExistenZ* (David Cronenberg, 1999), but as doubt about humanity and the reality of others ('Are you for real?' the replicant Zhora amusingly asks Deckard when he comes to flush her out). The hunt for replicants begins with their detection, a matter of proving (or not) that they are not human: the essential point of the film from its opening scenes is thus these 'Voight-Kampff' tests supposed to detect abnormal and 'non-empathetic' reactions of the androids—a test that Deckard-Descartes makes Rachael, an employee of Tyrrel (the android producing company), undergo to prove, rather laboriously, that she is a replicant. Since replicants are capable of emotion, humour, self-awareness (Rachael understands what she is and is deeply distressed by it; the rebellious Nexus 6 are aware of their situation and want to overthrow it), interaction with others, and therefore of progression, it makes no sense to deny them the status of human (which is defined not by criteria or any mode of production, but by these very capabilities). Rather, it is the procedures for defining and limiting the human (which leads to the elimination of replicants) that are themselves inhumane.

In the trajectories of Rachael or Roy in the first *Blade Runner*, we find the tragedy of someone who knows they are doomed, programmed to end. At the same time, in *The Claim of Reason* (1979), Cavell drew a now classic parallel between scepticism and tragedy: at the origin of scepticism, there is the attempt to transform humanity into a theoretical difficulty. The tragedy of Othello or Lear, for instance, lies not in the doubt that assails them, but in their refusal to acknowledge and recognize the other. Othello is lost as soon as he tries to know; that is, as soon as he wants 'proof', as soon as his questioning takes the form of scepticism. Science fiction movies are the contemporary expression of scepticism. In *Blade Runner*, doubt is radicalized because it is extended to the subject itself: in the final moments (in the 2008 version) Deckard understands, and we with him, that he too is a replicant. But is that the most important thing? What the film has taught us is that it is not.

The best response to doubt is our relationship with and attachment to these characters, including the androids, who are the most strongly human presences in the film. Likewise, the answer to scepticism is the humanity of these beings that is once again present in the aesthetics of the film, for instance in the very real and striking presence of Roy (Rutger Hauer), Pris (Daryl Hannah), and Zhora (Joanna Cassidy). These women in particular are of superhuman strength, and their domination of the image, in the same vein of feminism of *Thelma and Louise* (Ridley Scott, 1991), is certainly the most compelling answer to doubt about humanity. It is thus a new power of cinema that *Blade Runner* explores, creating the gloomy backdrop against which carnal, strange, and lively figures emerge: Pris with her white mask and punk-like made-up eyes; Joanna Cassidy's six minutes on-screen as a snake charmer and then as a fearsome killer, finally shot down as if in mid-air in her transparent blood-spattered mackintosh, are as unforgettable as Rutger Hauer's famous last words. Showing that real humanity lies in this capacity to suffer, to bleed, cry, and refuse death, the film offers us characters that will mark us through these life-memories that are movies, and then 'will be lost in time like tears in rain'.

Though we knew we would be, we are still disappointed by *Blade Runner 2049* because Villeneuve's film is too perfect: a pretty, smooth hero, K, the-replicant played by Ryan Gosling (as subtly inexpressive as in *La La Land*, Damien Chazelle, 2016), and accompanied by his cute comfort hologram (there is no reason to accuse a film with so many wonderful and strong female characters of sexism, not to mention its main narrative: it follows a false male lead to a female revelation); beautiful images of lunar and devastated landscapes; an complex script; and the touching return of Harrison Ford as Rick Deckard.

One is reminded, with a nostalgia compounded by flashbacks—particularly of a real crackling recording of Deckard's first test interview with Rachael—of the original *Blade Runner* and its imperfections. But it is the confusing character of the original that *Blade Runner 2049* lacks. Though we find Ford (who as in *Star Wars* Episode VII thus returns to the two roles of his debut) as if to complete a cycle, here the return is less joyful.

Similarly, the original science fiction aesthetic is here clean, depressing, and basically less vivid in *Blade Runner 2049*. Where *Blade Runner* featured the pre-apocalyptic, *Blade Runner 2049* plays the well-worn dystopia card, regurgitating all the films that have imitated its model, from *12 Monkeys* (Terry Gilliam, 1995) to *The Terminator* (James Cameron, 1984), or *Oblivion* (Joseph Kosinski, 2013). Just because we don't have flying cars and the sun is still over our heads doesn't mean we have to reboot *Blade Runner*, because the *Blade Runner* of 2019 is not outdated. It is definitely our time because the question it asked is ours more than ever: the human being, its definitions, and its limits. A metaphysical question that takes the form of a sceptical interrogation—How do I know that I am dealing with a human being? What are the criteria of the human?, *Blade Runner* was a pioneer of philosophical scepticism in cinematic expression (not as doubt about the reality of the world—the theme of the brilliant *The Matrix* or *Existenz*), but about humanity and the reality of others.) In *Blade Runner 2049*, the hunt for 'replicants' no longer even requires their behavioural detection by the so-called Voight-Kampff test, which was the point of *Blade Runner*.

Scepticism about the humanity of the 'other' is, in *Blade Runner 2049*, suppressed in favour of traditional cognitive scepticism about the reality of an experience or representation, which is the strong point of the film, with the 'confirmation' of K's childhood memory. But *Blade Runner 2049* expresses, through continuity with the conclusion of the first *Blade Runner*, the individual question of our own nature as replicants or machines—just as in *Westworld*, where the new scepticism is not about the existence of reality (*The Matrix*), about the threat of robots (*The Terminator*) and their ability to replace humans, nor about the doubt that one can have about the humanity of others; but instead about one's doubt about one's own humanity, which has become a certainty that is impossible to assume.

Blade Runner's radical thesis of the moral superiority of androids, and of the inhumanity of humans as revealed in the procedures of human criterionization, is transformed into conformist epistemological reflection in *Blade Runner 2049*. The non-humans that were grandiose in *Blade Runner* become ectoplasmic or megalomaniacal in *Blade Runner 2049*; the *2049* clones of Pris or Zhora are weak reminders of their physical presence on-screen, which was so unforgettable in *Blade Runner*—so much so that a Rick Deckard at the end of his rope becomes, contrary to the original, the most human character of the film. *Blade Runner* was its own answer to doubts about humanity: a Voight-Kampff test in itself, by attaching us to its characters, and making its world real. The flashy *2049* is unlikely to make the same impression, even if it plays on the same attachment and world. It is a matter of aesthetics and metaphysics.

Twin Peaks: The Uncanniness of The Ordinary

The question of whether television series should still be excluded from the field of cinephilia is largely settled, but so is the latent confrontation that has developed over the last decade between films and series—or rather between their followers and specialists proclaiming the essential inferiority of the former or the programmed disappearance of the latter. In both cases, it is first and foremost a question of ignorance. Jean-Michel Frodon recently showed us the effervescence of international film production; as for series, we must learn to take them seriously as an aesthetic production, something in which the cinema, in particular great Hollywood cinema, can educate us. *Twin Peaks: The Return*, by Mark Frost and David Lynch, picks up the thread of the 1990–1991 cult series and leaves no room for debate: it is clearly a major cinematographic work, whether as a television series or an eighteen-hour film—for such is the claim of David Lynch, who directed all the 'parts', in contrast to the remarkable plurality of scriptwriters and directors on the first two seasons. In this *Return*, which is much more than merely a sequel, Lynch unabashedly combines both cinema and TV, as demonstrated by the vertiginous passage at the end of part seventeen, where he replays both the conclusion of the film *Fire Walk with Me* a few moments before Laura Palmer's death; and the first images of the first episode of the first season of *Twin Peaks* with the return of FBI agent Dale Cooper to Laura (finally found and then lost again, plunging into the dark forest where her destiny is played out).

Lynch and Frost had invented the innovative and magnificent first season of *Twin Peaks* after the success of *Blue Velvet* (1986), a film starring the same lead actor, Kyle McLachlan, who returns under various identities in *The Return*. Lynch had chosen to be fully involved in the TV medium, exploiting all the cinematographic and serial genres of the twentieth century (detective, melodrama, high-school intrigue, soap opera, small-town chronicle, romantic comedy, horror film) in the style, or more precisely the mood, of the comic and disquieting strangeness that is his signature. The unexpected success of the first season, which kept a large audience transfixed by the show (Who killed Laura Palmer? was only one mystery, solved between the fourteenth and sixteenth episode, which raised so many others), led to a second season that was just as brilliant (albeit less popular), and finally to the abandonment of the series by ABC. By 1990, *Twin Peaks* had demonstrated that personal style and systematic strangeness were compatible with the success of a series, and with the seduction of a diverse audience—an audience the show respected by the very fact of demanding something of it, as a way of addressing everyone. From this point of view, *Twin Peaks* has been echoed in highly diverse, sometimes more standard productions, such as *Lost*, *The Killing*, *The Leftovers*,

---

* This article first appeared in *AOC*, at https://aoc.media/critique/2018/02/05/twin-peaks-retour-serie-methode/, 5 February 2018.

Ally McBeal, or *Top of the Lake*, a series directed by another great filmmaker, Jane Campion, and which also features a policewoman.

In 1990, the duality between cinema and series was already over. The film *Fire Walk with Me*—a prequel to the series released in 1992 and totally scorned, particularly in France—is naturally inhabited by series, as is all the rest of Lynch's work, whether we think of *Mulholland Drive* (2001) or *Inland Empire* (2006). Beyond the articulation of cinema and television, what *Twin Peaks* was implementing in 1990 was the universe of infinite possibilities of the series—something that its return pushes to the extreme—in terms of aesthetic, visual, and sound radicality, managing to film the detail, for example three minutes of sweeping the floor of the Roadhouse in a fixed shot (part seven) or two minutes of a silent cigarette break between Gordon Cole (Lynch himself), Diane (Laura Dern), and Tamara (Chrysta Bell) (part nine), and time being stretched to the extreme—as in the last moments of the episodes that feature languid artists and music over which the anticipated and abrupt end credits are displayed; or in the Dantesque part eight, where the creation of evil is played out to the sound of the Moonlight Sonata, distended to the point of being unrecognizably terrifying. The aesthetics of *Twin Peaks*, here more than ever, is what Stanley Cavell calls the uncanniness of the ordinary—the disturbing feeling that arises not or not only from horror or the catastrophic, but from the everyday. *Twin Peaks* was certainly the first series to implement and provoke the viewer's attention to the details of life—a powerful mark and crucial method of the series format. Something of this was already present in *Columbo*, as well as in great series of the 2000s, such as *Six Feet Under*, *The Wire*, or in the following decade, *The Affair* and *The Leftovers*. Lynch is a fan of detail, admitting: 'On television you can afford to play with detail, lots of detail. Films have a limited time frame. Focusing on a crumb of cherry pie or the smoke from a black coffee while the characters are talking is something you can only do in series.'[3]

The duration and recurrence (the regular return of episodes and seasons) of series allows time to be distended as paradoxically (and in a completely different style) in the series *24*, which, through the device of real time, made a day in the life of agent Jack Bauer fit a TV season. On the other hand, time may also be condensed in such a way as to reconfigure a season in a few minutes, such as in the delightful episode sixteen, where we are reunited with our old friend Dale Cooper. The first two seasons of *Twin Peaks* were savoured (by my generation) in the classic mode, with the weekly expectation of the revelations of the next episode, as were *ER*, *The White House*, *24*. For *The Return*, as well as for those who discover the first two seasons today, the possibility, if not of binge-watching (which Lynch would like to be able to forbid), at least of stringing two or three episodes together, creates a much different experience.

---

3 *Who Killed Laura Palmer?*, interview with F. Coignard, 1991, *Cahiers du Cinéma*.

Return to what?

It is against the background of our experience of the first two seasons of *Twin Peaks* that we see and experience *The Return*. This is not simply a background of knowledge, or even reminiscence, but something of our life—that is to say, something of ourselves that is returned to us alive as a part of ourselves that was asleep or comatose, rather like Cooper locked up for twenty-five years in the red room. Lynch's method is thus to make the experience of the series an exploration and reappropriation of the self (the first image of the first season, and the last of the second, was a reflection in a mirror), and rather than to recover or regain an identity or a certainty, to awaken something disturbing and subjective, which with *The Return* returns, like a dream: 'For me, it is very precious that everyone has their own feeling, their own dream about what happened. I don't want to spoil that.'[4]

It is a capacity of the series to locate its realism in our concern (which may be called care) for the characters over time, whose transformations and ageing are the visible mark of our attachment. From this point of view, some feel the same jubilation when they hear Cooper asking for his coffee to the sound of Badalamenti's original theme, as they do when they see R2D2 in The *Force Awakens* wake up and blink at the approach of Rey, the new Jedi (or the old Han Solo, who, in *The Force Awakens*, is reunited with his ship, the *Millennium Falcon*, in the company of his faithful Chewbacca: 'We're home'). The serialization of popular cinema that allows for the attachment of heroes through the evolution of actors is also an element of the hybridization between series and films.

The moment of Dale Cooper's actual return to the series is incredibly delayed (until part sixteen!) when he finally wakes up, thanks to a self-administered electric shock. Here Lynch's method is to make us look forward to the return of the 1990s hero, and at the heart of that very anticipation to give us another extraordinary and unexpected experience—the meeting of the series', and, for many it seems, 2017 as a whole's, most endearing character: Dougie Jones, who appears in the third episode of the third season, a 'tulpa' (corporeal husk) via which the good Cooper re-enters the human world once he has successfully left the 'Red Room'. Lynch and Frost have the luxury of putting this character, who has two doubles—the evil Cooper (inhabited by Bob, Laura's killer) and Dougie, the 'good Cooper' who has become catatonic—on-screen for thirteen episodes. Once again, this is a form of education: the vegetative Cooper is upsetting because he lacks all the elements of the human life form, a form that the series reveals its metaphysical ambition to display in its nakedness (symmetrically, in the famous episode eight).

Lynch and Frost radicalize the alien characters of science fiction films: not only can Dougie not speak or socialize, he can't even walk or go to the

---

4 Ibid.

toilet. The character's effect on us owes nothing to the traditional mythology of a Cooper trapped in another body, or even to our attachment to his model; in this respect Dougie is an entire aesthetic innovation. Even catatonic, he is a deeply alive character: he ecstatically discovers coffee, cherry pie, sexuality, and family affection with his wife Janey-E (Naomi Watts), and their son Sonny Jim. The character's strength is also linked to a kind of ethical talent that makes this season cathartic—though it is rooted in Agent Cooper's famous bonhomie, with Dougie bringing out the buried goodness in a pair of mobsters (the Mitchums), thus enabling the redemption of a fellow crook, and ultimately doing good for everyone—including us as viewers, who, ever taken seriously, are led beyond ourselves by this contact.

In the Heart of Darkness

This is also why Dale Cooper's return to full form will not lead to a happy ending, despite the jubilation of the moment. One of the most touching moments of the whole series is when Dougie finally returns home at the beginning of the final part (Cooper or Lynch having decided to recreate him to give him back to his family) and says 'Home' in his standard style of expression. This return to ordinary, domestic life finally recovered is the last happy moment of *Twin Peaks*: everything that happens afterwards occurs as if Cooper had left his joviality and lightness, quite simply a crucial part of himself, with Dougie.

That the ordinary form of life is both familiar, like the police station in Twin Peaks, and strange and uncomfortable (*unheimlich*) is confirmed in the conclusion of this eighteenth part, which gradually separates us from everything we have just found and value. Cooper, as mentioned above, attempts to save Laura by returning to the time and place of her disappearance, and it seems, as in time travel films, that he has succeeded: no plastic-wrapped corpse on the beach; the day goes on as 'normal'. But the next stages—a creepy journey in search of Laura into, one might say, into the heart of darkness—are ones of disorientation that see our gradual disassociation from the character we were happy to find (who even loses even his name, becoming 'Richard' and taking on an unsympathetic aspect). He does find Laura, far from Twin Peaks, but everything is odd in the squalid house in which he comes across her: her name is Carrie, and though she doesn't know who she is, she follows him. Back in Twin Peaks in the night, Richard and Carrie go to the Palmer house to find it inhabited by puzzled strangers who have never heard of Laura Palmer. Laura is thus merely a fragment who remains in Carrie—and in her final howl of terror, which chills us for ever. Our experience goes beyond Lynch's usual eerie strangeness, for in this episode we lose touch with the series' most important characters, those who have structured its vision from the beginning. The meaning of the 'return' of the title is thus tragically turned upside down, as the world that Cooper's return gave us is again torn away, made uninhabitable for us as for them.

According to Cavell, the characteristic of twentieth-century cinema (see *Pursuits of Happiness*) was to make us doubt the world or to erase our presence from it—as in Capra's iconic *It's a Wonderful Life* (1946)—so as to better return it to us through the film's proximity to experience, the taste of happiness, and the acceptance of the ordinary. If Frost and Lynch inscribe the series in this sceptical heritage, it is in order to better strip us of it: the reappropriation of the world, and of its vital intensity, has the effect of making us strangers to it. This is certainly *Twin Peaks'* method of paradoxically merging series and cinema.

The Americans: With and Without You

The end of a great series is always a difficult parting, especially when we must leave behind characters as strong as those of *The Americans*, one of the best, and now classic, series of the century. *The Americans* illustrated what may be called a third wave of ambitious series after the HBO classics of the beginning of the century, such as *The Sopranos*, *Six Feet Under*, and *The Wire*, along with the remarkable *Buffy* (and after the second wave, carried by other networks such as FX and AMC (*Lost*, *Breaking Bad*, *Mad Men*). This third wave is now at the end of its course, with the conclusion of *Hannibal*, *Girls*, and *The Leftovers* as well as *Game of Thrones*, *Homeland*, and *The Walking Dead*. Appearing in the middle of a peak period for other more addictive series, *The Americans* never broke out in terms of ratings or analysis, but it did create a deep attachment.

This was largely because of the quality and extreme charm of its actors, Keri Russell—much appreciated in *Felicity*—and Matthew Rhys, already a fine character in *Brothers & Sisters*, who together play a KGB spy couple under the names Elizabeth and Philip Jennings in the United States of the 1980s. There is also the excellent Noah Emmerich (their neighbour and FBI agent, Stan Beeman) who gives the full measure of his talent in this season, as well as the exceptional roles of the children, Paige and Henry, both characters in their own right. In addition to the actors, there was also the meticulous reconstruction of the 1980s universe, which takes over from *Mad Men* in terms of precise history and aesthetics; the Cold War and Reaganist atmosphere, which we are encountering again today under other aspects that are different but more worrying; the beauty and language of the Russian characters, Nina and Oleg; the hilarious disguises and low-tech tools of the heroes; the realistic way of describing the murders carried out by the spies on their missions—always laborious, long-winded, and horrible—and finally for its ability to transform us by taking us totally by surprise: Americans are able to love these Americans, spies, and KGB assassins, trembling for them when they are finally burned.

This love is directly related to the temporal realism induced by the form of consumption of the series. *The Americans*, like many third-wave series, will have had as its audience those who have become so attached to it that they impatiently await the return of the seasons and, for two or three months, wait each week for the next episode; an old-fashioned way of watching, far removed from the binge-watching induced by Netflix. The series has been consumed in the actual temporality of its six years (with the acceleration of the last one), becoming part of the viewer's routine and daily life that mirrors those of our heroes. This realism means seeing the children grow up, and Elizabeth and Philip transform and harden physically (both of them) and morally (her). *The Americans* also broke new ground by introducing an

---

* This article first appeared in *Libération*, 21 June 2018.

unlovable, radical, and violent female character, who existed far from any stereotype—as Keri Russell said, it's exciting and rare to be 'the tough one', whereas Philip was the more vulnerable and accessible. Another taboo broken by the series was, let's not forget, that of the adultery—normally, a more unforgivable TV crime than paedophilia or murder—required for the storyline, since Elizabeth and Philip necessarily had to have sex or become romantically involved with other people (poor Martha), as part of their missions.

The viewer understands and accepts the Hollywood structure of remarriage that is acted out at least three times in the couple's story: right at the beginning, when after years of pretend living together, including raising children, they genuinely fall in love with each other; at the time of their 'real' clandestine, orthodox marriage, which leads them to be discovered by the FBI; and at the very end, when they have to imagine a new life together back 'at home' (a home that no longer exists). This final reunion, a tragic version of the comedy of remarriage (a concept invented by Cavell in his masterpiece *Pursuits of Happiness*) is the result of a final subversion: the abandonment of the children in both senses of the term. Elizabeth and Philip abandon their son to a life they know will be better and are themselves abandoned by their daughter on a station platform, in one of the most moving scenes of the series. We understand here that the true 'Americans' will be Paige and Henry, and it is at this moment, as well as in the key scene before it (the terrible eleven-minute exchange in a car park between Stan and Philip), that the series establishes our ability as viewers to separate ourselves from the characters, and from the show. For the first time, we identify with Stan, who lets go of Elizabeth and Philip, as if to teach us to let go and carry on without them too… all to the tune of U2's 1987 song, 'With or Without You'.

Game of Thrones Education

Game of Thrones (*GoT*) is a series built on waiting (and what a wait we've had for the episodes over the past eighteen months), as if to better make us feel the passage of time in an era where miniseries of six episodes watched in two days are multiplying (although excellent sometimes, this hardly gives any opportunity for seeing protagonists mature or to settle into their universe). A major reason for its success that has nothing to do with its usual excess, records, or even with its singularity, *GoT*, in this sense, is a classic series that is one of the last of its kind, with its history and stories; seasons; families (the great subject of series); its beloved characters (even if we lose many of them along the way); and its episodic format, which means that we see its actors change and age, a far less common phenomenon than the packages of episodes bundled together on Netflix. All these are features that give the series an exceptional place in our lives—and which the producers have evidently thought about when considering how the public will manage to part with it without too much damage.

This beginning of the last season in Winterfell, the stronghold of the Stark family, also reminds us that *GoT*, which has a reputation as an action series—and, in fact, has promoted the series genre from 'family', or intimate, to grand spectacle—is essentially made up of conversations (sometimes monologues), which is a characteristic feature of most of the great classic series (from *Buffy* to *The Wire*). It is this individual and interactional expressiveness that builds the characters of *GoT*, with their particular ways of being, as well as the bonds that gradually constitute, as Wittgenstein would write, 'the background against which we perceive the action'—often collective and joint.

The quality of the writing and dialogues and the genius of the actors and actresses to 'deliver' them in the right tone, is the first and foremost richness of *GoT*. A particularly pertinent example of this is episode two of the last season, which is entirely made up of these exchanges, contextualized by the temporal thickness of the eight years spent with them. Speech is action.

The beginning of the season is, as is often the case with *GoT*, slow and meditative, focused on the anticipation of the great battle of the Living versus the Dead. The first episode certainly had its share of revelations and reunions, as well as a return to hard violence and soft porn, as if to remind us that this is HBO. The following episodes are decidedly different, with the second entirely focused on exchanges between people, and the evocation and confirmation of the strong and weak links that unite them—including antagonistic ones (when it comes to Clegane and Arya, who each tried to massacre the other, or the heavyweight Tormund with his advances to Brienne, or Bran and Jaime Lannister, whose chance meeting in season one, episode one sealed the fate of so many characters).

---

* This article first appeared as a short version in *Libération*, 24 May 2019.

That first episode of *GoT*, which many of us are rewatching with nostalgia these days, so impressive is the amount of material that proves crucial afterwards, already provided a method of reading: this series, however, will invent a different ethic, extreme and real characters, and a sense that anything can happen.

In episode two of season eight, set entirely in Winterfell, it's Bran and Jaime's first reunion since the day the cruel couple threw little Bran out of a tower window, after he had caught Cersei and Jaime in intense sexual activity. The cute little Stark kids from season one are now grown up, and Bran and Arya may hold Jaime, freshly arrived at Winterfell to join the fight of the living against the dead, to account. But in a beautiful polyphonic scene reminiscent of other, less fair trials (that of the dwarf Tyrion summarily condemned by his own family, s4e6), the great Brienne of Tarth (Gwendoline Christie), certainly one of the most wonderful characters on *GoT*, convinces all present (we are now in a quasi-matriarchy) of the loyalty of her friend, who protected the Stark girls out of a commitment to Catelyn Stark, and saved her from death.

Bran hilariously echoes the words Jaime spoke after ratting him out: 'The things I'd do for love' ('The things I wouldn't do for love'). This applies to us. How can we forgive Jaime and love him? In this sense, Jaime is a true TV hero because we get attached to him despite his flaws (and his successive hairstyle changes). This is because he has changed over time, both physically (the loss of his hand) and morally—and because, as the incredible actress Gwendoline Christie (who appeared in the feminist *Top of the Lake*, season two) said in a recent interview, Brienne 'has deconstructed this stereotypical, patriarchal male'. Brienne and Jaime's relationship is the most remarkable and subversive in *GoT*, initially based on the intense pleasure of being together, before becoming sexual (and not entirely convincing as such) in episodes four and five.

The women of Westeros are often beauties, embodied by stars (in the full sense: we contemplate them, we are enlightened by them). They are also often strong, powerful women—whether it is Catelyn, who is not a traditional mother, or Daenerys, who becomes a formidable warrior. *GoT* is truly a women's show; indeed, they are the only ones left in the credits for season eight. However, Arya and Brienne are unique in that they reject heterosexual seduction in principle (although both make one-off exceptions in the final season), and, above all, the role of reproducers. Having both lost their mothers, like the heroines in remarriage comedies, they must somehow re-create themselves, and be reborn purely of themselves.

The strength and uniqueness of Brienne lies in her combination of loyalty, great sensitivity, and humanity, a paradox that the actress Gwendoline Christie embodies magnificently. This role is subversive because it allows for the combination of feminine and masculine qualities in a character (admittedly a little atypical), and thus creates a character with strong individuality in terms of how her chivalry is embodied: Brienne combines physical courage and care. There is, as she says to Catelyn in a memorable conversation, a 'woman's courage', a feminine style of bravery (s2e5) that Brienne is able to assume while also preserving a manly dimension. She doesn't give up.

In the first season, during a fencing session, Arya Stark explains to her father, who saw her as the head of a line of little princes and princesses: 'That's not me' (s1e4). While Brienne is ironic (and terrifying) because she is so raw and 'manly', Arya has decided from the start that she is not interested in seduction, and her fate is individualistic. Singular, gifted, and mysterious, Arya is a true heroine in the classical sense from the very beginning, and her romantic departure to the West at the end makes her a character to follow—largely because we do not understand her, and thus follow her in the final seasons with increasing curiosity. As in Shakespeare's tragedies, she must go through a death and rebirth in order to find herself—death here being represented by the loss of face and sight, a radical form of marginalization and anonymity. It is in overcoming this loss that she regains her identity—or rather creates a new one. When she leaves the Faceless, saying to Jaqen H'ghar 'A girl is Arya Stark of Winterfell. And I am going home' (s6e8), she finds the 'I', and claims her identity in its gratuity, one of the most beautiful moments of the series.

Arya, during the Long Night, seeks out Gendry so as not to risk dying without sexual experience; Sansa flirts with Theon or Tyrion depending on the moment... all the twisted couples who are products of this night of waiting for almost certain death, and who have more charm than the flamboyant star duo of Daenerys and Jon, in full decay (the one limping, the other megalomaniac). But by reactivating the various ties that bind them to each other (and us to them), *GoT* season eight episode two also allows us to prepare ourselves for what is already certain—the inevitable separation from the characters at the end of the show. The recognizable atmosphere of the Lannister brothers' wake—a sentimental and fatalistic end to the evening in its acceptance of human mortality—allows everyone to say goodbye to characters who are each trying to be their best.

That Jaime, at the very end, returns to Cersei is not (or not only) to give in fatally to his dark side. It is also, in a complex way, part of his moral trajectory, which leads him to protect others. As Brienne writes in the last episode, in a particularly moving moment that is a sort of encyclopaedia of valiant knights, 'Died protecting his queen'. Far from being a reversal, Jaime's journey to King's Landing and Cersei remains a perfectionist one, as is indicated in the help he receives from his brother Tyrion, and Tyrion's grief when he discovers the corpses of the Lannister twins.

Who would have thought a few years ago that one day we *GoT* viewers would be heartbroken by the deaths of Cersei and Jaime Lannister, crushed in the collapse of King's Landing? Maybe more likely for Jaime, whose rehabilitation we've seen over the seasons; but the dreaded Cersei, the enemy to be slain forever, who our favourite Arya had at the top of her list? So it is with *GoT*, with its ability to turn its fans. This genius is not so much in the famous surprises they imagine themselves to have, but rather in the long-prepared transformations: Jaime who is morally educated and ennobled by meeting Catelyn and then Brienne; young Arya as a stealthy and fearsome slayer; little Daenerys as a megalomaniac monster. All has been present from the beginning in the details that the series has taught us to see: the pleasure of *GoT* is based on the audience's attention span, which it has mobilized and developed over the years. In the sadness of the show's closure, one consolation is that the collective spoiler phobia is over. We can also hope that the pleasure of seeing *GoT* again will be a further lesson in the future.

A characteristic of *GoT* from the beginning has been that, while you can expect a certain amount from the narrative, and from yourself and your own reactions, you can still surprise yourself in the variety of people and situations that are offered, which is what makes watching the series an enhanced personal experience. *GoT* has done away with the devaluing conception of the show as a 'mirror' of a society, while remaining realistic in its humanity and its characters.

It's never easy to part with a series, as we saw—and more unexpectedly—with *The Americans*; for *GoT*, it is particularly difficult, given the structural expectation of the series and the deep attachment of the viewers to the characters of the saga. Paradoxically, it was this attachment that gave rise (along with the fake buzz clues, of course) to the idea that almost everyone would die in a bloodbath worthy of season three—as if we'd rather lose our favourite heroes in a massacre than imagine them going on without us. 'Winter is coming' has taken on a new, concrete meaning (far from the worn-out climatic interpretations), and it is the anxiety of loss that has been expressed in recent weeks, including in the touching petition calling for the rewrite of season eight. Attachment to the show is an appropriation of the characters and their trajectories, which form such a strong part of fans' lives that they consider themselves to know them better than the creators who built that very attachment. In this sense, the multiple criticisms that have plagued this last season represent one of the show's successes.

These final episodes, seemingly sloppy in the highly cinematic acceleration towards the conclusion, did take their time: they constantly offered occasion for meditation and dialogue, and certainly never lacked reflexivity—particularly with the series returning to itself in a very clear way in the final episode (the dwarf Tyrion, in a most Shakespearean moment, praises the great stories that bring humans together and keep them alive to his transfixed audience of Westeros chieftains). The farewells are repeated throughout the season, including, in the final episode, our own: the grimoire that supposedly tells the whole story, presented in a hilarious royal council scene; the knight's ledger, where Brienne, recently promoted, completes Jaime's Wikipedia page; Tyrion, noting that he has been heard from a lot on the show, also reminds us that *GoT* is a series woven of conversations, which remain its true life form.

The surprise (again well prepared) is that it is the Starks who win in the end, resilient after being decimated. The magnificent conclusion seems 'all wrapped up', tracing the fates of each—Sansa's coronation, Arya's departure for something like America, Jon's return to the Wall, and beyond. But these fates are a separation. Reunited in a final image, they are then filmed in strict parallel movement, lines that will never meet again. This is the image of separation, not as a one-off event, but rather an essential state. The beauty and the final shock of the ending, with Jon Snow's return to his starting point, is that it brings each of us back to ourselves, and to the mysterious individuality of these heroes. This is in no way the smallest paradox of the most extraordinary series of our century, which, having created such a collective of characters with so many links to its viewers and between its different audiences, now finally teaches us to return to ourselves.

God save *The Crown*

The Crown is not really a historical series, but a fine articulation of aesthetics and politics. I have no taste for 'British series', and did not warm up to *Downton Abbey*. I know nothing about the British royal family, and only recently understood the lineage of Princess Anne, who competed on horseback in the 1970s; I have no expertise in historical series, preferring to focus instead on post-apocalyptic, crime, feminist, security, and romance genres. And yet I am among those who have been looking forward to the third season of *The Crown*—already the most expensive series in Netflix's history—which tells the story of the life of Elizabeth II of England. Rather than being 'historical', despite the settings, costumes, and Winston Churchill (the great John Lithgow), it is a realistic fiction whose success stems from the unexpected attachment we feel for unknown and peculiar characters. True, it educates us fairly regularly (on the family tree of the teratological Windsor family, on the Labour and Conservative parties, and the great traumas of the country in the second half of the twentieth century), but the series is anchored less in contemporary history than in other famous works such as *The Queen* (Stephen Frears, 2006, with Helen Mirren), which presented Elizabeth grappling with the national crisis of Diana's accidental death; and *The King's Speech* (Tom Hopper, 2010, with Colin Firth and Helena Bonham Carter, whom we see again in season three of *The Crown* as Princess Margaret, a bizarre genealogy in which the same actress plays both the Queen Mother and her youngest daughter), which featured Elizabeth's father, George VI, and the resolution of his speech impediments during his 1939 speech. We particularly appreciate finding this king in the first season of *The Crown*, this time in the guise of Jared Harris (always an extraordinary actor, as we have since seen in the blockbuster miniseries *Chernobyl*), where his moral sense, his earthy complexion, and ravaged skin make him stand out.

The Crown first confirmed the extent to which attention (care) paid to a series—its actors, documentation, and writing (with the immense resources of Netflix)—is a sure way of making it a cinematic work. The artistic paradigm of this series is not only British; it is *Mad Men*, which succeeded in revisiting the history of the 1960s–1980s through the same fine articulation of the aesthetic and the social (social modernity through the objects of advertising and the design of the 1960s; social mobility through the professionalization of women and the fragility of men). This political aesthetic is also that of *The Crown*, which particularly emphasizes the contrast and the back and forth between the spectacle of the monarchy and everyday life in the palaces: Elizabeth's coronation in season one, for instance, is a mythical media moment, viewed banally on television from the Parisian home of a bitter Duke of Windsor; the reportage in season three on the ordinary life

---

* This is a compilation of articles first appeared in *Libération*, 5 December 2019, 3 December 2020, 9 September 2022.

of the royal family that is intended to improve its image turns out to be ultra-depressing and ridiculous—only saved afterwards by the emergence of Prince Philip's mother as a crazy old nun.

The reflexivity of *The Crown* is, as with so many other series, its primary strength: out of explicitly cheesy and boring characters, as well as an outdated and too well-known public image, a real series and magnificent fiction is made—a miracle that takes place in each episode. A further strength in it is also the series format, which leads us to wait patiently for the seasons, and to obediently conform to the specific temporality of one decade per season. There are no spoilers, as we know what will happen to Churchill and Kennedy, Charles and Camilla, and to Elizabeth at the end; and yet the tension is extreme at every moment. Here the mystery is the ordinary mystery of the characters, with their emotion and action visible as they are reduced to their simplest expression—for instance, Elizabeth's ability to express suffering, conformity, or anger within a character who is totally conventional and ultimately unknowable. One thinks of the episode about Elizabeth's rivalry with the brilliant and anorexic Jackie Kennedy, who, after allegedly chumming up with her, spouts off at society dinners about an uncultured, frumpy, and outdated queen and royalty. The scene in which Elizabeth summons her to tea and subsequently humiliates her symbolizes the reversal that is constantly taking place in the series. Equally, the narcissistic Margaret, sometimes seen by the public as more interesting and pretty than her sister, is regularly put in her place—by the show itself.

This structural upheaval for the viewer is the result of the exceptional talent of the actors, and particularly of Claire Foy's ability, in the first two seasons, to embody (literally) both the very absence of charisma and the almost sacred force of female power. This physical, sensitive, and moral texture is so unforgettable and particular that it was difficult—despite the principle stated from the start, and of the necessity for a change of cast every two years—to accept a new Elizabeth. The violence of the change can be seen at the opening of season three, when the queen reviews her image on a new stamp placed next to the previous one featuring Claire Foy's profile. 'Quite a change, but here we are,' she says. 'Age is rarely kind to anyone.' But the ageing is less unforgiving for the viewer, for Olivia Colman is an immensely popular English actress, and is, in fact, more suited to the role (she picked up an Oscar for her portrayal of another queen (Anne) in *The Favourite*), yet she nevertheless fails to possess the same mystery or insecurity, as well as the disquieting strangeness, that is the charm of the series' character, and which has now become inseparable from the actress. The opening of the third season of *The Crown* has been both eagerly awaited and feared by viewers, who have become attached to the moving and mysterious character of the young queen played by Claire Foy in the first two seasons. In the cast change to Olivia Coleman, *The Crown* thus 'officially' assumes what series fans have been observing since the beginning of the century: the time has come for women in their fifties. These are everywhere in the classic series, from *Six Feet Under* (with the wonderful character of Ruth Fisher), *Damages* (with the formidable Patty Hewes played by Glenn Close), to *Top of the Lake* (with Holly Hunter), *House of Cards* (which features Robin Wright as the US president, Claire Underwood, replacing her fired husband), and Catelyn Stark in *Game of Thrones*. Indeed, the new fourth season of *The Crown*—set in the 1980s—goes one step further with a fine portrait of Margaret Thatcher (Gillian Anderson). The constant thread that runs through the season is the quiet rivalry between the queen and the prime minister—'two menopausal women' as Thatcher's husband bluntly describes them. The two women nevertheless shine on-screen—through their styles of exercising power and mutual respect—without conventional seduction tools. We can see what is at stake in bringing to the forefront these fifty-year-old characters, who no longer care (or care less) about motherhood, and can devote themselves, like their male counterparts, to following their own path.

In the magnificent portrait of Margaret Thatcher, the fourth season, like *Mrs. America*, deals with the difficulty of honouring an ultra-conservative woman. Realistic in its description of a destructive antisocial policy, the series humanizes Thatcher through her complex relationship with the queen, an empathy that culminates in the scene in which Elizabeth presents a humiliated Margaret with the Order of Merit. This mutual respect and the implicit recognition of the sexism of the 'coup' that led to Thatcher's ouster does not negate her sexism (just appointed, she tells the queen that there will be no women in her cabinet, 'obviously'), a classic example of a woman who succeeds in pulling up the ladder behind her, and, in compensation for her gender, devalues other women.

Just as the political reality of the twenty-first century is affected by the aesthetic background of the images of 9/11, so *The Crown* now determines our experience and knowledge of Queen Elizabeth. The deepest mystery of *The Crown* remains the relationship between the queen as a historical (and now deceased) figure and her embodiment by an actress (in our case, serial holders of the role: Claire Foy, Olivia Colman, and Imelda Staunton).

Even if there are many splendid actors throughout the seasons, the power of *The Crown* is initially thanks to one actress, who created it in the first place: Claire Foy. By replacing the person who plays the queen after twenty hours, *The Crown* actually makes a radical and reflective choice. Despite all the time spent with Foy as the queen, our attachment to her, our concern for her marriage, we are cruelly reminded—at the first episode of season three—that she is a (superb) actress. Given the advances in prosthetics and special effects—we may think of the end of *The Affair* (2014–2019) or the time-warping of the beautiful contemporary series *This Is Us* (2016–2022) or of the actors of *For All Mankind*, preserved for decades—it is perfectly conceivable that Morgan could have kept Foy for all six seasons and 'aged her out'. To use three actresses, to have them appear serially, in equal parts, educates the audience on how the very nature of the actresses informs the creation of a fictional person on-screen. Through seriality, we learn that each of them is Elizabeth—and none of them is. The sacred (expressed every time in the credits) remains the same from one end to the other. Certainly, this is one of the most powerful and hard lessons of *The Crown*.

Very Spacey Heroes

Who knows whether the death of Prince Philip, Duke of Edinburgh, who died on 9 April 2021 just before his 100th birthday, would have had the same public impact without *The Crown?* Across the first four seasons, the series managed to give exceptional consistency to this central figure of the British royal family. For the British, he was already (to quote the phrase we heard most often in tearful speeches) 'part of the family'; but it was via *The Crown* that Philip became part of the family of all the show's viewers, once again underlining a key theme of the great long-running series (from The *Sopranos* and *Six Feet Under*, to *Ozark* and *This Is Us*). It is as a fictional character that Philip has most mattered to us—including those of us who have no interest in the royals at all—specifically through his portrayal by the excellent Matt Smith (s1 and s2) and Tobias Menzies (s3 and s4), proving once again that the power of TV series often comes through the regular return of characters inseparable from the expressiveness of actors. From the opening episode, Philip has humanized a series based on the mystery and power of the Crown through his imperfections, his vivacity, his art of speech, and his perfect retorts—which also made him a comic character—as well as by his often-unnecessary resistance to the royal matriarchy, which made him a paradoxical model of emancipation. Though he has spent his life 'in the background', three steps behind Elizabeth, he is a scene stealer over the four seasons of the series (he's what we see and enjoy most when he is on-screen, even in a corner of the shot). Philip is a seductive operator for *The Crown*, introducing a romantic and even sexy dimension through his trajectory (the abandoned and fallen prince, 'chosen' by Elizabeth), the mysteries and infidelities heavily suggested by the narration, and the allusions and sexual scenes that are iconoclastic in their representation of the royal couple's relationship. Everything contributes to making this historical series fit into the classic remarriage genre, characterized by the conversation and reconciliation of the protagonists against the backdrop of ordinary life—but also in the constant battle for equality of speech, fought this time from the male point of view. For some viewers, it may be more painful to lose the actors Matt Smith and Tobias Menzies, who will be succeeded in seasons five and six by Jonathan Pryce, seen in the excellent Netflix miniseries *Two Popes*, than it is to lose the historical Philip, whose adventure continues in the series.

We have to wait until 2022 for the return of *The Crown*, and the best kept secret in the world at the moment is that right now there are no more series—or at least no more of those series that make us wait for the ritual return of the seasons and get us attached to characters that we see grow old or grow up. The pandemic has struck here too, after two glorious decades started with HBO and continued on Netflix. Although we're waiting for the last season of *Succession*, the laborious sequel to *The Handmaid's Tale*, and the interminable end of *The Walking Dead* (the last mythical opus of the genre),

---

* This article first appeared in *Libération*, 8 May 2021.

there is nothing new on the horizon—hence the pitiful question at the end of this lockdown: 'Can you recommend something to watch?' This leads either to scouring the platforms like dating sites, or to contenting oneself with numerous and very good miniseries, but which are series in name only, and only register on the surface of our experience as viewers.

While waiting for season five of *The Crown*, we can pay homage to the fictional Philip by rewatching 'Moondust', one of the richest episodes of season three, in which the prince is seized by a sort of midlife crisis, and questions the meaning of his life on the occasion of the Apollo 11 moon landing in 1969. Fixated on his TV and obsessed by the heroism of the American astronauts, he suddenly sees his life as a renunciation of any real action. While being a total narrative invention (apart from the American astronauts' visit to the queen during their world tour), this episode reflects our contemporary preoccupation with space by pointing to its metaphysical dimension. Philip will find his way back by realizing that his American heroes are fairly average, cold, and boring humans, and by joining an all-male therapy group—a return to ordinary life. This plotline echoes the many recent cinematic fictions that describe life in space as a way of finding oneself at the end of the journey: *First Man* (Damien Chazelle, 2019), in which Neil Armstrong goes to the moon to overcome the mourning of his child; *Interstellar* (Christopher Nolan, 2014), in which humanity tries to rediscover its taste for technological adventure in the search for a planet B; *Ad Astra* (James Gray, 2019), in which the hero goes to meet his father and finally lets him go into space; and the feminine heroism of *Proxima* (Alice Winocour, 2019), and *Gravity* (Alfonso Cuarón, 2013). The latter film provides the key to the space genre with the image of the astronaut landing and feeling the weight of gravity after his harrowing journey. The experience, extraordinarily visible in the final moments of the film, represents a feature of the ordinary form of life—of being 'on earth'. Wittgenstein remarked that in order to walk we do not need ideal conditions, but 'friction', and the roughness and heaviness of the ordinary is inherent in the dream of space as human achievement.

The newest and greatest illustration of this calling into space is the beautiful, clever, and underestimated show *For All Mankind*, based on an intriguing premise: what would have happened to space exploration if the USSR had not conceded defeat so soon? The first season begins with cosmonaut Alexei Leonov beating Neil Armstrong to the moon by a few days. In the years following this event, the United States tries to regain lost ground, establishing a permanent base on the Moon in the early 1970s. To this alternative history, the creator of the series, Ronald D. Moore, a veteran of space series (*Star Trek*, *Battlestar Galactica*), adds the everyday lives of characters—borrowed from history (Wernher von Braun, Deke Slayton) or produced by the imagination of a talented writing room. Together, all these fictional characters give life to this alternative history of humanity: Joel Kinnaman as Ed Baldwin, Michael Dorman as Gordo Stevens, Krys Marshall as Danielle Poole, Sonya Walger as Molly Cobb.

For All Mankind references all the codes of pop culture of the last forty years, from *The Right Stuff* (Philip Kaufman, 1983) to *Mrs. America*; it quotes from *The West Wing, Mad Men, American Crime Story, The Americans*, and thereby claims to be a summation of classic TV, as well as a new vision of history. The series is explicitly feminist, with women included on the astronaut team almost from the outset, thanks to the Soviets who send a woman to the moon in the second episode. The small step for man becomes a leap for women, thereby changing the whole history of gender and the concept of mankind. This fictional early opening of the space programme to women not only supports a feminist claim (asking: why weren't they included?), but it also expands the cast's possibilities, equally involving women and men while inventing an alternative history. Hence the show's powerful characters: Margo Madison (Wrenn Schmidt, eerily extracted from the CIA offices of *The Looming Tower*), who rises to head of command at NASA and finds herself at the heart of a new Cold War; Ellen Wilson (Jodi Balfour), a star astronaut, who becomes head of NASA and is a closeted lesbian, in a fiction where social advances have not extended to gay people or to ethnic and racial minorities. The characters who start as (desperate) housewives—Karen Baldwin (Shantel VanSanten) and Tracy Stevens (Sarah Jones)—become independent, always through divorce, and find their way into space, one as an astronaut, competing with her husband (Stevens), the other as a businesswoman, joining the new project led by a more charming version of Elon Musk (Edi Cathegi).

Though it has remained low-key so far, *For All Mankind* is further proof, akin to Volodymyr Zelensky's rise to political power after he played the president in his *Servant of the People* series, of the forward-thinking or predictive power of television series. *For All Mankind* is neither space science fiction nor one of those dystopias that have shaped our TV and political culture in recent years, such as *The Handmaid's Tale, Westworld*, or *House of Cards*. This fictional reality, in contrast to, for example, *The Man in the High Castle* (inspired by Philip K. Dick) does not wear itself out over the seasons: leaping ten years forward in time with each season, *For All Mankind* shows America, and beyond that humanity, taking a different path, transformed by the pursuit of space conquest and structured by an East–West rivalry that induces radical political changes. The series describes the astronauts' constant transition from space life to ordinary life; a capacity extended to all, in a process of democratization of space that opens up new forms of life.

For All Mankind is based on ordinary human qualities, 'the right stuff'; but it is not a virile ode to America. Ed Baldwin learns the hard way that his values do not necessarily bring happiness. Men are vulnerable… and women are taking over. An element of fictional storytelling (women on the moon) leads to widening the initially male cast of *For All Mankind* by introducing an entire group of female characters: women are wives, astronauts, engineers, heroines, and soon president! This expansion cleverly leads to question the concept of humanity, which we find in the title of the series.

What is 'Mankind' in Armstrong's famous statement? Instead, we could speak of womankind, through strong characters, such as geek-spy Margo Madison; Molly Cobb, a true hero; Ellen Wilson, an astronaut turned president. One of the most subtle lessons of the series is its differentiation between the fate of women, who are promoted quite readily (in this sense we are indeed in science fiction!) and that of gay people, as if these were two radically different issues. In the alternate reality of *For All Mankind* women are everywhere, in power, on an equal footing with men, but there are just a handful of black astronauts. By staging ordinary lives within alternate presents, reinvented pasts, or bifurcated futures, TV series offer a field for experimentation and political criticism, for the gradual visibilization of minorities, and also a place for complex interrogations on inequalities in emancipation.

5

Serial Care

Security Series as a Popular Genre

Lockdown gave us an occasion to discover new television series and to revisit others. TV series accompany us in our ordinary lives, but they can also be a resource or refuge in extraordinary situations. As the success of *Friends* proves, they provide us with universes of comfort, full of things that now seem like distant memories: enduring worlds in which people go to the coffee shop, travel, touch each other. They allow us to see both the value and charm of an everyday life we might take for granted—and that we might seek to escape by immersing ourselves in more or less exotic professional worlds: the worlds of cops, undertakers, millionaires, or spies. They have offered us continuity through the ruptures and upheavals of these past months, keeping us connected to characters whose return we await, such as those on *This Is Us*, and the somewhat less lovable ones on *Succession*—and those we got to see again for the last time during lockdown: those on *The Bureau*.

The question of the relevance and importance of series is not only aesthetic, or sociological, or communicational. It is, rather, the question of how the presence of these images and givens (a wide-ranging presence, because there are now series in all countries, and they circulate far beyond their countries of origin), change not only our visions of the world but also the world itself. Series produce the given of what we may call elementary forms of shared experience, and security series provide a particularly exciting demonstration of the power of TV series; of the grip reality has on them, and their grip—the grip of cultural data—on reality.

One of the innovations of the new series of the turn of the twenty-first century is the way they confront viewers with a work environment, a mysterious vocabulary, and a world whose elements cannot be immediately understood, so that the viewer is obliged to pay attention, to gain familiarity,

---

* This article, first published in *Open Philosophy*, n°5, 2021, Topical issue: Ethics and Politics of TV Series, ed. Sandra Laugier, pp. 155–167, under the title 'Series under Threat', has been translated by Daniela Ginsburg.

and little by little, through this attention, to become educated—just like the child Wittgenstein describes at the beginning of the *Philosophical Investigations* who gradually becomes integrated into a form of life. The viewer is educated and cared for, as well as cared about in their moral capacity. Moral competence is not a matter of reasoning alone: it involves learning fitting expressions and educating one's sensibility—as, for example, a reader's sensibility is educated by an author, who makes certain situations and characters perceptible by placing (or depicting) them in the appropriate context. This is why the model of perception, based on the idea of description or vision, no longer suffices for explaining moral vision, which consists in seeing not objects or situations but rather the possibilities and meanings that emerge from them; in anticipating and improvising at every moment of perception.

In France, the UK, Germany, the US, and Israel, a growing number of films and television series are set 'behind the scenes' of democratic regimes faced with terrorist threats (in addition to *Homeland* and *The Bureau* we may cite *Hatufim*, *The Looming Tower*, *False Flag*, *Kalifat*, and *Teheran*, for example). These works reveal a moral state of the world. They may be analysed as mirrors of society or as ideological tools. But they can also be understood as new resources for the education, creativity, and perfectibility of their audiences, as the emergence of a form of 'soft power' that can serve as a resource for public policies and democratic conversation.

Because of their format (weekly/seasonal regularity, home viewing) and the participatory qualities of the Internet (tweeting, sharing, liking, chat forums), series allow for a new form of education by expressing complex issues through narrative and characters. However, their aesthetic potential for making ethical issues visible and their capacity to enable the democratic empowerment of viewers has not yet been analysed, nor has their power for confronting cultural and social upheavals, and for developing a collective inquiry into democratic values and human security. By elucidating how these series are conceived by their creators and audiences, we can understand if and how they might play a crucial role in building the awareness necessary for the safety of individuals and societies, and in creating shared and shareable values.

The wave of attacks that began in January 2015, and the more recent attacks of 2020, have reminded Europe and the world of the permanence of the terrorist threat. The entertainment industry has acknowledged this state of affairs as mainstream movies and television series represent and express the threats and risks that make up the current security context. Movies and series sometimes even anticipate threats, as *Homeland* did, when, in its fifth season, written in 2014, it portrayed European jihadist terrorist cells. When the show was broadcast, the day after the November 2015 attacks in Paris, the creators changed the dialogue to include the attacks that had just struck the French capital. Thanks to their wide reach, such fictions provide strong common cultural references, which populate ordinary conversations and political debates. Moreover, their influence is not limited to only one country or area: current revolutions in the modes of production, distribution, and consumption of these fictions encourage circulation between cultural zones. Thus, even if US productions are dominant, the French series *The Bureau* is shown internationally, and several British (*The State, Spooks*), German (*Berlin Station, Deutschland 83*), and Israeli series (*Hatufim, Fauda, False Flag, Our Boys*) are distributed globally. The porousness of the boundaries between the factual and the fictional facilitates the integration of these fictions into understandings of the world, systems of knowledge, and ways of envisioning a shared future. TV series shape common understandings of the controversial topic of security.

The importance that intangible components of power—so-called soft power—have taken on over the past thirty years constitutes an obvious transformation in forms of war. Information warfare, influence, manipulation, and counter-propaganda are at the heart of strategies to respond to, for example, propaganda from the Islamic State. Though forms of soft power may seek to use fictional representations of terrorism to attempt to influence the enemy's decision-making processes or as forms of internal propaganda, movies and TV series can play a subtler, significant, and so far under-studied role in shaping scholarly analysis, education, and collective understandings of terrorist violence.

Thus far, these cultural objects have been considered in two main fashions: they have been either simply ignored as negligible and as mere entertainment, or analysed through the lens of propaganda, influence, and manipulation. What has been missing until now is a more nuanced and exhaustive account of their impact on both the public and on defence actors, and of the consequences and risks of this impact. Filling in this gap means taking into account and demonstrating their degree of reflexivity, and their integration of the audience's moral capabilities.

My aim is to shift philosophical, political, and moral perspectives on the productions of popular culture by showing how popular culture operates when it comes to the topics of security and terrorism. In my perspective, popular culture is neither a primal stage nor an inferior or alienating version of culture: it creates shared and shareable values through the circulation and discussion of material that is available to all, and as such it is a major factor in the creation and nurturing of new democratic spaces. In the United States and France, the relationships between the entertainment industries and institutions of national security are being reshaped in new ways that attest to the importance cinematographic productions have taken on within state institutions.

Popular fiction is taken seriously by national security institutions: a few days after the 9/11 attacks, the CIA initiated a series of meetings with film and TV creators (directors, screenwriters, producers) to help the agency imagine future attack scenarios and anticipate threats. Security institutions (defence, intelligence) are opening up to the entertainment industry in Europe. In 2016, the French minister of defence Le Drian announced the launch of a 'Mission Cinéma' to encourage fiction creators to focus on subjects connected to the defence world. These developments have sparked fears that such works will be used as propaganda. They have also demonstrated that the scientific and political stakes of such initiatives have not yet been addressed either in public debate or in scholarly research. In the United States, the partnership is well established. In 1948, the Pentagon created a liaison office with Hollywood—a move the CIA imitated in 1996, not without controversy, in order to increase the realism of film and TV productions as well as to improve the agency's public image and attract new recruits (a good example of the results of this liaison is the character Sydney Bristow, the hero of the show *Alias*, played by Jennifer Garner).

The movie *Zero Dark Thirty* (Kathryn Bigelow, 2012), which depicts the CIA's hunt for and eventual elimination of Osama Bin Laden on 1 May 2011, sparked debate over so-called enhanced interrogation techniques. More than a hundred emails were declassified in 2014 as the result of a Freedom of Information Act request, revealing the closeness between the film's crew and the CIA. This was particularly problematic because the film has been read as defending the effectiveness of torture. Such cooperation inevitably raises political, ethical, and aesthetic questions. On the other hand, the Israeli show *Fauda*, which depicts both sides of the Israeli–Palestinian conflict through the work of an undercover Israeli unit operating inside Palestinian territories, was (at least at first) appreciated both by Israeli and Palestinian audiences, opening a previously unimaginable space for shared understanding and pluralism in a violent context. However, it quickly became apparent that the show is rather biased.

Security series open viewers to sympathy/empathy with characters at first seen as 'enemies', and to difficult, no-win moral choices and situations. In representing terrorism and counter-terrorism in action, these fictions give audiences a specific experience of the contemporary security world. They can be seen as attempts at collective reflection, as a democratic inquiry (in Dewey's sense) into an increasingly complex reality. They give unprecedented visibility to a dimension of democratic life usually hidden from the public: secrecy, espionage, the 'reason of state' in action.

The Endings of Two Classic Security Shows

It has always been difficult for fans of a series to say goodbye, and for some, the recent end of two major shows has been one more disaster on top of the catastrophe of the pandemic. *The Bureau* is probably not in its final season, but we have reached the end of the series as we knew and loved it, under the leadership of Eric Rochant, with his ever-endearing characters. *Homeland* ended quietly after eight seasons; in contrast, *The Bureau*, initially overlooked because of its arid and highly pedagogical style, is now lauded by critics and fans. However, the latter were not at all pleased with the last two episodes of season five, which Rochant entrusted to director Jacques Audiard, and they have expressed their indignation on social media.

This is reminiscent of the final season of *Game of Thrones*, which also sparked irritated commentary from fans; a sign not only of separation anxiety, but also of viewers' attachment to the show, their appropriation of the characters and their trajectories—characters who were so much a part of fans' lives that they felt as if they knew them better than the creators who constructed this attachment in the first place. In this respect, the criticism that marked the series' final season and the many alternative endings fans proposed for it were the ultimate sign of the show's success. Similarly, the outcry from fans of *The Bureau* who cannot bear the break in style between the bulk of the series and its latest episodes, or who lament the fact that various characters have been abandoned mid-course (what will become of Pacemaker?) indicates the intensity of their relationship to the series and its heroes, constructed over the years, and to the very aesthetic of the show. This tendency of the audience to appropriate characters, to find it difficult to let go of them, to not know what will happen to them, is proof—if any were needed—of the extent to which TV series are part of our lives, especially when we have seen characters evolve and change, including physically, over the years.[2]

Homeland belongs to a new Hollywood tradition in which a series can have a strong and beautiful ending even after a slight drop in quality (the same can be said of *The Americans* and *The Affair*, two extraordinary shows). Created by Alex Gansa and Howard Gordon, *Homeland* received a great deal of criticism after an aesthetically, morally, and politically innovative first season, which brought together a high-level American soldier, Nicholas Brody, a Marine Corps sergeant and prisoner of war who converted to terrorism during his captivity, was 'released' by an Islamist leader, and welcomed home as a hero, and the CIA agent Carrie Mathison, who is suspicious of him and decides to watch him around the clock at home. *Homeland* was abandoned by a large part of its audience after its second season, when the plot between Carrie and Brody stalled; this is unfortunate, because the series became fascinating once again beginning in the fifth season, which closely tracked the security issues of the moment. The first shot of the show's final episode—entitled 'Prisoners of War', a translation of the title of the Israeli series *Hatufim* that inspired the show—is of Brody, thus closing the circle.

Homeland and *The Bureau* are paradigmatic examples of the security genre, which was born in 2001: the 9/11 attacks on New York and Washington happened to coincide with the release of the major series *24*, which had been shot and scheduled well before. By presenting the constitutive stakes of a permanent state of insecurity, characterized by multiform threats and deterritorialized enemies, security series are not only sites onto which this new state of insecurity is projected but are fully constitutive of it. In this way, security series directly raise the question of the relationship between reality and fiction.

---

2 This is the argument of my book *TV-Philosophy* (Exeter: University of Exeter Press, 2023).

Even when they are fictional and dramatized, reality sometimes catches up with them. In the case of *Homeland*, it is not the real that influences fiction, but rather reality and fiction co-determine one another. Thus, it is necessary to take into account and demonstrate their degree of reflexivity, while at the same time reconsidering the question of realism—understood not as a resemblance to reality, but rather in terms of impact and action on the real.

This unprecedented relationship between reality and fiction results, in part, from a revolution in how these series are made: connections between television professionals and security actors in the United States, the United Kingdom, and France (the Pentagon, the CIA, MI6, DGSE) have proliferated. The question is not how these series echo a certain political climate, but rather, conversely, what the impact of these series may be on democratic regimes, understood as spaces of deliberation and contestation, spaces where conflict is framed. TV series provide strong common cultural referents, which populate both ordinary conversations and political debates. The revolution in narrative practices in the twenty-first century, which has gone along with true inventiveness on the part of series creators, has led to a change in the moral ambition of series. This has also allowed production to expand beyond the US classics. Here, we may note, in addition to Israeli series, which can be said to have created the subject, the quality and originality of European political series: the Danish *Borgen*, the French *Baron Noir*, *No Man's Land*; the Spanish *La Casa de Papel*; the Norwegian *Occupied*; the Swedish *Kalifat*. It seems that the security genre—and political series more broadly—represents an opportunity to challenge American dominance in television by multiplying political points of view and demanding more of the viewer. From the outset, it was the ambition of *The Bureau* to do better, and be truer, than *Homeland*.

By immersing us in specific worlds, security series modify the viewer's experience: their virtual topography influences the viewer's opinion or judgement of the situations they present. Other factors are also at play here: the actors' acting, the viewer's attachment to characters and frequent contact with them over the long duration of the series, the polyphony that makes it possible to hear diverging points of view and to become interested in a character initially perceived as an 'enemy' or as inscrutable. A logic of empowerment is at work, allowing the viewer to perfect themselves within a context with which few are familiar, and to gain a better understanding of political situations. If we miss *Homeland* or *The Bureau* it is as 'matrices of intelligibility' that allow their viewers to understand the world around them, as well as to demonstrate their own creativity (by creating pastiches, writing summaries of imaginary episodes, reinventing characters' trajectories, etc.). This ambition of security series has paralleled the practical ethical reflection that all series have developed—an 'ordinary' ethics, anchored in attention to the particularities of situations and human personalities, which we find at work in *24*, *Homeland*, *Fauda*, *The Bureau*, and in *The Looming*

Tower, which presents the conflicts and human errors that handicapped the FBI and CIA in the years leading up to 9/11. These are traits shared by many important series, but security series make elements of political analysis. In Europe and Israel, the security genre—now led by *The Bureau*—is flourishing, but for the moment, the United States has no homegrown successor to *Homeland*.

The Enemy Within: From 24 to Homeland

24 was launched the day after 9/11; *Homeland* began ten years later, in 2011, after the death of Bin Laden and at the moment when *24* had temporarily ended. *Homeland* took on part of *24*'s team, as well as its mission, and 9/11 is omnipresent within it, as its famous opening credits show. It must be said that things have changed since *24*'s melancholic ending, and that security series have become dominant as a genre that goes beyond suspense and characters' personal plot twists to express a veritable vision of national security, and, more broadly, of human security—a shared goal of democracies. *Homeland*, like *The Bureau*, is a realist production that, by way of the Israeli series that inspired it, takes part in the globalization of the security genre.

Homeland belongs to a category of works addressed to a mainstream audience that represent and express the multiform risks that make up the current security environment and that seek to describe and anticipate these threats. Whereas *24*, its predecessor in many ways, sought above all to conjure the terrorist threat in the wake of 9/11, *Homeland*, while remaining a work of fiction that does not hesitate to veer into the fantastic, is more concerned with adhering as close to the real as possible, and thereby informing, educating, and preventing; its showrunners work in cooperation with intelligence experts. Its originality lies in its redefinition of the contemporary terrorist threat through the figure of the homegrown terrorist—a marginal subject in *24*.

It is fascinating to observe how *Homeland*, which depicts a (strong) female president—who was also written and planned well in advance—was able to operate a turnaround after Trump's election, taking the new stakes into account by transforming this character into a megalomaniac dictator who decides to silence the opposition and imprison the majority of independent officials in her administration. The most lucid and educational aspect of the new season concerns the fatal, targeted circulation of fake news (a fabricated image supposedly revealing the FBI's responsibility for the death of a child) at a moment of crisis. The expression 'fake news' has become a hallmark of Trump's communication, but *Homeland* demonstrates the relevance of 'fake news' to forms of manipulation that involve casting suspicion on certain communities or governments, and thereby destroying national solidarity. The true enemies from within are the divisions and tensions that are heightened by fake news and weaken the social fabric.

Thus, *Homeland* has emerged as a concentrate of the security genre, a fusion of *24* and the Israeli series that inspired it. It has always been excessively dramatic, in particular in terms of Carrie's personal adventures, but it has also been remarkably well suited to the political moment: season seven depicts fake news in the service of fascism; season eight has an incompetent president more concerned with his image than with catastrophe. These series are written in the face of threats; no longer 'merely' the threat of terrorism, but also that of self-destruction by dangerous leaders. Henceforth, the enemy is no longer a particular person or group, but the inability of rulers to respond to threats, to the chaos—to use the title of another major series in the security genre, *Fauda* ('chaos' in Hebrew)—created by lies, war, disorganization, and mutual trust. This makes *Homeland* and other series in the genre particularly appropriate to the moment of the COVID-19 pandemic. Thus, it is somehow fitting that *Homeland* ended in the midst of another major crisis and in the face of a new enemy. In the United States, the figure of 3,000 dead from COVID-19 in New York—exceeding the death toll from the 9/11 attacks—marked a symbolic threshold and was announced in dramatic fashion. The various themes that run through and define the security genre have never been so strong and visible as they are during COVID, when vulnerability has become universal and security has become our shared responsibility.

The final episode of *Homeland* is entitled 'Prisoners of War'—a translation of the name of the Israeli series that originally inspired it—and it opens with a shot of Brody, at a moment when Carrie appears to be about to betray her country. We don't know what the future of the security genre will bring, but *Homeland* changed how the fight against terrorism is seen: from the overactive, patriotic, and sometimes Manichean vision of *24*, the genre moved toward ambivalence, by means of its unstable heroine (Carrie's bipolar disorder represents the impossibility of global equilibrium) and a complex view of geopolitics, of violence in the Middle East, and of the role American politicians play in it.

Homeland, like *24*, proclaims itself as fiction, and uses the audience's attachment to fictional characters to implicate us in political matters. But its role goes beyond creating a fictional universe that corresponds to global threats, beyond the topic of terrorism. The series has endeavoured not only to make the terrorist threat known and to remind us that the worst is always to come (a theme already taken up by *24*), but also to make us attentive to the invisible threat, rather than to highly visible signals, to teach us the always alert gaze.

Homeland set for itself the task of making the American public see and understand the causes—and not merely the consequences—of terror, including its own terror; of demonstrating the United States' role in and responsibility for attacks on its soil; of showing the dangers that heightened surveillance poses to democratic life and to the ideals of the nation; and of displaying the internal dangers posed by an incapable and ideologized government. Thus, fiction plays a crucial role in constituting post-attack culture, and now, in constituting crisis culture. It is interesting to see how the series has affected political reality, giving the public a way to interpret events that occur after it. If *24* was a response to terror, *Homeland* redefines the nation (whence its title, which has taken on increasing significance), by showing the causes of it. It expresses the end of innocence and sounds the alarm against an erroneous—even egotistic—feeling of safety within democracies on the precipice of disaster.

Homeland was the first indication that these series could begin to not only represent but also analyse foreign conflicts—and the role of the United States in them—in a new way. During its eight seasons, *Homeland* confronted its audience with a complex vision of global conflicts, a view of violence in the Middle East, as well as the American political violence that influenced and encouraged it. Over these eight seasons, Carrie Mathison led a tumultuous professional life, changed posts and continents approximately every season, had a child, and was involved in several significant relationships after Brody. But the relationship that defines *Homeland* is the one between Carrie (Claire Danes) and Saul Berenson (Mandy Patinkin), who has gone from being head of the Middle Eastern division of the CIA to the interim director to the president's national security advisor, while always being Carrie's strongest ally. It would be simplistic (and sexist) to say that Saul is Carrie's mentor, for she constantly pushes him in new and impossible directions, and theirs is truly a relationship of mutual education. This unstable balance, in which Carrie always goes too far (including for her own mental health, which thus plays a crucial role in the dynamic of the series), and in which Saul supports and encourages her nevertheless, is constitutive of the series and its moral tone.

Carrie and Saul often try to solve the same security problem from different angles, and their partnership became—and remained until the end—the true aesthetic and political framework of the series, through to their final, radical moral disagreement: can one sacrifice someone to save the world? This question—the response to which is clear for both *24* and for utilitarian moral philosophy—is finally itself questioned in the final episodes of the final season, in which Saul teaches one last lesson to Carrie and to the audience: no, there is never any reason to decide to sacrifice someone, and especially not if that person has your trust, is a friend, and has saved your life. And even if Carrie does not agree, the entirety of the series is devoted to the theme of such trust and the unbreakable bonds of friendship in a world of betrayals (Quinn, Max, and, ultimately, Yevgeny).

It is revealing, and quite magnificent, that the series ends with this partnership still in place, even if Carrie and Saul will undoubtedly never see one another again in person. Carrie is in Russia, sending information to Saul—just as his best Russian double agent, an official government translator, had done for decades, and using the same method (sending books with a note inserted; a representation of the cultural tradition to which security series refer). Although Carrie came close to assassinating Saul to get to this point, she continues her career, living on into a future that goes beyond the series, the last words of which are: 'Stay tuned.'

Homeland takes on almost surreal relevance within our current climate by depicting a world confronting an international crisis. In this sense, it is a better illustration of our situation today than the many epidemic or contagion films that have been made. The creators of *Homeland* do not try to end the wars in the Middle East, nor do they have the series end with the end of the world. To conclude the series, they based themselves on what was always the driver of this atypical series, the difficult relationship of absolute trust between Saul and Carrie. It is significant that the series ends with a sort of remarriage, in keeping with the Hollywood tradition of remarriage comedies: a remarriage of friendship, a confirmation of Saul's and Carrie's alliance, which is still in place, even at a distance.

In the last episode, Carrie shows her Russian friend Yevgeny (played by Costa Ronin, straight out of *The Americans*) the video Saul has left in case he dies, in which he says, 'In the end, who you trust in this life is all that matters.' *Homeland* doesn't end with a field of ruins or an assassination, or with a departure into the setting sun, like *24*, but with what has always been the heart of the series: the trust between these two characters, a delicate feeling but one that turns out to be the only solid connection within the threats of the present. Ultimately, this trust extends to the viewer, whom the series has educated over all these years, and to whom the two main characters entrust the responsibility of continuing to reflect on the world; entrusting to them a world much more dangerous, false, and vicious than the world of 2011, or even 2001.

The Bureau

Trust is not the central element of *The Bureau*, whose hero spends his time betraying and deceiving others. The relationships between characters are not transparent, and it is the absence of transparency between various circuits that is constantly revealed in the series, especially in the fifth season. Some characters are aware that Malotru is not dead and that his mission continues; others suspect it; others are unaware and are very upset. As Raymond says to Marina, when she expresses surprise at not hearing from her former colleagues at the Bureau once she is transferred to a different department: 'We're not family.' And yet viewers care deeply about these characters as they would care about a family member; we care about Malotru, who disappears in flames in the last images of season four, about the undercover agent 'Pacemaker' in Russia—who bears a name borrowed from another agent—and, in season five, which shows the danger each character, scattered across the world, is facing, we care about Marie-Jeanne, about Malotru who resurfaces, and about the bizarre new character Andrea/Mille Sabords. But such intense care for the characters is not to be seen in the relations between them, even if it becomes evident in moments of danger.

Eric Rochant's series is exemplary of security series, and there is no doubt it is the best show in the genre. It takes a relatively distant point of view from its subject matter and has pedagogical and documentary elements. The show, no more than *Homeland*, is not a mirror of society, nor an ideological base for it, but rather a concrete and realist tool of democratic action by virtue of its educational value and the political and moral training it provides its audience, a task that it takes extremely seriously. From its first episode, the series has led the viewer step by step through the (fictional) operations of the DGSE and has clearly and expertly presented the dimensions of major geopolitical crises in the Middle East. The stakes of the war in Syria and of the radicalized young people who go there (also the subject of two other excellent series, *The State* and *Kalifat*), are carefully laid out, but never in a way that feels heavy-handed, because everything is communicated through dialogue and situations. Seasons four and five add extra layers of complexity and anxiety by depicting cyberattacks and digital spying.

The show's aesthetic and pedagogical ambition is also to anchor political analysis in the human: it is a series about 'human intelligence' (HUMINT). 'Human is best', Sylvain Ellenstein declares to his geek acolytes, and this is not a humanist declaration but a technical one: beyond the various forms of technology the show depicts, the best sources of information are the infiltrated agents, their contacts, and their ways of being and interactions. Thus, the latest seasons of *Homeland* and of *The Bureau* conclude with stories about double agents—an inexhaustible subject ever since Le Carré, but here updated for the Russia of today. This human material gives *The Bureau* its particular moral density, and the best vehicles for its ultimately challenging goals are its endearing characters: Malotru, Marie-Jeanne, JJA, Marina, Raymond, as well as the apparently secondary characters to whom the viewer becomes attached over the course of the seasons. They make it possible for the show to express moral conflicts, which proliferate over the last two seasons. But they are also the electrifying vectors of the tension that fills the show, and the genre as a whole: the tension between personal feelings and professional obligations, between loyalty to the rules and loyalty to friends and family—in other words, between politics and care. These characters' humanity is signalled by the omnipresence of their sexuality in the last season, which points beyond the relative coolness of the narrative to their human vulnerability (see, for example, the analyst Jonas in the field in the Middle East and on the much more difficult battlefield of human seduction).

The Bureau, like its counter-model *Homeland*, describes the enmeshment of abstract geopolitics and the bloody reality of sacrificed lives. The fifth season shows the harshness of the relations between agents (Sisteron betrays JJA and sets a trap for Marie-Jean when she applies to become head of intelligence) as well as the trust that is subtly established between two characters, Marina and Andrea, over the course of two conversations. It is no small paradox that this highly masculine series (with its male-dominated hierarchy and the impressive figures of Duflot, Malotru, and Sisteron) ends not only with the ascension of Marie-Jeanne, but also through her: it is she who proposes closing the Bureau when she is recruited to be head of intelligence at the DGSE; she is the one who brings the series to an end. This was an act the show's creator, Eric Rochant, did not feel capable of carrying out—hence the change of director for the last two episodes. It is remarkable that the show that tried to be the most 'objective' and anti-spectacular of the security genre expresses, in the structure of the writing of its final episode—that is, in its aesthetic—the deep suffering that comes from leaving these characters. Unless, perhaps, this is a difficulty particular to the genre, and one that ultimately sets it apart: the violent attachment it creates to characters whose own humanity is constantly under threat. Much work still remains to be done around the concept of point of view in security series and the usages of popular TV series.

Like all series, but especially those in this corpus, the study of security series requires special resources in moral and ethical philosophy—no longer a 'liberal' or normative ethics but an ethics anchored in values, vulnerability, and care. Security series paradoxically allow the emergence of a heterodox ethics that constitutes a real alternative to the mainstream ethics of decisions and behaviours, which are far removed from everyday realities as from political realities. The alternative and context-based moral conceptions they present constitute the moral element of these public works and define the form of education that they inspire in the public. The question of a morality expressed by contemporary media, and of the educational potential of series, is therefore entangled in all dimensions of private and public life.

Series Care for the Audience

One unexpected success has been *En thérapie*, which apparently won over even viewers who 'don't usually like series', but who find a strange comfort in compulsively following the appointments with the psychoanalyst that occupy each episode of the series. *En thérapie* is Eric Toledano and Olivier Nakache's adaptation of the cult Israeli series *BeTipul*, already adapted for HBO by the same director, Hagai Levi, with *In Treatment*. It is an adaptation, in the strongest sense, in that it scrupulously takes the structure, the characters, and the painful jokes of the Israeli series into a French context without fear of the discrepancies that this brings about: the patient's declaration of love that might be conceivable in an Israeli or American context, but is strange here; the policeman, traumatized in *BeTipul* because he killed civilians in the West Bank, and, in *En thérapie*, in great discomfort after the Bataclan; the analyst and interventionist Philippe Dayan (the formidable Frédéric Pierrot) explaining life to his patients. Never mind the implausibilities, the series is worthwhile because of the care it establishes in multiple ways: the viewer's care for the tried and tested characters, to whom they become attached as they repeatedly return to the couch; and the care that the series provides, throughout its thirty-five episodes, for its traumatized audience. But what then?

The question is complex, and one may wonder about the ambiguity of this masterpiece. *In Therapy* actually takes care of a confined audience who are deprived, by the curfew, of social contacts and the end of leisure activities, and are both distanced and depressed (as shown by the surveys carried out during the broadcast of the series, at the lowest point of French morale). The daily or at least regular appointment with the shrink is a comfort, free of charge moreover, and does not expose us since we are literally hidden behind a screen. The fascinating element of both the original series and its adaptations—from all countries—is this unprecedented rupture between the private and the public that makes it similar to pornography; it is this way of revealing human expressivity—of faces, bodies, and speech—which simultaneously reveals and conceals. The therapy of *En thérapie* is indeed in the shot of expression it provides at a time when, except in the domestic world, we scrutinize the look over the mask, and no longer know how to hear the tone or perceive the grain of the voice.

The intense reception of *En thérapie* is a product of the extreme and caricatured form of the relationship to TV series that confinement over the past year has established. The series that used to accompany ordinary lives are now a resource or a refuge in extraordinary situations, presenting universes of comfort that have become memories—of going to coffee shops, travelling, meeting, and touching each other... They allow their viewers, like the

---

* This article first appeared in *AOC*, at https://aoc.media/critique/2021/03/14/en-confinement-du-care-en-series/, 15 March 2021.

characters in a disaster film or a dystopian series, to perceive the price and the charm of an everyday life that we took for granted. Where series used to provide an escape from everyday life by delving into more or less exotic professional worlds—cops, doctors, undertakers, mobsters, billionaires, and spies—now it is ordinary life that becomes precious and unattainable.

The series offered a semblance of continuity in the radical disruption of the pandemic by maintaining the link with the characters of the series we were looking forward to seeing again (such as those of *This Is Us* whom we found masked and keeping their distance in September for the return of the fifth season). Nevertheless, we've also been awaiting the return of much-loved series such as *The Walking Dead*, long overdue but which the pandemic and its production delays have deprived us of all too unfairly. As a consequence, there has resulted the exponential multiplication of miniseries (often very successful, as recently, among others, *The Plot Against America*, *Mrs. America*, and *The Queen's Gambit*), though this poorly hides the progressive defection of the long-running series that have accompanied us over the last few decades—who will take over from *GoT*, *Engrenages*, *Homeland*—and now *This Is Us*?

Series literally took care of us during the lockdown: they were an element of regularity in chaotic and anxious lives, allowing us to enlarge the family circle by allowing us to see 'friends' such as Elizabeth II, Malotru, Berthaud every day, creating a continuity where these characters settled. A fan who has followed a series from the beginning, and who thus lives with the characters for three to seven years, cares about these characters—they become objects of care for us. Netflix too has consolidated its hold on our lives by caring for us, in the form of series that are about care in several modes: subject (the series often represents care as an attitude or a job, and medical series remain a major serial genre), medium (the series elicits our care for characters, and we don't like to remain uncertain about their fate: will we ever know what happens to Mille Sabords and Pacemaker?), and agency (the series exercise, practise care).

The great classic *ER* permanently articulated the demands of private life and work, as well as the conflicts of care (ethical and medical care). Similarly, *Six Feet Under* was an extension of the realm of care to the dead; as is evident in *Cold Case*, which was rerun during the lockdown, and which manifested a care for forgotten victims, giving a tactile context to their lives. One is also reminded of the obsession of fans with the trajectories of the heroes of *Game of Thrones* in the final season in 2018, where the expressions of bitterness and proposals for alternative endings were really symptoms of abandonment anxiety. The heart of series is the affection we have for characters built over years, carefully written, and hard to part with: we care about what happens to them, even if (or because) it's not our life. The shared passion for the characters in *En thérapie*—and their return to and from the shrink's office—is one serious manifestation of this affection.

This appears most clearly at the moment of separation, for which the best series (those that have withstood the shock of duration and manage to 'wrap up') carefully prepares us (again a form of concern for us), in the same way as one recalls the gradual departures and farewells to the viewers of each of the surviving characters in *Game of Thrones*. Enduring series, often reviewed in containment, educate us in separating ourselves from their characters in masterful conclusions (*The Wire*, *Mad Men*, *Six Feet Under*, and *The Americans* are such paradigms); something that miniseries are not required to do, as they do not allow time for the characters time to settle into our lives.

The cult series *Banshee* exemplarily devotes its entire last episode to the hero's melancholic farewell to each of the characters—a way for him to free himself from the actors in his life, and thus to find autonomy. Likewise, *The Americans* works to make us leave Elizabeth and Philip Jennings in the same way as Stan Beeman, FBI agent and neighbour, who, in the last episode, both discovers them and subsequently lets them go, as if to teach us to go on without them in the same way. These terrible eleven minutes of exchange between Philip and Stan constitute, in pain, our capacity as spectators to separate ourselves from the characters, and this learning of loss is certainly one of the unexpected forms of care of and by the series—how appropriate today.

TV series have long dealt with pandemics and the destruction of normal life. *The Walking Dead* and *Fear the Walking Dead* both foreshadow life on a continent devastated by an epidemic since 2010, while other series—such as *The Leftovers*—have prepared us for the end of ordinary life. Similarly, in 2014 the Belgian series *Cordon* described a deadly epidemic in Antwerp— contained by 'containers'—and the immanent organization of the confined society. But since 2020, TV series, even medical ones, have not been able to take the shock of COVID-19; only *This Is Us* displayed, in the first episode of season five, masked characters, as well as the link between the pandemic and the Black Lives Matter movement, whose slogan took on a more precise and painful meaning with the toll paid by blacks on the front line in the fight against the virus. The series has yet to respond to the pandemic in the same way it has responded to terrorism since 2001.

The singularity of this umpteenth adaptation of *BeTipul* is that it is set in the aftermath of the 2015 attacks, allowing, for the first time, a return in fiction to traumatic events that continue to weigh on culture and politics in France today. The series thus succeeds in responding to both the anxiety of confinement, as well as the terrorist threat, by dealing with an essential question of today: human security. Since 2001 (for *Homeland* whose credits opened with the image of the gutted towers of the World Trade Center), and since 2015 (for *En thérapie*, the French version, which begins in the aftermath of 13 November), we live in a vulnerable world, a vulnerability that has only deepened with COVID-19.

It should be recalled that *Homeland* was also an adaptation of a great Israeli series, *Hatufim*, with its latest episode, released at the peak of the pandemic in 2020, entitled 'Prisoners of War', a literal translation of *Hatufim*. In France, Israel, and the United States, the number of films and series revealing the backstage of democratic regimes dealing with the terrorist threat has thus increased significantly since 2001 (in addition to *Homeland* and *The Bureau* there have been *The Looming Tower, Fauda, False Flag, Kalifat, Occupied, No Man's Land, The Girl from Oslo, Teheran*), indicative of the moral state of a world now living under threat. But they are also intended to be instruments of education and information for the public, as was made clear in the first episode of *The Bureau*, which introduced a new recruit to the workings of the DGSE. The reflexive capacity of these works, which often offer strong analyses of the situation in the Middle East, thus gives them a role in the democratic conversation. They provide strong common cultural referents, which populate ordinary discussions and political debates, something that has enabled a global expansion of their output beyond the United States. Through their aesthetic format, the particular attachment they arouse to characters who are opaque and constantly on the edge, and the democratization and diversification of their viewing methods (internet, streaming, discussion forums), these series work to build up a public in Dewey's sense (a group concerned and able to decide) by their immersion in very particular universes, modifying the spectator's experience. If we miss *Homeland* and *The Bureau*, it is evidence that series can not only represent, but also analyse and foresee international as well as national conflicts. America does not even have a homegrown successor to *Homeland* for the moment; rather, it is France that, in lockdown is undertaking the post-attacks work with *The Bureau, No Man's Land*, and, last but not least, *En thérapie*.

The genius of *Homeland* was that, after presenting domestic terrorism in an unprecedented way, it exposed the manipulations of power that exploit the terrorist threat—for the real enemy within is the divisions and tensions that fake news stirs up to weaken the social fabric. The enemy now is not a particular person or group, but the inability of those in power to respond to the threat—or to the chaos, to use *Fauda*'s title. *Homeland* ended in the midst of a major new crisis, in the face of a new invisible enemy that is no longer terrorism, but a vulnerability that is becoming universalized, and security that is becoming a shared and human issue. These series are written under the threat, which now includes the excessive security response determined by leaders who are themselves increasingly dangerous in the violence they provoke by their policies and words.

24 still had villains—whether terrorists or traitors (Nina Meyers in season one, President Logan in season five)—but *Homeland* changed the game by humanizing Brody, alongside other enemies. Security series have relativized the figure of the 'bad guy' by embodying him in a variety of characters, the pinnacle of which was reached by the aforementioned *The Americans*), in creating an unexpected attachment in the American public for spies, communists, atheists, killers, and (worst of all) occasional adulterers.

The global containment and the health crisis will therefore not have seen an explosion of medical or epidemic series, nor of security series in the 'anxiety' climate, where it is a depersonalized and invisible enemy that attacks humanity... but a reflexive return to the 1980s. How can we fail to notice the number of recent series set in the Reagan years? To mention only the best known, they include *The Americans, Halt and Catch Fire, Show Me a Hero, Stranger Things, Glow, The Deuce, Dark, Chernobyl, Cobra Kai, When They See Us, Deutschland 83, 86, 89*, and even the stars of 2020 *The Queen's Gambit* and *The Crown*, which won several awards for its fourth season at the Golden Globes.

Similarly, the moving French series *Je te promets*, an adaptation of *This Is Us*, touches us by going back and forth between a neurotic family of the present day and its formation in the 1980s around the birth of twins and the adoption of a black baby abandoned on the day of Mitterrand's election. Likewise, *I Promise You* creates its emotional backdrop and draws its emotional power not only from the narrative and beautifully played characters, but also from references to the collective moments of the last century that have shaped our personal history.

The form of care that these series offer is created by living off our past—showing, though irretrievably past, that it is the source of our present insecurity, as asking in all sorts of ways where it went wrong (a *Back to the Future* style of returning to the past, but being unable to change anything about the present). What is shown to us on the small screen is then, as Cavell noted of the big screen, a world from which we are excluded: 'The screen is a barrier. It screens me from the world it contains—in other words, it makes me invisible. And it hides the world from me.'[3]

The world projected in the cinema does not exist (any more) and we cannot be part of it—it is for this reason that the film critic Victor Perkins noted that 'we are powerless over the image because it presents actions already performed and recorded; it gives us no influence and allows no possibility of intervention'.[4] These series set in the 1980s present us with a nostalgic but relentless unfolding of action and history, in the way that the 1980s scenes in *This Is Us* and *Je te promets* lead irrevocably to the death of the father.

In this respect, the 2020 series have become, like the cinema, 'a moving image of scepticism'. They don't just make us appreciate the life we had before, and fictitiously widen our range of experience and our circle of confined relationships—if they take care of us, it is not by putting us back into the world, but by separating us from it, by shielding us from it, and showing us a reality in which we are radically absent and powerless—but which we can dream about and regret, like a mythical period. Certainly, these series often aim to make us revise our vision of the past (*When They See Us*

---

3 Stanley Cavell, *The World Viewed: Reflections on the Ontology of Film* (Cambridge, MA: Harvard University Press, 1979 [1971]), p. 58.
4 Victor F. Perkins, *Film as Film: Understanding and Judging Movies* (Boston, MA: Da Capo Press, 1993), p. 71.

is the best example), and to repair, if possible, past mistakes, breaking with an implicit historicism and the illusion of a global and shared progress of humanity. They succeed, for instance, in demonstrating the influence of the 1980s, the boom years of capitalism, on present catastrophes, and, in doing so, show us a vanished world that we are no longer sure was a legitimate step towards a better future.

With No Hope of Return

Lost in the mass of miniseries that we are able to watch in a single weekend, we are fortunately left with a few 'real' series whose characters we have been following for years (depending on how long they have been in our lives), to a degree that we can already imagine the sadness of separation. *The Walking Dead* is approaching a form of conclusion or resolution in season ten, since season eleven will be the finale… and preparing its spin-offs to follow certain characters (such as Carol and Daryl). *Fear the Walking Dead*, the first *The Walking Dead* spin-off, after having remarkably shown, in its first season, the beginnings of the epidemic and the gradual disappearance of everyday life and all security, does not have the same resilience as *The Walking Dead*—which essentially holds us by our attachment to the characters, alive (Negan), but also dead (Glenn), or passed out (Rick?). Indeed, *The Walking Dead* is the series that best prepared us for this last year of disaster. Apocalyptic films or television series, like works of epidemic horror, have prepared us for events that we could not have foreseen or conceived of through 'intellectual' channels—just as post-attack security series, from *Homeland* to *In Therapy*, lead us to other forms of destruction and disruption of the ordinary form of life: a study of 310 volunteers concluded that fans of apocalyptic films were better prepared for the COVID-19 pandemic than other individuals. The period has thus established the cultural centrality of the zombie genre (even if the word is never uttered in *The Walking Dead*), recently illustrated by the excellent and curiously invigorating *Army of the Dead* (Jack Snyder, 2021).

The (not great) series *War of the Worlds*, a little depressing in season one, but striking and powerful in season two, continues in the same vein, with passage through an apocalypse allowing us to grasp the vulnerability, texture, and quality of ordinary life, suddenly perceptible in its loss and in its return. In fact, it is also the return to normal that these series prepare us for: a normal that we will never have again. Like *Lost*, they fast-forward us into a radically or subtly transformed future, with no possibility of turning back.

The Handmaid's Tale is no exception; yet another apocalyptic series, its political setting, the Republic of Gilead, evokes reality in all its potential for horror: dictatorship, crushing hierarchies, and the violent control of bodies. The series, regularly said to be at the end of its course, continues to be carried by its heroine, June (Elisabeth Moss), and has succeeded in shifting its narrative: escaped from Boston, June leaves for Chicago, tragically loses her servant friends on the way, and ends up being taken in by an NGO. The current season four continues the exploration and illustration of radical feminism undertaken by the *Tale*—both through its direction, taken over by Moss for several episodes; the complex and multiply antagonistic relationships between the women, whose analysis supplements and supersedes that of patriarchy; the inversion of the care relationship between June and Janine;

---

* This article first appeared in *Libération*, 3 June 2021.

Rita's quiet revolt against Serena; and the resentful background of the friendship between June and Moira. June's arrival as a political refugee in Canada and her reunion with her husband Luke is imbued with a disquieting strangeness and a radical philosophical scepticism—the return episode (e7s4), entitled 'Home', is truly a creepy conclusion worthy of *Twin Peaks* and *Twin Peaks: The Return*. Here, above all, it is as if, once again, no return to normal (to home) is possible.

The sceptical atmosphere expresses June's inability to regain contact with reality, and conversation with others—she has to confront and abuse Serena (now detained in Canada) in the middle of the night to regain speech and action. This is followed by the creepiest scene of the season, June's sexual reunion with Luke: back 'at home' and excited by the confrontation with Serena, she approaches Luke, pulls down his trousers, kisses and straddles him brutally—and, with all the hallmarks of rape, she immobilizes and chokes him, with her hand over his mouth. The camera zooms in on June's orgasmic face, an image of both a powerful woman and the climax of trauma.

This episode, in contrast to the feminist washing and Girl Power myths that run through most current fiction, deals with the issue of female violence—in the same way as a very different miniseries, *A Teacher*, whose final minutes turn our vision of the story around. *The Handmaid's Tale* comes to analyse all sides of the topic by, in season four, articulating it to race—for this is also what is at stake in the painful scene of Luke's rape by his beloved wife.

To Be Born or not to Be

House of the Dragon, the sequel to the legendary *Game of Thrones*, although set two hundred years earlier, is different in many ways from its parent series—including, for the moment, a relative lack of major geopolitical struggles or military battles/engagements. Most of the politics is played out as a war of succession and, for this reason, the series has been likened to Jesse Armstrong's magnificent *Succession*, also produced by HBO, which features the rivalries between the children of a media mogul. In this first season of *House of the Dragon*, we find a similar plot, with multiple betrayals, animosities, and shifting alliances within a quasi-nuclear family revolving around the father, Viserys (Paddy Considine, in a striking role), whose end is foretold in a way that creates an interminable wait over the course of the episodes (like that of another father, the one from *This Is Us*, whose death underlies that show's first two seasons and haunts the following ones).

It is not surprising, then, that this obsessive theme of succession is also that of generation, which materializes in *House of the Dragon* in the most concrete way. For another astonishing difference between this new series and *Game of Thrones* is the proliferation of birth scenes—I count four of them, each one more harrowing than the last. In the first episode, Queen Aemma, wife of Viserys, does not survive a caesarean section ordered by her dear husband to 'save the child' (the heir, Baelon, who will only survive a few hours). Episode six—set much later and featuring a different actress—opens with their grown-up daughter, Rhaenyra, giving birth. We learn that this is not her first birth, but it is the only one in the season that goes smoothly, apart from the harrowing scene in which Rhaenyra, still bleeding, drags herself through the palace to bring her newborn to her vindictive stepmother, Queen Alicent. In the same episode, Laena, second wife of Daemon (Viserys' brother and Rhaenyra's uncle), finds herself in the same situation as Aemma, with a baby who is not doing well during the birth. Daemon (though far from perfect), unlike Viserys, offers to sacrifice the child and to save her. Laena, however, prefers to get it over with and be charred by her dragon (Dracarys). The final birth scene is in the season finale: in shock at her father's death and Alicent's betrayal, Rhaenyra gives birth prematurely, without any help. In a shocking scene, she reaches her bare hands between her legs, extracting the lifeless body of the baby herself.

House of the Dragon, faithful to an increasingly well-known historical reality, presents motherhood as an extreme risk, one that regularly leads to the death of the mother (episode one), the child (episode ten), or both (episode six). These scenes have provoked puzzled, even indignant, commentary, not only because they represent death and violence, but also because they have shown a very wide audience the reality and violence of all births and the burden

---

* This article first appeared in *L'école des parents*, December 2022.

carried by women, made explicit by Aemma in a conversation with Rhaenyra in the first episode.

These births also tell us a story about women. Aemma does not have autonomy over her body (Viserys chooses for her). In the next generation, Laena, and especially Rhaenyra, somehow manage to. Note that the numerous heroic women of *Game of Thrones* were little affected by the pangs of motherhood: neither Sansa nor Arya bore children. Daenerys does, again in a memorable season finale, but it's a rather particular birth (she gives birth to dragons—via eggs, which still have a crucial symbolic place in *House of the Dragon*).

Game of Thrones was a pioneer in showcasing female heroines of all ages and styles in their multiplicity; *House of the Dragon* effectively continues this unveiling, by putting women's reproductive work on-screen, for a generation of viewers who have already learned to talk about menstruation more freely (something demonstrated, not insignificantly, by advertisements for menstrual protection that have begun to depict red menstrual blood instead of a demure blue liquid).

A few months before *House of the Dragon*, we had the opportunity to discover the excellent, more discreet miniseries *This is Going to Hurt*, starring actor Ben Whishaw, consistently hilarious since 2012 as Q in the James Bond saga. Here, he plays a tormented gynaecologist. The title refers simultaneously to the daily work of the hero, Adam Kay, in the obstetrics department of a London hospital; to the suffering and risks of women at different moments in their reproductive journeys; and to the shock that viewers, who are unaccustomed to such raw representations, will bear. The originality of the series lies in its recognition of, to use Freud's words, the 'dark continent' of women's reproductive and sexual health, and in its focus on a sector of health care that is even more neglected than others—for reasons of gender. *This is Going to Hurt* also offers a ruthless depiction of working conditions in the British health system: a baby delivered in a lift, lack of uniforms for medical workers, ridiculously low wages—conditions that became even more apparent during a recent and unprecedented nurses' strike in England.

In a key episode, Adam, doing a trial run at a private maternity hospital, is flabbergasted and ecstatic at the conditions of comfort reserved for privileged patients and the staff at their service, only to realize—once again—on the occasion of a childbirth that goes wrong the lamentable level of care in this profit-based establishment, and to find himself forced to bring a woman in distress to the public hospital that she had done everything to avoid. The subject matter of this series converges with that of such French examples as the beautiful *Hippocrate*, which shows a despised, underfunded, and undervalued public hospital that nonetheless accomplishes unimaginable daily feats—thanks to the skills and dedication of its professionals. The latter are not without their limits, as shown by the heartbreaking trajectory of the character of Shruti on the British series or the fate of Igor on *Hippocrate*.

In cinema, where men and their preoccupations have historically dominated, maternity and birth are still largely absent. The issue of abortion has been addressed in a few films, but rarely that of childbirth. But, like many subaltern themes, these topics are very much present in TV series. From this point of view, Adam Kay's striking series is not only an illustration of the durability of the medical series, an essential genre since *ER*, but also constitutes a new stage in the representation of women.

The theme of childbirth becomes more radical in the fifth season of *The Handmaid's Tale*. Bruce Miller's series, starring Elizabeth Moss, was certainly the first to address these issues, in a way that was as direct as it was traumatic, by presenting 'handmaids'—women known to be fertile, in a world where the birth rate has fallen sharply. Handmaids, charged with producing babies for the infertile women of the ruling class, are dispossessed of their bodies, which become the property of their masters. It is this theme of state control over the reproductive function, and thus over women's bodies, that gives *The Handmaid's Tale* its consistency. This fifth season offers a situation reversal when Serena, the former boss of June, the heroine, gives birth, in highly precarious conditions (again!), with only June's help. The relationship between these two great female characters acquires a different dimension and comes to constitute a new heart of the series, as shown in the final, almost jubilant, shot of their meeting on the train: each having had the opportunity to choose, each with her baby in her arms.

It should not be forgotten that it was the threat to women's autonomy and control over their bodies, with anti-abortion measures decided by a Supreme Court dominated by the most reactionary and bigoted Republicans, that mobilized youth and women in the recent mid-term elections in the United States, averting the anticipated disaster for President Biden's Democratic party.

This Is Us: A Lesson in Care

Do we have to see reality on a series for it to be fully real? That's the feeling I had when I was reunited with the heroes of the beautiful series *This Is Us* after their seven-month absence from the screen (with the subsequent shock of seeing them with masks and hand sanitizer in the first episode of season five). The series is built across different temporalities—that of the childhood of the central characters, the 'Big Three', Kate, Kevin, and Randall, false triplets who are supposed to celebrate their fortieth birthday during this episode; that of the youth of their parents, Rebecca and Jack Pearson; and finally, that of the parallel tragedy of Randall's biological father, William (which led the latter to abandon the new-born child, dropping him off in great melodramatic tradition in front of a fire station).

The series thus returns to its pilot, which already mixed the present and the past—Kate, Kevin, and Randall's thirty-sixth birthday and the day of their birth—and displayed its method—to loop back to the events of the past, allowing us to understand them in many new ways. It gradually revealed the bond between these three very different people (a black man, a white woman, and a white man): the founding events of the series—Rebecca's delivery of triplets, the birth of the twins Kate and Kevin, the tragedy of the third baby's death, and the Pearson couple's adoption of the abandoned black baby on the same day.

This fifth season, which began filming in September, is surprisingly (even for this highly realistic series) connected to current events. Although *This Is Us* has never before touched on the political context, the first episode plunges us into it through a statement from Madison, pregnant with Kevin's child after a one-night stand: 'This is happening just as the whole world is falling apart.' 'You mean the virus?' asks Kevin. This may be understood in multiple ways: the world is falling apart with the murder of George Floyd by Minneapolis police officers and the ensuing riots; with wildfires; with the catastrophic presidency of Donald Trump; and of course, with the virus. The wearing of masks by the show's characters is a gesture that is thus both political and educational.

The many meanings of this statement are indicated in a second scene between Beth and Randall that looks like a public health spot. On what is usually an emotionally close show, all the characters keep their distance—including Kate, who is moved by the news of Kevin's paternity (twins, by the way, which is a bit heavy-handed), but merely mimes an air hug.

Shot in the middle of the presidential campaign, the episode reminds us that masking is a political marker, as clearly expressed by Donald Trump's contempt during his first debate with Joe Biden, by his tearing off his mask on his return to the White House after his COVID-19 episode as a gesture

---

* This article first appeared in *Libération*, 5 November 2020.

of defiance, and with his supporters systematically unmasked at rallies. The mask, a symbol of concern for others, confirms the moral stance of the series, which is centred on care. Despite the disquieting strangeness that its presence creates for the characters, the feeling is no stranger than the one we feel when watching current series and films that bear no trace of the pandemic.

And the show's pedagogy goes even further, with a third instance: Randall discovers the news of George Floyd's death, which upsets him in a specific way. From this point on, *This Is Us* confronts the question of race through a reflexive return to the trajectory of Randall, a black child raised in a white, loving, and 'colour-blind' family: we remember the embarrassing scenes at the swimming pool when Rebecca insisted on spreading sun cream on him like his brother and sister; the phase when Randall flabbergasted his family by wanting to go to talk with a black family, or to study at Howard University. The realism of *This Is Us* is present in this individual relationship to social reality, with George Floyd's death adding further weight to the charge carried by Randall (by the brilliant Sterling K. Brown) and the show's other black characters, William, Beth, Déjà, and Malik.

Recall that the reflexivity of *The Walking Dead* lay in what the series made us understand about ourselves and our gradual moral transformation. *This Is Us* makes us reconsider our own attachment to the Pearson family, rooted in the caring act of Randall's adoption, which subsequently results in a denial of his colour. Randall is thus placed in a moment of scepticism— of doubt about who he is and where he comes from, and it is the George Floyd affair on his birthday that makes him realize that for him it's not a birthday—he doesn't even know what his real day of birth is, as he simply ended up in hospital at the same time as Kevin and Kate. Celebrating his birthday with them feels not only like a chore, but also like violence. As a result, we as fans realize that what we saw from the beginning as a beautiful story of integration and love has also been a story of denial, and thus grasp the lesson of *This Is Us*, which is both about its characters and about ourselves.

Randall, in a key scene at the end of the episode, reminds his sister of what it was like to be black and raised in a white family that didn't talk about race—to have to fend for himself and to think about the 1995 murder of Jonny Gammage by Pittsburgh police. Kate has just become aware of the systemic racism of America, but for Randall this is nothing new... except that he 'can't take it any more, to try to please them' and 'avoid the discomfort'—a dizzying moment in which the show also addresses us and our own moral comfort.

This moment of rupture joins other gestures by series, such as *Mrs. America*—which depicts the treatment of the first black presidential candidate, Shirley Chisholm, by well-known white feminists—or *Watchmen* and *Lovecraft Country*, both of which revisit collectively repressed episodes from American history (e.g. the Tulsa massacre). *The Comey Rule* ironizes on politicians' delusions of moral superiority (self-righteousness) during Trump's election in 2016, convinced that he would not dare to take on American institutions—or them. It is important that a series such as *This Is Us*, aired by NBC (as *The West Wing* once was), and with a wide and popular audience, reclaims the 'us' not as consensus or majority, but as a reckoning with silenced voices.

The World Viewed, Once and Again

When the credits roll and before the lights come back up, there is scattered applause—and then a bit more, although without any general outburst—a scene that has been repeated at many cinema screenings since the reopening of theatres, including at the end of *Drive My Car* (Ryusuke Hamaguchi, 2021), *No Time to Die* (Cary Joji Fukunaga, 2021), *La Fracture* (Catherine Corsini, 2021), and of course, Ruffin's *Debout les femmes* (Gilles Perret and François Ruffin, 2021), which naturally calls for it. Are viewers applauding the pleasure of being back in a cinema, a place that had been forbidden since 2020? Or the sharing of the experience of a film with others? Or finally seeing the credits roll in their entirety? We are reinventing the companionable nature of the cinematic experience: masks and health passes are still with us, but to find ourselves in a darkened room with strangers, sharing a viewing of the same film, is an experience we were missing.

It is all the more depressing to learn from the Harris survey on French cultural outings after the crisis that audiences have not returned to the cinema in great numbers (only 41 per cent have), and, above all, that many do not intend to do so again any time soon—even (and especially!) those who say they used to go before (a third even plan to reduce their cinema attendance by the end of 2021). The reasons most often given are a fear of crowded places, as well as preference for digital content (which is less obviously available in the case of 'live performances' as opposed to movies), which makes it all the more striking that, according to the Harris survey, it is the cinemagoers themselves who have unlearned the practice of going to the cinema, now preferring the setting of their own homes to view films that are readily available and cheaper. Films, like series, seem to have entered the domestic space, a consequence of lockdowns, during which series have played the role of comforter or therapist: the intense reception of the series *En thérapie* in France exemplifies this relationship to TV series that lockdown established, and is just one example of the 'privatization' of cultural life, a radical modification of those 'lives where we go to the movies'.

One can only wonder whether the transformation of social and private life introduced in the last century by the invention of cinema and the practice of moviegoing still remains—indeed, whether 'the cinema' still exists any more, when there are so many film libraries, classics readily available on various platforms, and numerous film channels on TV. What so many regular or occasional cinema-goers appear to be giving up are not films as such, but a form of life: passing in front of a movie theatre on the way home from work or coming out of the metro or café and deciding to 'catch a movie'— making a social or family outing out of a trip to the cinema, or waiting for films to come out… all part of a distant life, when cinema was an integral part of daily existence, mixing public and private space. As Emmanuel

---

* This article first appeared in *Le Monde*, 13 November 2021.

Bourdieu said in 2001, 'Cinema is common and ordinary aesthetic experience; shared, involved, and intertwined with everyday life: a movie before or after dinner; returning home and perhaps spending the night dreaming of it, thinking about it at breakfast the next morning, etc.'[5]

We must not neglect the rupture constituted by this globalized 'lockdown'—the magnitude and irreversibility of the change in our cultural habits, and, in particular, in the 'weak ties' that unite us with people we do not know, but with whom we share space for a limited time.

Going to the movies is the primary, primitive experience of film. At the same time, the strangeness of the situation in which one finds oneself alongside masked strangers in a darkened theatre makes us aware of its social as well as aesthetic radicality: to be in a space open to all, yet closed; to perceive these strangers no longer as a threat, but as a group of 'co-experiencers' with whom one enters into the same subjective space.

Whether we go to the cinema with others or by ourselves, our memory of a film is affected by those we saw it with. It is this intimate company that determines our vision and memory of the film and inscribes it in our personal history. The companionship of the experience of cinema is central to Cavell's analysis in *The World Viewed*. In reality, going back to the movies is not a return to the normal, but to the abnormal: it means recovering an experience and a relationship to the world that is new, and which exemplifies the way in which a technology transformed the human experience in the twentieth century. It is true that a significant proportion of humans, for reasons of taste or situation, never went to the cinema (or watched TV), but it was nevertheless present in everyone's lives and everyone cared about it:

> Rich and poor, those who care about no (other) art and those who live on the promise of art, those whose pride is education and those whose pride is power or practicality—all care about movies, await them, respond to them, remember them, talk about them, hate some of them, are grateful for some of them.[6]

This experience was so ordinary in the life of a film lover (as well as of the occasional viewer), that one would never have imagined it could become impossible. Indeed, it should be noted that the format of movie showings has not fundamentally changed for the last hundred years, since the advent of talking pictures and colour—apart from a few variants (twelve-hour

---

5 Emmanuel Bourdieu, "Stanley Cavell—pour une esthétique d'un art impur," in Marc Cerisuelo and Sandra Laugier, eds., *Stanley Cavell, Cinéma et philosophie* (Paris: Presses de la Sorbonne Nouvelle, 2000), p. 57.
6 Cavell, *The World Viewed*, pp. 4–5.

films, 3D) that have remained marginal. We went to the cinema on New Year's Eve, on days of general strikes, or even the day after a disaster.

Such moviegoing is the ontology of cinema, a practice both mysterious and ordinary; ordinary because nothing is—or was—more sharable and obvious, in so many places in the world, than going to see films; mysterious because of the evanescence and magnetism of the film experience, which was never negated by the many means of recording them—from our old video tapes to DVD collections and hard drives, all of which have been rendered obsolete in recent years by the availability of thousands of works on streaming platforms. The films that matter, that figure in our lives as memorable public events, constitute fragments of experiences and memories of a lifetime.

To this experience of exploration is added a new definition of privacy—a form of anonymity. It is this intimate company that determines our vision and memory of the film: even if we go to the cinema alone, the experience has nothing to do with watching a film alone on TV (which also has its charm). It is an experience that is individual yet not private (in the sense of secret), as it remains shareable, and includes the company of those with whom one has seen the film—if not with the friends or relatives with whom one goes to see the film, then with those strangers with whom one shares a simultaneously intimate and public moment.

I can still remember the tall, tearful teenager a few seats to my right during the final fight between Anakin and Obi-wan in *Revenge of the Sith*, as well as the howls of laughter from the audience at the Filmothèque du Quartier Latin when discovering *The Lady Eve* (Preston Sturges, 1941).

This is an element that was noted by Erwin Panofsky: if cinema is important, it is because it, unlike other major art forms, has not lost contact with a wide audience. For me, it is not a matter of some outdated and elitist hierarchy between TV series and films; television series and films can be seen on television—even if, as I write this sentence, I realize its weakness, at a time when series are watched on computers, on phones, and taken on public transport. TV series are thus progressively detaching themselves from the domestic medium that has historically defined them (and which relegated them to a subaltern place within the arts). Series accompanied ordinary lives during COVID-19, proving a resource or refuge in extraordinary situations by offering universes of solace—indeed, they offered a semblance of continuity during the disruption of the pandemic, particularly given its destruction of the ordinary public spaces in which everyday, anonymous, and public exchanges forge 'weak ties' and nurture democracy. They literally took care of us during lockdown and proved essential to our collective moral survival. It is not accidental (even if there are all sorts of practical reasons for this) that series are not shown in cinemas, whereas digital platforms produce their own films (most often pure by-products of a contemporary corpus exploited to the bone and more diluted than a good series episode). Even if cinema educates, transforms, comforts, and makes us (feel) better, it doesn't care in the same way series do. It offers the unsettling experience of a world and characters larger than oneself, on a screen that cuts off the world while simultaneously projecting it. So many great shows, our companions over the past decade (*Homeland*, *Veep*, *This is Us*, *The Walking Dead*, *Better Call Saul*, *Ozark*, must now be mourned—since coming to an end during COVID-19 or right after. Which series will take care of us now?

Bibliography

Allouche, Sylvie and Laugier, Sandra (eds), *Buffy, tueuse de vampires* (Paris: Bragelonne, 2014).
Bourdieu, Emmanuel, 'Stanley Cavell—Pour Une Esthétique d'un Art Impur', in *Stanley Cavell: Cinema et Philosophie*, edited by Marc Cerisuelo and Sandra Laugier (Paris: Presses de la Sorbonne Nouvelle, 2001).
Cavell, Stanley, *A Pitch of Philosophy: Autobiographical Exercises* (Cambridge, MA: Harvard University Press, 1994).
———, *Cavell on Film*, edited by William Rothman (New York: SUNY Press, 2005).
———, *Cities of Words: Pedagogical Letters on a Register of the Moral Life* (Cambridge, MA: Belknap Press of Harvard University Press, 2004).
———, *Contesting Tears: The Hollywood Melodrama of the Unknown Woman* (Chicago, IL: University of Chicago Press, 1996).
———, *Here and There. Sites of Philosophy* (Cambridge, MA: Harvard University Press, 2022)
———, *In Quest of the Ordinary: Lines of Skepticism and Romanticism* (Chicago, IL: University of Chicago Press, 1988).
———, *Little Did I Know: Excerpts from Memory* (Stanford, CA: Stanford University Press, 2010).
———, *Pursuits of Happiness: The Hollywood Comedy of Remarriage* (Cambridge, MA: Harvard University Press, 1981).
———, 'The Thought of Movies', in *Themes out of School: Effects and Causes*, pp. 3–26 (Chicago, IL: University of Chicago Press, 1988).
———, *The World Viewed: Reflections on the Ontology of Film*, enlarged edition (Cambridge, MA, and London: Viking Press, 1971).
Dewey, John, *Art as Experience* (New York: Perigree, 1980).
———, *The Public and Its Problems* (New York: Henry Holt and Company, 1927).
Diamond, Cora, *The Realistic Spirit: Wittgenstein, Philosophy, and the Mind*, reprint (Cambridge, MA: MIT Press, 1995 [1991]).
———, *L'importance d'être humain et autres essais de philosophie morale*, edited and translated by Sandra Laugier, Emmanuel Halais, and Jean-Yves Mondon (Paris: Presses Universitaires de France, 2011).
Emerson, Ralph Waldo, *The Essential Writings of Ralph Waldo Emerson*, edited by Brooks Atkinson (New York: Modern Library, 2000).
Gefen, A. and S. Laugier (eds), *Le pouvoir des liens faibles* (Paris: CNRS editions, 2020).

Gilligan, Carol, *In a Different Voice: Psychological Theory and Women's Development* (Cambridge, MA: Harvard University Press, 1982).

Gilligan, Carol and Snider, Naomi, *Why Does Patriarchy Persist?* (Cambridge: Polity Press, 2018).

Laugier, Sandra (ed.), *Éthique, littérature, vie humaine* (Paris: Presses universitaires de France, 2006).

—— (ed.), *La voix et la vertu. Variétés du perfectionnisme moral* (Paris: PUF, 2010).

——*Why We Need Ordinary Language Philosophy*, trans. D. Ginsburg (Chicago: Chicago University Press, 2013).

——The Ethics of Care as a Politics of the Ordinary, *New Literary History*, 46, 2015, pp. 217–240.

—— "What Matters: Ethics and Aesthetics of Importance," in *Stanley Cavell on Aesthetic Understanding*, ed. Garry L. Hagberg (New York: Palgrave Macmillan, 2018.

——, 'The Conception of Film for the Subject of Television: Moral Education of the Public and a Return to an Aesthetics of the Ordinary', in *The Thought of Stanley Cavell and Cinema: Turning Anew to the Ontology of Film a Half-Century after The World Viewed*, edited by David LaRocca (London: Bloomsbury, 2020), pp. 210–227.

——, *Nos Vies en Séries: Philosophie et Morale D'une Culture Populaire* (Paris: Climats Flammarion, 2019).

—— (ed.), *Series TV, laboratoires d'éveil politique* (Paris: CNRS Editions, 2023).

—— and Marc Cerisuelo (eds), *Stanley Cavell, cinéma et philosophie* (Paris: Presses de la Sorbonne Nouvelle, 2001).

Paperman, Patricia, and Sandra Laugier (eds), *Le Souci des autres: éthique et politique du care* (Paris: Éditions de l'Écoles des hautes études en sciences sociales, 2005).

Rothman, William, 'Cavell on Film, Television, and Opera', in *Stanley Cavell*, edited by Richard Eldridge, pp. 206–38 (Cambridge: Cambridge University Press, 2003).

Rothman, William, *The 'I' of the camera, Essays in Film Criticism, History, and Aesthetics*, 2nd ed. (Cambridge: Cambridge University Press, 2004 [1988]).

Saint Maurice, Thibaut de, *Philosophie en séries* (Paris: Ellipses, 2015).

——, 'Portrait du sériephile en philosophe', in *Le pouvoir des liens faibles*, edited by Alexandre Gefen and Sandra Laugier (Paris: CNRS editions, 2020).

Shuster, Martin, *New Television: The Aesthetics and Politics of a Genre*, illustrated edition (Chicago, IL: University of Chicago Press, 2017).

Sinnerbrink, Robert, *Cinematic Ethics: Exploring Ethical Experience through Film* (London and New York: Routledge, 2016).

Thiellement, Pacôme, *Pop Yoga* (Paris: Sonatine Éditions, 2013).

Warshow, Robert, *The Immediate Experience: Movies, Comics, Theatre & Other Aspects of Popular Culture*, enlarged edition (Cambridge, MA: Harvard University Press, 2001).

Wittgenstein, Ludwig, *Philosophical Investigations*, translated by G.E.M. Anscombe (Englewood Cliffs, NJ: Prentice Hall, 1958).

Serigraphy and Filmography

24 (Joel Surnow & Robert Cochran, Fox, 2001–2014)
The Affair (Sarah Treem & Hagai Levi, Showtime, 2014–2019)
Alias (J.J. Abrams, ABC, 2001–2006)
Allegiance (George Nolfi, NBC, 2015)
Ally McBeal (David E. Kelley, Fox, 1997–2002)
American Crime (John Ridley, ABC, 2015–2017)
American Crime Story (Alexander, Karaszewski, Smith & Burgess, FX, 2016–)
American Horror Story (Murphy & Falchuk, FX, 2011–)
The Americans (Joe Weisberg, FX, 2013–2018)
Angel (Joss Whedon, WB, 1999–2004)
Banshee (Cinemax, 2013–2016)
Baron Noir (Ziad Doueiri, Canal+, 2016–)
Barry (Alec Berg & Bill Hader, HBO, 2018–)
Battlestar Galactica (Ronald D. Moore, Sky One/SyFy, 2004–2009)
BeTipul (Levi, Bergman, & Sivan, Hot 3, 2005–2008)
Berlin Station (Olen Steinhauer, Epix, 2016–2018)
Better Things (Pamela Adlon, Louis C.K, FX, 2016–2022)
Bewitched (Sol Saks, ABC, 1964–1972)
The Big Bang Theory (Chuck Lorre and Bill Prady, CBS, 2007–2019)
Big Little Lies (David E. Kelley, HBO, 2017–2019)
Bodyguard (Jed Mercurio, BBC One, 2018)
Borgen (Adam Price, DR1, 2010–2013)
Boss (Farhad Safinia, Starz, 2011–2012)
Breaking Bad (Vince Gilligan, AMC, 2008–2013)
Broen (Hans Rosenfeldt, SVT1/DR1, 2011–2018)
Brothers & Sisters (J.R. Baitz, ABC, 2006–2011)
Buffy the Vampire Slayer (Joss Whedon, UPN, 1997–2003)
The Bureau/Le Bureau des legendes (Eric Rochant, Canal+, 2015–2020)
The Chair (Amanda Peet & Annie Julia Wyman, Netflix, 2021)
Chernobyl (Craig Mazin, HBO, 2019)
Cobra Kai (Jon Hurwitz, Hayden Schlossberg and Josh Heald, Netflix, 2018–)
Cold Case (Meredith Stiehm, CBS, 2003–2010)
Columbo (Richard Levinson and William Link, NBCABC, 1968–2003)
Cordon (Carl Joos, Eyeworks, 2014)
The Comey Rule (Billy Ray, Showtime, 2020)
The Crown (Peter Morgan, Netflix, 2016–)
Counterpart (Justin Marks, Starz, 2017–2019)

Dallas (David Jacobs, CBS, 1978–1991)
Damages (Todd A. Kessler, Glenn Kessler, & Daniel Zelman, FX/Audience, 2007–2012)
Dark (Jantse Friese, Netflix 2017–2020)
Deadwood (David Milch, HBO, 2004–2006)
Designated Survivor (David Guggenheim, ABC/Netflix, 2016–2019)
Desperate Housewives (Marc Cherry, ABC, 2004–2012)
The Deuce (George Pelecanos and David Simon, HBO, 2017–2019)
Deutschland 83, 86, 89 (Anna Winger and Joerg Winger, AMC, 2015–2020)
Dexter (James Manos, Showtime, 2006–2013)
Dollhouse (Joss Whedon, Fox, 2009–2010)
Downton Abbey (Julian Fellowes, ITV, 2010–2015)
Dream On (Martha Kauffman and David Crane, HBO, 1990–96)
Dr. Quinn, Medicine Woman (Beth Sullivan, CBS, 1993–1998)
Emily in Paris (Darren Star, Netflix, 2020–)
En thérapie (Eric Toledano and Olivier Nakache, Arte, 2021–). See *BeTipul*
Engrenages/*Spiral* (Anne Landois et al., Canal+, 2005–2020)
ER (Michael Crichton, NBC, 1994–2009)
Everwood (Greg Berlanti, The WB, 2002–2006)
The Fall (Allan Cubitt, BBC Two, 2014–)
False Flag (Feldman & Cohen, Channel 2, 2015–)
Fargo (Noah Hawley, FX, 2014–)
Fauda (Raz & Issacharoff, Yes Oh/ Netflix, 2015–)
Fear the Walking Dead (Kirkman & Erickson, AMC, 2015–)
Felicity (J.J. Abrams and Matt Reeves, 1998–2001)
Firefly (Joss Whedon, Fox, 2002)
Fleabag (Phoebe Waller-Bridge, Two Brothers Picture, BBC, 2016–2019)
For All Mankind (Moore, Wolpert, Nedivi, Apple TV, 2019–)
Foxcatcher (Bennett Miller, 2014)
Friends (Martha Kauffman and David Crane, NBC, 1994–2004)
Fringe (Abrams, Kurtzman & Orci, Fox, 2008–2013)
Game of Thrones (Benioff & Weiss, HBO, 2011–2019)
The Girl from Oslo (Stian Kristiansen, Uri Barbash Netflix, 2021)
Girls (Lena Dunham, HBO, 2011–2017)
Glow (Liz Flahive and Carly Mensch, Netflix 2017–2019)
Golden Girls (Susan Harris, NBC, 1985–1992)
Gomorrah (Roberto Saviano, Sky Atlantic, 2014–2021)
Grey's Anatomy (Shonda Rhimes, ABC, 2005–)
Halt and Catch Fire (Christopher Cantwell and Christopher C. Rogers, AMC 2014–2017)
The Handmaid's Tale (Bruce Miller, Hulu, 2017–)
Hannibal (Bryan Fuller, NBC, 2013–2015)
Hatufim (Gideon Raff, Aroutz 2, 2010–2012)
High Fidelity (Nick Hornby, Hulu, 2020).
Hippocrate (Thomas Lilti, Canal+, 2018–)
Homeland (Gordon & Gansa, Showtime, 2011–2020)
House of Cards (Beau Willimon, Netflix, 2013–2018)

How I Met Your Mother (Cater Bays and Craig Thomas, CBS, 2005–2014)
House of the Dragon (George R. R. Martin and Ryan Condal, HBO, 2022–)
I May Destroy You (Michaela Coel, BBC One, HBO 2020)
In Treatment (Rodrigo Garcia, HBO, 2008–2021).
Je te promets (TF1, 2021–)
Kalifat (Netflix, 2020)
Kate & Allie (Sherry Coben, CBS, 1984–1989)
The Killing (Veena Sud, AMC/Netflix, 2011–2014)
Killing Eve (Phoebe Waller-Bridge and alii, BBC, 2018–2022)
The Kingdom (Lars von Trier, DR, 1994–)
The L Word (Ilene Chaiken, Showtime, 2004–2009)
La Casa de Papel (Alex Pina, Netflix, 2017–2021)
The Leftovers (Damon Lindelof and Tom Perrotta, HBO, 2014–2017)
Little Fires Everywhere (Liz Tigelaar, Hulu, 2020)
The Looming Tower (Dan Futterman, Alex Gibney, Lawrence Wright, Hulu, 2018)
Lost (Jeffrey Lieber, J.J. Abrams & Damon Lindelof, ABC, 2004–2010)
Lovecraft Country (Misha Green, Damon Lindelof, J.J. Abrams, HBO, 2019)
Lupin (George Kay & François Uzan, Netflix, 2021–)
Mad Men (Matthew Weiner, AMC, 2007–2015)
Maid (Land, Metzler, Netflix, 2021)
The Man in the High Castle (Frank Spotnitz, Amazon Prime, 2015–2020)
Mare of Easttown (Brad Ingelsby, HBO, 2021)
The Marvelous Mrs. Maisel (Amy Sherman-Palladino, Amazon Prime, 2017–2022)
The Mary Tyler Moore Show (James L. Brooks & Allan Burns, CBS, 1970–1977)
Miami Vice (Anthony Yerkoich, NBC, 1984–1989)
Mindhunter (Joe Penhall, Netflix, 2017–2019)
Modern Family (Christopher Lloyd, ABC, 2009–2020)
Mr. Robot (Sam Esmail, USA Network, 2015–2019)
Mrs. America (Dahvi Waller, Hulu, 2020)
The Marvelous Mrs. Maisel (Amy Sherman-Palladino, Amazon Prime, 2017–)
Narcos (Chris Brancato, Carlo Bernard and Doug Miro, Netflix, 2015–2018)
The NIght Of (Steven Zaillian and James Marsh, HBO, 2016)
No Man's Land (Maria Feldman and Eitan Mansuri, Arte 2020)
NYPD Blue (Steven Bochco and David Mills, ABC, 1993–2005)
Occupied (Jo Nesbo, Eric Skojoldbjaerg and Karianne Lund, TV2, 2015–2019)
Orange Is the New Black (Jenji Kohan, Netflix, 2013–2019)
Our Boys (Hagai Levi, Joseph Cedar and Tawfik Abu-Wael, HBO, 2019)
OVNI(s) (Clémence Dargent and Martin Douaire, Canal+, 2020–2022)
Ozark (Chris Mundy, Netflix, 2017–2022)
Paris, etc. (Zabou Breitman, Canal+, 2017)
The People v. O.J. Simpson: American Crime Story (Alexander & Karaszewski, FX, 2016)
The Persuaders! (Robert S. Baker, ITV, 1971–1972)
The Plot Against America (Simon & Burns, HBO, 2020)
Pose (Ryan Murphy, Brad Falchuk and Steven Canals, FX, 2018–2021)
Prime Suspect (Lynda La Plante, ITV, 1991–2002)
The Persuaders (Robert S. Baker, ITV/ABC, 1971–1972)

The Queen's Gambit (Scott Frank and Allan Scott, Netflix, 2020)
Scandal (Shonda Rhimes, ABC, 2012–2018)
Servant of the People (Volodymyr Zelensky, Kvartal 95 Studio, 2015–2019)
Seven Seconds (Veena Sud, Netflix, 2018)
Sex and the City (Darren Star, HBO, 1998–2004)
Show Me a Hero (David Simon & William F. Zorzi, HBO, 2015)
The Simpsons (Matt Groening, Fox, 1989–)
Six Feet Under (Alan Ball, HBO, 2001–2005)
The Social Network (David Fincher, 2010)
The Sopranos (David Chase, HBO, 1999–2007)
Spies of Warsaw (Clement, Furst, & La Frenais, BBX Four, 2013)
Spooks (David Wolstencroft, BBC, 2005–2011)
Squid Game (Hwang Dong-hyuk, Netflix, 2021–)
The State (Peter Kosminsky, Channel 4, 2017)
Stateless (Blanchett, Ayres & McCredie, ABC, 2020)
Starsky and Hutch (William Blinn, ABC, 1975–1979)
Stranger Things (Duffer Brothers, Netflix, 2016–)
Suburra (Daniele Cesarano and Barbara Petronio, Netflix, 2017–2020)
Succession (Jesse Armstrong, HBO, 2018–2023)
A Teacher (Hannah Fidel, 2020)
Teheran (Moshe Zonder, Dana Eden, Maor Kohn, Apple TV, 2020–2022)
This is Going to Hurt (Adam Kay, BBC, 2022)
This Is Us (Dan Fogelman, NBC, 2016–2022)
Top of the Lake (Campion & Lee, BBC, 2013)
Transparent (Joey Soloway, Amazon Prime, 2014–2019)
True Blood (Alan Ball, HBO, 2008–2014)
True Detective (Nic Pizzolato, HBO, 2014–)
Twin Peaks (Frost & Lynch, ABC, 1991–1992)
Twin Peaks: The Return (Frost & Lynch, Showtime, 2017)
Unbelievable (Grant, Waldman, and Chabon, Netflix, 2019)
Unorthodox (Winger & Karolinski, Netflix, 2020)
The Walking Dead (Frank Darabont, AMC, 2010–2021)
War of the Worlds (H. Overman, 2019–)
Watchmen (Damon Lindelof, HBO, 2019)
The West Wing (Aaron Sorkin, NBC, 1999–2006)
Westworld (Jonathan Nolan and Lisa Joy, HBO, 2016–2022)
When They See Us (Ava DuVernay, Netflix, 2019)
The Wire (David Simon, HBO, 2002–2008)
X-Files (Chris Carter, Fox, 1993–2018)

Index

12 Monkeys 148
12 Years 57
24 18, 35, 42, 44, 49, 110, 112–13, 144, 151, 173–8
30 Going on 13 59

A
Abdul-Mateen, Yahya 82
Abrams, J.J. 59
Abzug, Bella 81
Ad Astra 166
Adlon, Pamela 63
Aduba, Uzo 80
Affair, The 60, 94, 103, 107, 142–4, 151, 173
Akinnagbe, Gbenga 112
Alias 13, 59, 108, 172
Alien 146
Allegiance 16
Allouche, Sylvie 6n4, 26
Ally McBeal 12, 75, 88, 151
A.I. 146
American Crime 7, 58, 60, 62, 66–7, 91
American Crime Story 66, 70, 85–6, 167
American Crime Story: Impeachment 85
American Horror Story 60
Americans, The 16–17, 70, 73, 85, 103–5, 130, 140, 155–6, 160, 167, 173, 183, 185
Anderson, Gillian 87
Andor 8
Angel 26, 134, 138
Annette 132
Argo 16
Armstrong, Jesse 189

Army of the Dead 187
Assassination of Gianni Versace, The 70, 85
Auclert, Hubertine 35
Austin, J.L. viii, 14, 48
Awful Truth, The 145

B
Bagdikian, Ben 73
Bale, Christian 59
Banshee 183
Baron Noir 6, 25, 31–3, 35–6, 174
Barrett, Amy Coney 79
Barry 65
Bartlet, Jed 10, 35
Bauer, Jack 18, 42
Beasts of No Nation 58
Beautiful Mind, A 77
Benjamin, Walter viii
BeTipul 46, 181, 183
Better Call Saul 103
Better Things 63–5, 104–5
Bewitched 87
Biden, Joe 83, 192
Big Bang Theory, The 55, 79
Big Little Lies 61–2, 78, 80, 88–90
Big Short, The 59
Bildungsroman 137–9
Black Girls Matter: Pushed Out 93
Black Panther 74, 83
Blade Runner 137, 146–9
Blade Runner 2049 148–9
Blanchett, Cate 80
Blue Is the Warmest Colour 20
Blues Brothers 129

Blue Velvet 150
Body, The 135
Borgen 12, 31, 44, 46, 49, 174
Born on the Fourth of July 130
Borstein, Alex 65
Boseman, Chadwick 74
Bourdieu, Emmanuel 195–6, 196n5
Bradlee, Ben 73
Breaking Bad 6, 103, 118
Breitman, Zabou 62
Bridge of Spies 59
Broen 46
Brosnahan, Rachel 65
Brothers & Sisters 155
Brown, Sterling K. 74, 105
Buffy the Vampire Slayer ix, 6–7, 13–14, 22–3, 24–6, 36, 60, 75, 88, 107–8, 118, 120, 125, 133–5, 138, 155
Bureau, The 25, 30, 41, 44, 46, 49, 103, 104, 169–74, 178–80, 184
Byrde, Wendy 104

C

Cabral, Richard 60, 66
Call Me by Your Name 79
Cameron, David 29
Carson, Rachel 51
Cavell on Film xi
Cavell, Stanley vii, xi,1–2, 20, 108, 133, 185n3, 196n6
  Cities of Words xi
  Claim of Reason, The 147
  Conditions Handsome and Unhandsome 20
  Day After Tomorrow, The 51
  Little Did I Know... 108
  Must We Mean What We Say? viii
  Pursuits of Happiness 89, 145, 154
  World Viewed, The viii, ix–x, 108, 196
Chair, The 99–100
Cheadle, Don 57
Chernobyl 51–2, 55, 130, 185
Chisholm, Shirley 81–2, 193
Clinton, Hillary 82, 86
Cobra Kai, When They See Us 185

Cochran, Johnnie 19
Cold Case 182
Coleman, Olivia 163
Collateral 130
Color of Money, The 130
Columbo 151
Comer, Jodie 80
Comey Rule, The 80, 82, 193
Comment je me suis disputé... 108
Confirmation 70, 79, 85
Contesting Tears xi
Cordon 183
Counterpart 65
Creed 58
Cregg, C.J. 10, 12, 27, 89
Crenshaw, Kimberlé W. 92
Crown, The 52, 162–6, 185
Cruise, Tom 66, 132
Cullen, Edward 136

D

Dallas Buyers Club 16, 59
Damages 12, 112, 163
Danes, Claire 80
Darden, Christopher 19
Dargent, Clémence 96
Dark 185
Daumas, Cécile 3
Davis, Angela 92
Dayan, Philippe 181
Deadwood 122
Debout les femmes 195
Demarginalizing the Intersection of Race and Sex 92
Departed, The 60
Designated Survivor 18–19, 42–3, 66
Desperate Housewives 12, 66, 88
Desplechin, Arnaud 109
Deuce, The 62, 65, 70, 85, 185
Deutschland 83, 86, 89 85, 130, 185
DiCaprio, Leonardo 60
Dollhouse 26, 65, 137–9
Dolphin, Renate 71
Donovan, Tate 112
Dorendeu, Amélie 35–6

Douaire, Martin 96
Downton Abbey 12, 162
Dracula 133
Dream On 17
Drive My Car 195
Dr. Quinn, Medicine Woman 88
Dunham, Lena 118

E
Edge of Tomorrow 130
Elba, Idris 58
Elle 62
Ellsberg, Daniel 73
Emily in Paris 98
Engrenages 87–8, 103, 182
En thérapie 181, 184, 195
Entourage 118
ER 30, 67, 108, 151
Escobar, Pablo 116
ExistenZ 147
Ex Machina 146
Eyes Wide Shut 130

F
Fairley, Michelle 112
Fall, The 87
False Flag 170, 184
Fargo 140
Fauda 46, 172, 174, 176, 184
Favourite, The 163
Fear the Walking Dead (FTWD) 51, 183, 187
Felicity 155
Feminist Theory 92
Ferris Bueller's Day Off 29
Fincher, David 79
Firefly 26, 139
Fire Walk with Me 150–1
Firm, The 130
First Man 166
Fishburne, Laurence 58, 60, 82
Fitzpatrick, Carol 89
Fleabag 88
Floyd, George 106, 192–3
For All Mankind 3, 7, 164, 166–8

Force Awakens, The 152
Ford, Christine 71
Foundation 6
Foxcatcher 14, 16
Foxx, Jamie 57
Freeman, Morgan 57, 60
Friedan, Betty 81
Friends 12, 26, 75, 107–8, 142, 169
Fringe 142
Frodon, Jean-Michel 150
Frost, Mark 150

G
Gallardo, Miguel Angel Félix 117
Game of Thrones (GoT) 12, 25, 51–2, 55, 78–9, 87, 100, 103, 107–8, 112, 114, 118–21, 124, 140, 155, 157–61, 173, 182–3, 189–90
Gangs of New York 60
Gansa, Alex 173
Garner, Jennifer 59
Gatsby 60
gender theory with *The Simpsons* 53–4
Generation Q 76
Gilligan, Carol 36
Ginsburg, Ruth Bader 79
Girl from Oslo, The 184
Girls 118, 155
Gladiator 146
Glory 58
Glow 185
Godzilla 51
Goffman, Erwing 27
Goldberg, Whoopi 59
Golden Girls 88
Gomorrah 46
Gone Girl 114
Gone with the Wind 57
Gooding, Cuba, Jr. 66
Good Will Hunting 77
Gordon, Howard 173
Graham, Kay 73
Grantland 122
Gravity 140, 166
Grey's Anatomy 99

Grier, Pam 80
Guardians of the Galaxy 16

H
Halt and Catch Fire 185
Hambling, Joan 100
Handmaid's Tale, The 3, 6–7, 36, 65, 68–9, 78, 80, 88, 93, 165, 167, 187–8, 191
Hangover, The 52
Hanks, Tom 59, 73
Hannibal 155
Harding, Tonya 85
Harris, Kamala 81, 83
Harry Potter 125
Hatufim 44, 46, 170, 173
Heller, James 112
Hepburn, Katharine 12
Héritier, Françoise 62
High Fidelity 29
Hill, Anita 71, 93
Hippocrate 190
Homeland 12, 18, 30, 36, 39–41, 43–4, 49, 80, 103, 110, 140, 155, 170, 172–8, 182, 184, 187
Honoré, Christophe 145
Hounsou, Djimon 57
House, MD 13
House of Cards x, 1, 10–12, 16–17, 29–31, 33, 49, 66, 77, 79, 110, 116, 164, 167
House of the Dragon 189–90
How I Met Your Mother 12, 17, 26, 60
How to Do Things with Words 14
Huffman, Felicity 60, 66, 91
Hull, Akasha Gloria 92n6
Hunger Games 125
Hurston, Zora Neale 64
Hutton, Timothy 60, 66, 91

I
I May Destroy You 81
Impeachment 85–6
Iñárritu, Alejandro González 60
Inland Empire 151
Inside Man 46
Interstellar 140–1, 166
In Therapy 181, 187
In Treatment 181
I Promise You 185
It's a Wonderful Life 154

J
Jack Ryan 45
Jackson, Joshua 142
Jackson, Samuel L. 57–8
Jason Bourne 49
Jennings, Elizabeth 16
Jerome, Jharrel 55
Jerry Maguire 66, 130
Jessup, Connor 66
Je te promets 185
Ji-Yoon Kim 99–100
Jones, Felicity 79, 128
Jones, Paula 85
Jones, Ron Cephas 82
Jordan, Michael B. 58, 74
Joy 59
Justice League 74
Justified ix

K
Kalifat 170, 174, 179, 184
Kaluuya, Daniel 74
Kate & Allie 88
Kavanaugh, Brett 71, 86
Kelly, John 19
Kennedy, Anthony 71
Kidman, Nicole 80
Killing Eve 36, 64, 78, 80, 87–8, 99
Killing, The 12, 46, 150
Kingdom, The 25
King of the Hill 63
King, Martin Luther 58
King, Regina 58, 60, 66, 80, 82, 91
King's Speech, The 162
Kirkman, Tom 18

L
La Casa de Papel 47–8, 98, 174
L.A. Confidential 114

Lady Eve, The 197
La Fracture 195
Land, Stephanie 101
Langmore, Ruth 104
Lannister, Jaime 120
Lannister, Tyrion 121
Last Jedi, The 62
Lawrence, Jennifer 59
Lee, Spike 57
Leftovers, The 6, 16, 18, 67, 102, 107, 140–1, 150–1, 155, 183
Legend, John 58
Lennon, John 64
L'Esquive 20
Libération xi, 1–4
Lincoln 114
Lindelof, Damon 140
Linden, Sarah 12
Linney, Laura 104
Little Fires Everywhere 85
Live Another Day 110
Looming Tower, The 170, 174–5, 184
Lord of the Rings 120, 125
Lost 6, 25, 38, 49, 140, 147, 150, 187
Love 102
Lovecraft Country 7, 82–3, 193
Luna, Diego 117
Lupin 7, 95, 97–8
Lyman, Josh 10
Lynch, David 150
L Word: Generation Q, The 75
L Word, The 7, 11, 13, 75–6, 79–80, 88–9

M
MacDowell, Andie 102
Macray, Alice 82
Mad Max 59, 108
Mad Max: Fury Road 108
Mad Men 6, 68, 70, 88, 104, 107, 118, 162, 167, 183
Maid 7, 101–2
Man in the High Castle, The 167
Maps to the Stars 129
Mare of Easttown 101

Marianne 98
Martinez, Benito 66
Martin, George R.R. 122
Marvelous Mrs. Maisel, The 88
Mary Tyler Moore Show, The 87–8
Matrix, The 125, 147
Maverick 131
Mazin, Craig 52
McAdams, Rachel 64
McCarthy, Tom 59
McConaughey, Matthew 114
McGarry, Leo 27
McKinnon, Kate 79
McNamara, Robert 73
McNulty, Jimmy 103
McQueen, Steve 57
Melancholia 111
Menzies, Tobias 165
Metaphysics 133–68
#MeToo movement 7, 55, 61, 63–4, 71, 77, 79, 81–4, 86, 90, 93, 144
Miami Vice 65
Midnight in Paris 98
Millennium Falcon 152
Miller, Bruce 68
Mindhunter 85
Minority Report 130
Mirren, Helen 87
Mission Impossible 107, 130–1
Mission Impossible: Fallout 130
Modern Family 103, 105
Molinier, Pascale 135
Moneyball 77
Moore, Julianne 82
Moss, Elizabeth 68, 80, 93
Most Violent Year, A 16
Moura, Wagner 116
Mr. Robot 49
Mrs. America 79–82, 87, 164, 167, 182, 193
Mrs. Maisel 65
Mulholland Drive 151
Murphy, Eddie 57, 82
Murphy, Ryan 85
My Golden Years 124

N

Nakache, Olivier 181
Narcos 116
Narcos: Mexico 117
New Hope, A 124
Newman, Oscar 115
Night Of, The 83
No Man's Land 174, 184
No Time to Die 195
North by Northwest 16
Nyborg, Birgitte 12
Nyong'o, Lupita 57, 74
NYPD Blue 65

O

Oblivion 148
Occupied 174, 184
Occupy Wall Street 38
Ocean's Eleven 46
Once Upon a Time in America 131
Once Upon a Time in Hollywood 102
Ono, Yoko 63
On the Basis of Sex 79
On the Origin of Species 53
Orange Is the New Black 7, 13, 18, 58, 66, 68, 76, 79, 81, 88–9, 91, 103, 116
Organa, Leia 61
Outsiders, The 130
Overpoliced 93
OVNI(s) 130
Oyelowo, David 58
Ozark 103–4

P

Pailhas, Géraldine 96
Paperman, Patricia 28
Paris 62
Paulson, Sarah 85
Pearson, Jack 105
Penn, Kal 18
Pentagon Papers 73
Perkins, Victor F. 185n4
Perrotta, Tom 140
Philadelphia Story, The 17
Philip K. Dick 16
Philosophical Investigations viii, 170
Plot Against America, The 182
Poitier, Sidney 57
Pose 7, 85
Post, The 73–4
Poupaud, Melvil 96
Prime Suspect 87
Proust, Caroline 87
Proxima 166

Q

Qualley, Margaret 102
Queen's Gambit, The 77, 182, 185

R

Rashomon 91
Real Humans 146
Renck, Johan 52
Return of the Jedi 124, 128
Return, The 150–2
Revenant, The 60
Revenge of the Sith 197
Rhys, Matthew 73
Ridley, John 66
Right Stuff, The 131, 167
Risky Business 130
Robinson, Nick 102
Robot, I 146
Rochant, Eric 179–80
Rock, Chris 57, 59–60
Rogue One 61, 79, 117, 128–9
Romeo + Juliet 60
Room 212 145
Rothman, William 1–2, 5
Royal, Ségolène 63
Ruckelshaus, Jill 81
Rudolph, Maya 82
Ruffalo, Mark 59
Ruffin, François 195
Russell, Keri 73

S

Santos, Matt 33
Sartre, Jean-Paul 7

INDEX

Saturday Night Live 79
Scandal 18, 30, 42, 66, 79, 91
Scorsese 60
Scott, Ridley 146
Selma 58
Sense and Sensibilia 14
Servant of the People 167
Seven Seconds 55, 80
Sex and the City 12, 36, 75, 79, 88–9, 116, 118
Show Me a Hero 85, 115, 130, 185
Shuster, Martin 138
Silent Spring 51
Simmons, J.K. 65
Simon 102
Simon, David 62, 70, 73, 115
Simpson, O.J. 19, 70
Simpsons, The 53–4
Sinnerbrink, Robert 1–2
Six Feet Under 6–7, 18, 60, 88–9, 103, 105, 116, 118, 144, 151, 155, 163, 182–3
Sixth Sense 114
Smith, Gregory 18
Smith, Jada Pinkett 57
Smith, Matt 165
Smith, Will 57–8
Snow, Jon 121
Social Network, The 10, 79
Society Must be Defended 35
Sopranos, The 6, 13, 88, 103, 116, 118, 155
Soprano, Tony 100
Spielberg, Steven 59, 73
Spies of Warsaw 16
Spotlight 59
Squid Game 101
Stanwyck, Barbara 12
Stark, Arya 121
Stark, Ned 121
Starsky and Hutch 65
Star Wars 8, 61, 107, 124–9, 146
Star Wars VIII: The Last Jedi 61
Star Wars: The Last Jedi 64
State of the Union 17

State, The 179
Stateless 80
Station Eleven 6
Steinem, Gloria 81
Stigma 28
Straight Outta Compton 58
Stranger Things 73, 85, 116, 130, 185
Streep, Meryl 73, 80, 89
Suburra 46
Succession 80, 101, 103–4, 165, 169, 189
Sutherland, Kiefer 42, 111

T

Targaryen, Daenerys 121
Taylor, Lili 66
Teacher, A 102, 188
Teheran 170, 184
Terminator, The 107–8, 148
The Persuaders! 65
Thelma and Louise 146–7
Theron, Charlize 59
Thiellement, Pacôme 126n5
This is Going to Hurt 190
This Is Us 4, 7, 9, 74, 95–6, 103, 105–6, 164, 169, 182–3, 185, 192–4
Thomas, Clarence 93
Tierney, Maura 142
Titanic 60, 114
Toboni, Jacqueline 76
Toledano, Eric 181
Top Gun 130–2
Top Gun: Maverick 130
Top of the Lake 12, 18, 61–2, 80, 88, 151, 158, 164
Total Recall 146
Town, The 46
Transparent 7, 66
Tripp, Linda 85
True Blood 134
True Detective 56, 60, 80, 107, 114
Truman Show The 147
Trump, Donald 71, 73, 81, 192
Twilight 133

Twin Peaks 18, 108, 124, 150–4, 188
Twin Peaks: The Return 61, 150, 188
Two Popes 165

U
Unbelievable 7, 55–6, 65, 78, 80, 85, 87, 102
Underwood, Frank 29
Unorthodox 80, 87

V
Vallée, Jean-Marc 59
vampires 133–6
Vaughn, Vince 114
Veep 55
Very Bad Trip 52
Vikander, Alicia 82
von Trier, Lars 25

W
Walking Dead, The (*TWD*) 6, 37–8, 51, 74, 103, 121, 143, 155, 165, 182–3, 187, 193
Waller-Bridge, Phoebe 64, 88
War of the Worlds 187
Warshow, Robert 5n3, 133
Washington Post 73
Washington, Denzel 57–8
Washington, Kerry 79
Watchmen 6–7, 80, 82–3 193
Waterford, Frederick 69
Watergate 73

West Wing, The ix, x, 6, 10–12, 18–19, 27, 29–33, 35, 42, 49, 61, 67, 89, 108, 167
Westworld 146, 149, 167
Whedon, Joss 22, 26, 137
When Harry Met Sally 62, 129
When They See Us 6–7, 55, 83
Whitaker, Forest 57
White House, The 151
Wiley, Samira 93
Winick, Gary 59
Winslet, Kate 101
Wire, The 11, 27, 30, 58, 60, 67, 74–5, 83, 88, 99, 103, 112, 115–18, 151, 155, 183
Witherspoon, Reese 80
Wittgenstein, Ludwig viii
Wonder Woman 74
Woodley, Shailene 80
World Viewed, The viii, ix–x, 108, 196
Wright, Letitia 74
Wright, Seth 18

X
X-Files 87
X-Men 107
X-Men: First Class 124

Z
Zelensky, Volodymyr 167
Zero Dark Thirty 45, 172
Ziegler, Toby 10, 61